The Changing Landscape of Education in Africa:
quality, equality and democracy

The Changing Landscape of Education in Africa:
quality, equality and democracy

Edited by
David Johnson

Oxford Studies in Comparative Education
Series Editor: David Phillips

SYMPOSIUM
BOOKS

Symposium Books
PO Box 204 Didcot Oxford OX11 9ZQ United Kingdom
the book publishing division of wwwords Ltd
www.symposium-books.co.uk

Published in the United Kingdom, 2008

ISBN 978-1-873927-11-3

This publication is also available on a subscription basis
as Volume 19 Number 1 of *Oxford Studies in Comparative Education*
(ISSN 0961-2149)

Typeset by wwwords Ltd
Printed and bound in the United Kingdom by Cambridge University Press

Contents

The Changing Landscape of Education in Africa: quality, equality and democracy

DAVID JOHNSON & WILLIAM BEINART

Forty years ago Coombs (1968) first drew attention to the 'World Education Crisis', and specifically problems in the educational systems of countries in the developing world. Today, many of these problems remain, and are most visible in the educational systems of countries in sub-Saharan Africa. A large number of children remain out of school and for those who do enrol, less than half complete the primary education cycle. More worrying is the fact that of those who do complete primary schooling, many leave with unacceptably low levels of knowledge and skills. Further, the problems of access to education, and the quality of learning opportunities and learning outcomes, are unevenly spread between rural and urban areas, better-off and worse-off constituencies and between boys and girls. Ross et al (2005) illustrate graphically the relationship between income and educational outcomes in a number of African countries (see Figure 1): in a mathematics test for grade 6 students, Namibia, Zambia, Malawi, and Lesotho are the worst performers, but interestingly, when the socio-economic status of pupils is taken into account, there is less inequality in Lesotho and Malawi, possibly because the gaps between rich and poor are not as pronounced as elsewhere. Mauritius and the Seychelles, which are the top performing countries in the south-west Indian Ocean, are also amongst the most socially and economically divided in respect of those pupils who perform well and those who do less well. In South Africa, there is a big wealth divide but even so, both the poorer and better off groups do not perform as well as Mozambique, Swaziland or Kenya.

On the face of it, the news on educational development in Africa, especially when assessed against indicators such as 'a good quality of education for all', appears grim. Indeed, for many countries the sheer task of overhauling what are, to a large degree, dysfunctional systems of education is so overwhelming that it is difficult to think in terms of change and progress. Indeed, it is easy to overlook some of the efforts in this direction.

Thus, we have set ourselves the task in this volume to identify those signs and symbols of change, of resilience and the will to succeed. The study of signs – a sort of social semiotics of education in Africa – we hope will provide us with an important and compelling framework to identify features that define the changing landscape of education in Africa. We are quick to point out that signs and symbols of change are not in themselves hard evidence of progress. In fact, there are many chapters in this volume that will show that signs of change are sometimes complex to interpret (see Lemon on the issues of race, class and education in South Africa, and Unterhalter on masculinities in South Africa).

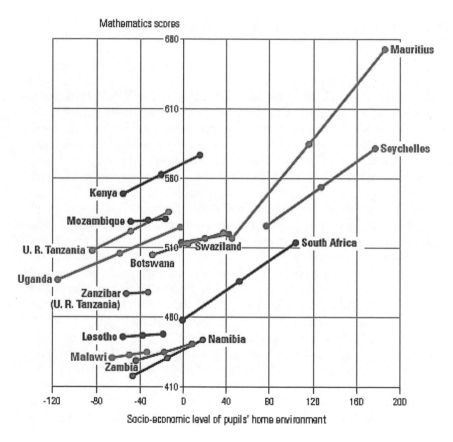

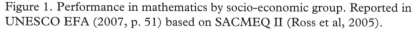

Figure 1. Performance in mathematics by socio-economic group. Reported in UNESCO EFA (2007, p. 51) based on SACMEQ II (Ross et al, 2005).

Hence, the volume is concerned with capturing some features of change in the educational systems of Africa; in some chapters, the explicit and visible policies that drive educational systems, their design and structure, their linguistic features and the content embodied in the curricula are discussed (see Verspoor on the features that define educational quality; Johnson on educational policies in Nigeria; and Crossley on the school management structure in Kenya). For other chapters, it is the less explicit features of the educational system that are important – their representational character or what Halliday (1985) calls 'ideational meanings'. Questions such as, 'what does education or knowledge mean or represent and what functions does it serve?' are important here (see Low on Khoisan healers in Namibia and Trudell on literacy in minority language communities in Cameroon). For yet others, it is the affordances and potentiality of the system to transform its own character and that of those within and around it, to (re)make a society in which justice, freedom and democratic participation are the defining features that are important (see Schweisfurth on The Gambia and Unterhalter on South Africa).

In his chapter, Verspoor provides an excellent overview of some of the factors that constrain the growth and qualitative improvement in many African countries, but he also points to those areas in which there have been promising signs (and symbols) of change, including devolution of largely centralised systems with many layers of bureaucracy, community involvement and social accountability both of political institutions and those public institutions responsible for the delivery of front line public services. Johnson takes up the theme of governance and social accountability in his chapter on Nigeria. Here the Federal Government of Nigeria has launched a community accountability and transparency initiative in an attempt to minimise corruption and the wastages and leakage of public funds. Whilst this is an important central policy imperative, questions about the extent to which communities will use this as a catalyst for change, as they did in Uganda, and to a more limited extent in Ghana and Tanzania, remains to be seen. But, as Crossley shows in his study on management and leadership in Kenya, it is possible to strengthen features of an educational system and in so doing enhance the possibility of wider change. Lemon, on the other hand, shows that regardless of intentions to achieve equality and fairness, changes in the physical characteristics of an educational system might be uneven and skewed. In a fascinating chapter that looks at the shifting geographies of education in South Africa, Lemon shows how previous racial and class inequalities are in danger of being transposed across new educational boundaries. This point is picked up in Unterhalter's chapter on South Africa, especially in her notion of 'resemblance' of the inequalities of the 'old' system. Crucially, these shifting boundaries of education do not lay a firm basis for citizenship and democracy, as discussed in an article on citizenship in fragmented societies (Johnson, 2007), a point picked up by Schweisfurth more generally.

In a searching chapter, Low questions how representative are the forms of knowledge that are assessed (perhaps because they can be assessed) of the cognitive functioning of African society. In defending the thesis that there are many ways of knowing, he gives a detailed account of the sociocultural meaning-making activities of the Khoisan in Namibia. In a similar fashion,

Trudell outlines the literacy practices of the Bafut, Kom and Nso' in Cameroon. These two chapters underline the increasing attention given to indigenous knowledge systems in Africa and their potential for social and economic regeneration in the context of rapidly changing needs of the global economy. Sadly, there appears to be little in the formal school curriculum and its associated methods of assessment that seeks to understand the creative capacities of youth in Africa. The educational system is reliant on one mode of assessment – linguistic.

The ideational or hidden meanings of educational systems are discussed in the chapter by Unterhalter. She examines four types of change in South Africa since its first democratic elections in 1994. These are reconstitution (of a previously segregated education system), repositioning (the changing role of the educational system in South Africa in respect of immigration and migration), recognition (the way in which the curriculum functions to sensitise children to the wrongs of discrimination and exploitation) and resemblance (a worrying similarity between the new and the old). Unterhalter argues:

> In my view the four forms of the reformed nation I have identified link with four different modalities of education. Education has been reconstituted with regard to the institutional form of national governance. South African education has been repositioned in relation to an international nexus through which people and ideas flow. It has moved from an outer periphery to a place close to the centre. The education system, and particularly the outcomes-based curriculum, seeks to structure knowledge in such a way that children can look again, (recognise) ideas and the ways they are utilised developing skills in communication and evaluation. But in many ways, with regard to the everyday experience of schools and classrooms, relations are changing much more slowly and the present often uncomfortably resembles the past. (p. 96)

This last point strikes a particularly disconcerting note, especially in view of the complex relationship between education, ethnicity and conflict (Johnson & Stewart, 2007).

The education system is a powerful influence over identities and is a source of power and of income in contemporary society. If educational systems do not change sufficiently and inherently retain the features of the past, there is a real danger of cementing other horizontal inequalities – in income, employment, nutrition and health as well as political position (see Johnson & Stewart, 2007). Importantly, since horizontal inequalities can be an important source of violent conflict, educational inequalities are politically provocative, even dangerous.

The importance, therefore, of nurturing the transformative capabilities of the educational system is strongly emphasised in the chapter by Schweisfurth. One way to achieve this is to maximise the potentiality of teachers in the system through in-service development. On the other hand, as Gallagher points out, 'simply changing the structure of schools today does not, in itself, solve all the problems of a divided society' (Gallagher, 2004, p. 11). Nonetheless, we would be hard pushed to disagree with the sentiment that prohibiting divisive education and education that stirs up cultural hostilities is desirable, especially in divided societies. And more positively, as Johnson & Stewart (2007) argue, 'providing knowledge of and respect for the other, can hardly be conflict-promoting and may make a contribution to improved attitudes'. This is powerfully argued by Neuberger:

> The role of the educational system in a democracy is to 'teach' coexistence, tolerance, cooperation, compromise and the capacity for at least some rational choice. In this way democratic education creates a 'democratic personality'. Democracy is built not only on constitutions, laws and institutions, but depends on a political culture of social trust, moderation and participation, and thus to a large extent on democratic socialisation, both at home and in school. (Neuberger, 2007, p. 292)

On the evidence of the chapters in this volume, there can be little doubt that there are signs and symbols of change in the educational systems of Africa. It is clear, however, that change is not linear and unidirectional, as we are strongly reminded by both Unterhalter and Lemon. Change is also slow and uncertain and policy imperatives (useful signs and symbols of change) alone are unlikely to have wide impact, unless coupled with wider societal imperatives. But there is also a new awakening in Africa – democracy is seen to be an intrinsic part of human development (Schweisfurth) and economic growth, and increasingly, many communities are becoming more vociferous in holding their governments and local authorities to account for the efficient delivery of public services like education (Johnson). There are also the first signs of a celebration of indigenous knowledge – a discovery and affirmation of the potentially powerful role that indigenous knowledge systems can play in explaining or complementing other forms of scientific knowledge (Low), and that local languages are not an impediment to higher forms of intellectual functioning (Trudell).

Yet, it is hard to ignore the many constraints upon African educational systems in achieving quality, equality and democracy. There is much to be done but we are confident, judging by the various signs and symbols of change, that African educational systems are on the road to recovery.

References

Coombs, P. (1968) *The World Educational Crisis: a systems analysis.* Oxford: Oxford University Press.

Gallagher, A.M. (2004) *Education in Divided Societies.* New York: Palgrave.

Halliday, M.A.K. (1985) *An Introduction to Functional Grammar.* London: Arnold.

Johnson, D. (2007) Building Citizenship in Fragmented Societies: the challenges of de-racialising and integrating schools in post-Apartheid South Africa, *International Journal of Education and Development*, 27(3), 306-317.

Johnson, D. & Stewart, F. (2007) Education, Ethnicity and Conflict, *International Journal of Educational Development*, 27(3), 247-251. http://dx.doi.org/10.1016/j.ijedudev.2006.10.017

Neuberger, B. (2007) Education for Democracy in Israel: structural impediments and basic dilemmas, *International Journal of Educational Development*, 27(3), 247-251. http://dx.doi.org/10.1016/j.ijedudev.2006.10.013

United Nations Educational, Scientific and Cultural Organisation (UNESCO) (2007) *EFA Global Monitoring Report: Strong Foundations*. Paris: UNESCO.

CHAPTER 1

The Challenge of Learning: improving the quality of basic education in sub-Saharan Africa[1]

ADRIAAN M. VERSPOOR

At the onset of the twenty-first century sub-Saharan Africa faces an unprecedented challenge, that of basic education development. All countries in sub-Saharan Africa recognise the critical importance of basic education for economic and social development. All have committed themselves to the goals of completion of primary schooling and learning for all set out at the World Education Forum in Dakar in 2000. But even after considerable efforts to expand access, most education systems in the region are far from reaching the Dakar goals. Unless the increase in admissions in grade one that has occurred in recent years in many countries is followed by improvements in quality and retention, the human resource base for sustained development will remain unacceptably weak. Less than one-third of the children of school leaving age currently acquire the knowledge and the skills specified in their national primary education curriculum. This jeopardises the very objectives of economic development, social progress, peace and democracy that are at the core of the New Partnership for African Development. The quest for quality is not just an issue of education policy, but is a key development challenge.

Improving the quality of education is arguably the most critical element of successful education for all (EFA) strategies in Africa. But real quality improvement, i.e. improvement in the teaching and learning process that results in enhanced learning outcomes, has been very difficult to bring about in both developing and industrialised countries. The experience of sub-Saharan Africa is no exception in this regard. To stimulate discussion and reflection on this issue, the Association for the Development of Education in Africa (ADEA) selected the issue of 'quality in basic education' as the central theme for its biannual meeting in 2003 and established a working group to

13

investigate the question: *How can the countries of sub-Saharan Africa improve, in a financially viable way, the quality of basic education and learning?*

Methodology of the Study

Quality is defined for the purpose of this study in terms of outcome: achievement by all children of learning objectives as defined in the national programmes –mediated by quality inputs and processes. Performances in the main subjects – languages, mathematics, science and social studies – are typically used to measure this outcome. But this is insufficient. The perceptions of the quality of education, especially beyond the basic skills, vary considerable among different stakeholders and may influence the demand for schooling.

The conceptual model that has guided the design of the study is based on the standard input–process–output approach that was presented in the 2002 Global Monitoring Report (United Nations Educational, Scientific and Cultural Organisation [UNESCO], 2002). It emphasises:

- classroom factors (time, grouping procedures, instructional strategies) as key determinants;
- school factors (leadership, emphasis on order and learning) that enable and reinforce;
- system factors (vision, standards, resources, relevant curriculum, incentives) that are necessary to provide direction; and
- community factors (home environment, support for education) that ensure local relevance and ownership.

The research methodology of the study is based on the praxis approach that was adopted for earlier work of ADEA. It is characterised by 'learning through action, learning from action to develop and improve action'. This approach emphasises the documentation and the exchange of experiences by participants in the reform processes, the sharing of knowledge between countries in order to develop a broadened vision, and the strengthening of institutional and technical capacities for the continuous improvement of the quality of education. This interactive process of learning is expected to ensure that each country learns from its own policies and actions by evaluating them and sharing the lessons with others in the region so that successful and/or promising experiences in improving the quality of basic education may be identified and analysed.

The 22 case studies carried out by country teams are the foundation of the analysis. The teams comprised national education specialists supported by an external resource person appointed by ADEA. In addition, most ADEA thematic working groups contributed background papers grounded in their experience. Education specialists were invited to write background papers, and reviews of the African literature by the researchers of the regional networks (Educational Research Network West and Central Africa

[ERNWACA] and Education Research Network East and Southern Africa [ERNESA]) were commissioned. These supporting documents have made it possible to add to the findings of the case studies and place them in a much broader context of African and international knowledge and practice.

This chapter explores the sub-Saharan Africa experience with quality improvement in basic education based on these documents. It briefly reviews the scope of the quality challenge in the region and summarises the promises and challenges documented by the country cases. It then proposes a framework for action that places these African experiences in the context of a broader international knowledge base documented in the background papers. Four strategic priorities are discussed: (i) moving towards a cost-effective allocation of resources; (ii) designing action programmes that are school based and learning focused; (iii) establishing a culture of quality that permeates the whole system; and (iv) adopting implementation strategies that aim at continuous learning and improvement. The last section of the chapter presents suggestions that countries may consider as they move to establish a national quality improvement agenda.

The Challenge of Learning for All

A large number of children on the continent remain out of school. The gross enrolment of sub-Saharan Africa stands at 81.2% (2000), lower than any other region in the world, while about 40% of the children of school age in sub-Saharan Africa remain out of school – proportionally more than in any other region of the world. Since about one-quarter of the students are over age, some 40% of the children of school age in sub-Saharan Africa remain out of school.

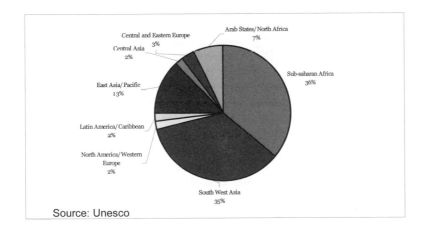

Figure 1. Distribution of out of school children in the world.

Learning Achievement is Unacceptably Low

In many schools in Africa, learning achievement is so low that after several years of schooling, the students still have not obtained basic literacy and numeracy skills (Figure 2). Therefore, if improvement of the quality of instruction is not emphasised, much of the EFA effort might be wasted; wasted because important resources will be invested without being translated into learning outcomes and because children – future adults – risk dropping out of school too soon or being illiterate despite completing primary school.

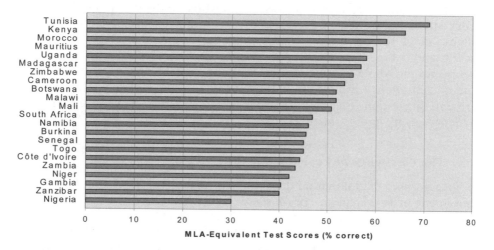

Figure 2. Percentage of correct answers on math and language tests of fourth graders.

Source: Data from UNESCO's Monitoring Learning Achievement (MLA) project supplemented with data collected through other international assessment exercises (e.g. Southern Africa Consortium for Monitoring Educational Quality [SACMEQ], Programme d'Analyse des Systèmes Éducatifs de la CONFEMEN [Programme of Analysis of Education Systems] [PASEC] and the Trends in International Mathematics and Science Study [TIMMS]) converted into MLA equivalents.

Of the children that enrol in grade 1, less than two-thirds reach the final grade and of these, only about half can demonstrate that they master the expected basic skills and knowledge (Figure 3). As a result, more than two out of every three children of primary school leaving age in sub-Saharan Africa enter the labour market with, at best, limited literacy and numeracy skills. The low level of education of the labour force constrains prospects for international competitiveness, economic growth and social development in many countries on the continent.

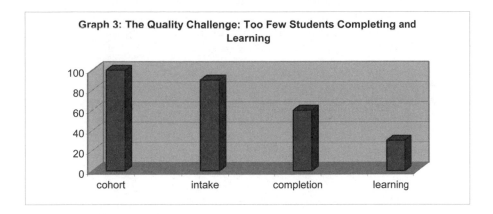

Figure 3. The quality challenge: too few students completing and learning.

The concerns about the quality of schooling are also apparent when the literacy levels of adults are examined. Six years of primary education should enable those who complete to be literate in the long term. Yet, the performance of school systems varies considerably. Figure 4 summarises the available data. They reflect the learning of people who attended primary school as it operated in the 1980s, as it is based on the reported literacy of adults whose average age is a little over 30. The data suggest that (i) time spent in school is a fundamental ingredient for learning; and (ii) the productivity of this time can vary greatly depending on how efficiently it is used.

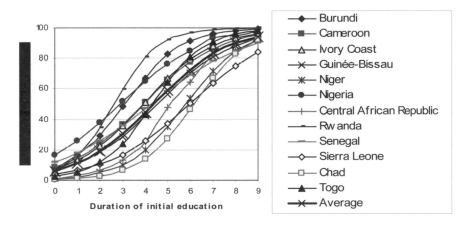

Figure 4. Percentage of adults who can read easily and their initial education.
Source: Mingat (2004).

Unsurprisingly, the inequitable access, the low retention and the low levels of learning achievement result in a level of education attainment in sub-Saharan Africa that is lower that in any other region of the world (Figure 5).

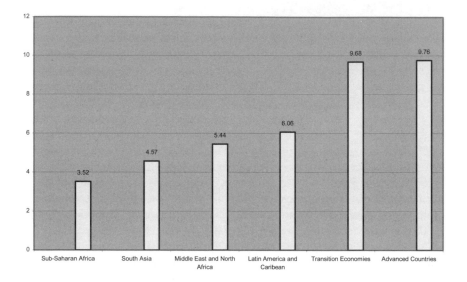

Figure 5. Average educational attainment by region.
Source: Barro & Lee (2000)

Quality and Equity: a concurrent challenge

The Dakar EFA goals call for an equitable opportunity to learn for all. Basic education policy, therefore, is not only confronted with a challenge of quality but also with one of equity, of equal opportunities to learn and achieve. The concept of equality has evolved considerably over time. After initially being construed as equality of access, the goal was redefined as equality of opportunity, implying the provision of the same teaching and learning conditions to all students. Even more ambitious equality concepts, reflecting the preoccupations highlighted during the Jomtien conference in 1990 and intensified at the World Education Forum in Dakar in 2002, concern the equality of results as measured by academic success. As a consequence, the indicator of progress towards education for all moved from a gross enrolment ratio of 100% to a net enrolment ratio of 100% [2], to a primary school completion rate of 100%. Even more demanding is the expectation that students who complete, master the skills and knowledge specified in the national curriculum. The latter perspective focuses on the inequalities of results and postulates that all students must have access to the opportunities to learn and pedagogic support that are necessary for them to attain at least the expected basic level of competence at the end of their schooling.

A Difficult Economic and Institutional Environment

Today, 30 out of the 36 least developed countries cited in the UNDP Human Development Report (2002) are in Africa. Over the 1990s, the annual per capita growth rate was negative in sub-Saharan Africa at -0.4%. The absence of economic growth partially explains the inability of many of these countries to fight poverty and build a human capital foundation for sustained economic growth. The proportion of individuals having only a dollar a day to live on increased over the period 1990-99, from 47.5% (241 million) to 49% (315 million) (UNDP, 2003). The weak economic growth of African countries weighs heavily on the availability of financial resources needed to meet the objectives of universal primary education (UPE).[3] This means that few countries will be able to finance UPE through their own resources and that the search for outside and private financing is imperative.

Many education reforms in sub-Saharan Africa have faltered on the shoals of implementation. In many countries the human capacity and institutions are not effectively used. In others the experience and skills are insufficient for the demanding and complex challenges of real education reform, i.e. programmes that impact on what students learn in the classroom. There is little doubt that the weak managerial and technical capacities of the ministries of national education, and other organisations and communities that act in the education sector are major obstacles to the improvement of education and learning (Moulton, 2003).

Conflicts and HIV/AIDS Add to the Challenge

The education for all challenge has become even more daunting as sub-Saharan countries suffer the consequences of conflict and HIV/AIDS. Conflicts usually have a severe negative impact on education. Often hundreds of thousands of people are internally displaced or become refugees, adding to the education challenges faced by the host country. Buildings are frequently damaged or destroyed; textbooks and instructional material also risk being spoiled. Parents and children are strongly marked by the violence that they have seen or experienced. Ministries of education are usually poorly prepared to face the challenge of rebuilding once peace returns.

The HIV/AIDS pandemic has stricken 28.5 million adults and children. HIV/AIDS has a serious negative impact on the ability of teachers to carry out their work with the expected regularity. It also affects students' ability to attend and learn, especially those who are HIV positive, live with sick people or whose parents or guardians have died of the disease. Considerable international financial support has been mobilized to help countries deal with the repercussions of morbidity and mortality linked to HIV/AIDS on the school systems of the countries in sub-Saharan Africa. Many African governments have organised awareness and information campaigns for their people and have also favoured access to antiretroviral drugs. Evidence is emerging (Bennell, 2003) that in several countries these efforts are beginning to pay off. The intensive efforts in Zambia, Botswana and Malawi to spread the knowledge of the cause and the methods of prevention of HIV/AIDS most likely have had a positive impact on teachers' behaviour, as recent estimates show that mortality rates are not as high as often had been projected. This clearly means that the actions undertaken must be continued and even reinforced over time.

Findings on Promising Practice

Countries and donor agencies have long recognised the critical importance of improvement in the quality of education. In almost every country innovations have been piloted and reforms initiated. There are several clear trends that are emerging and important lessons that can be distilled from these experiences. These are discussed in this section.

The Move towards De-concentration and School-Based Management is Ubiquitous

There is a widespread trend in the region towards decentralisation of non-personnel functions and increased school-level decision making. In most countries education has traditionally been managed through highly centralised systems with standardised models of schooling. This has often resulted in the inefficient application of resources, inequitable provision of access and unacceptable differences in quality of instruction and learning achievement between rich and poor, urban and rural and boys and girls, and has thwarted progress towards the EFA goals. In response, significant changes in the way education is managed are taking place. In many countries this takes the shape of a move towards school-based management. In others central functions are de-concentrated towards education offices at the district or regional level.

The trend towards school-based management gives schools more leeway to make decisions about curriculum, budgets and resource allocation, and staff and students. As a consequence they have increasing autonomy and flexibility to adapt school organisation and instructional practice to local conditions within broadly defined national standards and operational parameters. Teachers are being encouraged to adapt reforms and innovations to local conditions and student learning needs. In countries such as Uganda, Kenya, Tanzania and Mozambique the resource transfer takes place as conditional block grants; in others, for example, Madagascar, Senegal and Guinea, as support for school development projects developed at the school level; or as in Chad, through subsidies to community owned and operated schools.

The Ugandan devolution of financial management to school management committees is particularly interesting. Before decentralisation, the central government decided how funds were to be utilised and remitted them directly to the district education office, with the district authorities having no control over their use. With the UPE policy, school fees levied on parents have been abolished and the schools receive a UPE capitation grant from the Government. Uganda's grant system is calculated centrally and released as a conditional block grant to districts, which in turn, release all funds to schools on the basis of enrolment. The Ministry has also released guidelines to schools for allocation of funds; for example, 50% for instructional materials, 5% for administration, and so on. The grant system provides about US $4 per child per year for children in grades one through three and $6 per child per year for children in the next four years. The Government pays teachers' salaries and pays for textbooks, and the grants are used to fund other school needs. The School Management Committee (SMC) manages the money at school level. Efficient and transparent financial management is promoted through training and sensitisation workshops for all the actors to appreciate the structures and guidelines of record keeping and accountability. The programme aims to provide: (1) full community participation and decision making without making unrealistic and unfair demands on the poorest; (2) decentralised procurement which maximises use of the local expertise, and (3) targeting of the poorest communities through a system of ranking and prioritising neediest schools. At first there were problems with grants reaching schools in time, and parents' perceptions that they were not adequately involved in the SMC. To address this, amounts received from the district office are posted publicly in the school and any parent or community member can access the records of how the money is spent. Regular audits also ensure that the funds reach the schools and are utilised for the purposes intended. Problems that remain include: sharing information about allocations at all levels of the system; supporting SMCs; and lack of adequate funding to overburdened district education offices. Nevertheless, an effective means for the participation of parents in democratic decision making in education has been established.

Tanzania provided support to schools through the Community Education Fund (CEF), before moving to a block grant system in 2002. The programme expanded from 372 schools in 1999 to 1642 across 16 districts (reaching approximately 685,000 students) in 2001. The CEF matches funds mobilised at the community level with a government grant, to support implementation of a school plan developed by the community, in collaboration with the school staff. While the CEF was quite successful from the outset, it soon became clear that the poorest communities and weakest schools were not being reached, mainly due to the inability of poorer schools and communities to generate funds needed to receive the matching grant, weak school management, inexperienced community organisation, and bureaucratic rigidity in matching community contributions. To address the problems, a more flexible approach was adopted. The Ministry of Education in collaboration with the districts developed criteria to target the

21

economically poorest and organisationally weakest communities for matching funds. District councils were required to set aside funds for the weakest schools to attract matching grants at a slightly increased ratio (1:2, 1:3, etc.) Out of a total of 1642 CEF schools, 151 weak schools were identified, affecting district council pledges amounting to some Tshs 97,514,000 (about $100,000). This is about Tshs 500,000 per school ($500), but in some instances amounts to as much as Tshs 5 million (or $5000). For example, in a weak school in Kibaha, Kipangege school, parents raised $133, the district council then provided $2000, which was matched by the CEF at a 1:2 ratio, totalling $4200, from which the community is constructing two teachers' houses, and has purchased 20 desks and office materials. In July 2002, the following achievements of the CEF were reported:

(1) increased parental involvement and contributions: unit contribution per pupil increased from 1115 Tshs in 1996, to 3007 Tshs in 2000;
(2) increased enrolment: gross enrolment for CEF districts increased by 30% between 1998 and 2001, and 15% for non-CEF districts;
(3) improved attendance: from 82% in 1998 to 93% in 2001;
(4) improved student achievement: from 20% of students scoring A-C in the Primary School Leaving Examination in 1996, to 35% in 2001; and
(5) reduced drop-out rates: from 2.4% in 1995 to 1.5% in 2001.

Despite its successes, it is clear that even with additional support the poorest communities and weaker schools have struggled to implement their plans. Strategy to target the poor has tended to be over-general, and should have been aimed at specific poor communities and not the entire district.

Education decentralisation – in most instances more accurately described as de-concentration – is being implemented in many countries in the region. But most often it has not yet resulted in better quality education, improved governance, or greater efficiency in resource allocation or service delivery. This is not unexpected given that improving education quality while maintaining the integrity of the national education system and ensuring equity is a much greater challenge than administering expansion of enrolments (Chapman & Adams, 2002). The challenge is particularly daunting in sub-Saharan Africa because most education management changes, as initially conceived within the context of decentralisation, hardly touched key management issues relating to the organisation of instruction, planning of programmes, course content, financial management of funds, and personnel management. This is changing, with a greater focus on efficient management at all levels of the education system from the centre down to the school level, in support of quality improvement. The experiences to date show that:

• A large number of countries have embarked on education decentralisation, often within the context of a broader national policy. The process is mainly being implemented in three ways: administrative de-concentration, diversification of providers, and differentiation of programmes. It almost always includes administrative decentralisation but the evidence suggests that this is an important but far from sufficient element in improving the quality and efficiency of service delivery. The de-concentration process needs to be supported by deliberate efforts to involve communities in the process of schooling and the provision of direct support to schools.

- A range of alternative education structures and programme delivery mechanisms is being experimented with to ensure responsiveness to the needs and the priorities of people in different social, cultural and economic contexts. The diversification of providers has been primarily through private for-profit and not-for-profit providers (non-governmental organisations [NGOs] and churches). Some countries are exploring the potential of support from the business community, while others make extensive use of outsourcing to private providers.

- Separating financing and provision can allow governments to tap the contribution of multiple sources of provision, provided public financing is structured in such a way that equitable access to good-quality schooling for all is ensured.

- The restructuring of education management has important implications not only for the lower levels of the hierarchy, but also for the central services.

- A major challenge that few countries have tackled successfully is the improvement in the efficient management, the deployment and the professional development of teachers.

- Decentralisation and related changes at lower levels of the education system do not take place in a vacuum. The responsibilities of the different government levels and stakeholders in education need to be redefined and reallocated as new ideas emerge on what role the national government (ministry of education), sub-regional structures, schools, local communities and social partners should play in education. Significant changes in the role of central ministries of education in the management of education are a necessary part of decentralising education sector management.

- Effective restructuring will require sustained capacity development, including clear definition of roles and responsibilities, incentives for performance, continuous training and technical support at all levels of the system.

However, management reforms *alone* cannot be expected to improve quality. They have to be part of a comprehensive package that includes resources for essential inputs, and support for effective instruction. A mix of political will (policy makers working together with stakeholders), technical inputs (competent policies and personnel in education) and economic factors (adequate resources) is essential. At the same time, there has to be congruency between 'bottom-up' and 'top-down' principles, emphasising expertise, rights, and power of local communities while taking into account context and constraints. Decentralising responsibility to the district school administrators will only be successful if the increased responsibility of the district level is accompanied by increased resource availability. This in turn means that effective policies for supervision, support and monitoring become essential. Most important is the change in role of the head teachers, who, as school improvement becomes their central task, are increasingly asked to become transformational leaders instead of school administrators. The process of restructuring education sector management in sub-Saharan Africa must continue to emphasise flexibility and responsiveness to the needs of different populations and teaching staff while ensuring equity in access and results.

Community Involvement is Broadening

Community participation ranges from familiar forms of support – such as community involvement in construction – to more active involvement in management, planning, and learning. Community participation in sub-Saharan Africa is becoming multifaceted and more comprehensive, although the ability of communities to participate in and support education varies widely, and not surprisingly, its impact is often uneven. Some well-resourced, highly motivated, and cohesive communities are single-handedly financing and managing education on an ongoing basis. Other communities lack the resources to make anything more than a minor contribution to the costs of education, or are unable or unwilling to work together (Watt, 2001). Parent-Teacher Associations, and community-based School Management Committees, nevertheless, constitute one of the most striking features of the community's participation in basic education schooling.

In Mali, NGOs are supporting the operation of the Centers of Education for Development (CED), while the community, which set up a management committee, pays teachers. In Guinea, a seven-person management committee, designated by the community, oversees the NAFA centers, or second-chance schools for 10-16 year-olds not in regular schools. The management committee ensures the provision of premises and the enrolment of 60-90 children, and is responsible for payment of the organisers (Niane, 2003).

Local Community Schools (ECB) were initiated in Senegal in 1992/93 by two NGOs, ADEF-Afrique and Aide et Action, and were subsequently adopted in 1996 as a basic component of the alternative models tested by the Ministry responsible for alternative education programmes. They are currently in use by a number of private and community based operators subsidised by the Ministry and a large number of NGOs. They target youth aged 9-15 who were never enrolled in school (and are illiterate) or who left school early (school drop-outs and others not enrolled). There are three goals of the pedagogical approach used: the integration of young people into socio-economic activities in their environment; continuing secondary school study;

and pre-vocational training or integration into certain jobs. The model is based mainly on:

(1) the design and self-management of the school by the local community;
(2) the inclusion of children aged 9-15 who are not enrolled or have dropped out, in particular girls, designed to provide a four-year educational cycle, equivalent to six years of elementary school;
(3) the use of national languages as the main language of instruction and French as a second language;
(4) support for the 'basic adolescent education' programme by the 'adult literacy' programme;
(5) a coordinated 'parents school/children's school' approach; and
(6) the use of learning methods focused on promoting the environment.

Communities in Madagascar are supporting schools through programme contracts, based on local traditions of agreement and commitment.[4] The strategy is based on a bottom-up, participatory approach, with the steady empowerment of the community and its increasing involvement in the life of the school. The community is responsible for identifying its education needs. Each contract (which is a school project that defines each party's tasks and responsibilities) in principle concerns five parties: the village community, the teachers, the school principal, the school district ('CISCO') and the support project. Out of the 12,330 public elementary schools operating in Madagascar, about 4,330 (34%) in 63 'CISCO' (56% of 111 districts) have adopted the programme contract approach. Parents and the community have become more aware of their role and power in a fruitful partnership, which is reflected in improved follow-up of pupils by the families, who contact teachers more frequently.

The Madagascan experience suggests that successful scale up of the programme contract approach requires:

- mobilisation to create awareness of the importance of schooling and provide information to communities;
- adapting programme contracts to the realities of the local and/or regional context;
- clearly defining the roles and responsibilities of each contracting party;
- drawing on existing local structures to ensure contracts are met and the management (of money and supplies) is transparent;
- setting up monitoring systems that include administrators, school personnel, and community members; and
- a participatory approach to support community skills and motivate contracting parties at community level so as to encourage them to honour their commitments (e.g. providing classrooms in good condition, material for teaching and training, and enough qualified teachers.

Compelling Evidence of the Effectiveness of Bilingual Education

Connecting to the students' context means, in sub-Saharan Africa, first and foremost moving to mother-tongue instruction – at least in the early grades. The experience of Zambia, Mali and Burkina Faso with the use of African languages as the medium of instruction demonstrates how this challenge can be tackled. Two findings are consistently reported across these cases and others: (i) effective acquisition of early literacy in the mother tongue; and (ii) high performance in the second language in the upper primary grades. These findings are critically important, as reading ability is a precondition for effective learning and is one of the best predictors of educational achievement and survival (Juel, 1991; Hanson & Farrell, 1995; Carnine, 1998; National Reading Panel, 2000).

Yet, various multi-country evaluations indicate that literacy levels, especially reading ability, are very low among African students. For these reasons, the need to improve reading instruction and learning in sub-Saharan Africa cannot be emphasised enough. Bilingual education holds a lot of promise in this respect. At the same time there are, however, a number of challenges. The main one has to do with managing the switch from the first language to the second one. This is all the more important as the most common form of bilingual education adopted in sub-Saharan Africa is premised on the assumption that 'when students develop oral and written language aptitudes and skills in African languages, they can re-utilise these in learning other languages as well as to acquire knowledge in the latter' (Alidou & Maman, 2003). Evidence from several countries suggests that well-designed programmes can manage this challenge and that students in the upper grades who started their schooling in the African languages perform on average better than those that started in the 'colonial' language. The experience of Zambia provides strong evidence in this regard.

In 1995 Zambia organised a National Forum on Reading, in response to several studies that found children's performance in reading and writing to be significantly below desired levels. Among other things, the Forum recommended literacy for children in African languages while maintaining the English language component of the basic education curriculum. The Primary Reading Programme (PRP) resulted from the conclusions of this forum. The programme's main objective was to facilitate learning how to read and write. Therefore, the PRP teaches in the first year reading and writing of a Zambian language associated with the teaching of oral English. In the second year, students pursue education in the Zambian language, while oral and written English is taught based on what was learned in first year. From year three to year seven, the teaching of reading and writing of the Zambian language and English is consolidated. Teachers and pupils may express themselves in English or in one of the Zambian languages taught, to improve communication.

Textbooks and teachers' guides have prepared. Teachers were trained to teach the two chosen languages – the Zambian language and English. The content of the training is included in a manual, the *New Breakthrough to Literacy Training Manual*.

Launched in 1998 as a pilot project in two districts, involving 25 schools, 50 teachers and 2000 pupils, the PRP rapidly developed, and since the school year 2002-03 has covered all 4271 primary schools in Zambia. This rapid expansion is due to the excellent results recorded in terms of positive effects on learning. In the first year, an improvement of 780% was recorded for the test in Zambian languages in 2000 compared with the data from 1999. In the second year, a 575% improvement was recorded in the English language test. Finally, from year three to year five, the improvement in reading results varied between 165% and 484%. Overall, children read at the desired level in Zambian languages and are a year behind in English, whereas the previous data showed they were at least two years behind in both languages. These encouraging results have contributed to reinforcing the role of literacy, particularly in the first two years (Sampa, 2003).

As many African countries are highly multilingual, a critical aspect of language policy is language selection. This can be a highly sensitive issue, with socio-political implications. To develop a curriculum in a language presupposes that the latter has a written code and the capacity to convey key ideas from the collective knowledge base of humanity. For some, if not most African languages, this entails substantial background work, before writing curricula, launching textbook development, production and distribution, and initiating teacher development. The number of languages has implications for costs of textbook development and production, and these can be high if mass production is precluded by the size of the target population. A multi-country strategy may be a wise option in this respect, for languages that are spoken in more than one country, even when allowing for variation.[5]

Assessments of Student Learning are Spreading

Effective management of quality improvement in a system that is increasingly decentralised, involves multiple providers to deliver a programme adapted to a wide range of local conditions, and relies on multiple sources of financing cannot be done without reliable information to guide resource allocation and action. Assessments of student learning and statistics on key system performance indicators such as coverage, internal efficiency, teacher deployment and material input availability are the essential management information instruments in such a system. Information on student learning can come from (i) public examinations; (ii) national assessments; (iii) international assessments; and (iv) classroom assessment. Calls for reform of examinations are ubiquitous.

In the 1970s, steps were taken to reform examinations at the end of primary school in Kenya. The content of the examinations was changed to:

- include fewer items that measured the memorisation of factual information, and more that measured higher order skills (comprehension, application); and
- focus on the measurement of skills that could be applied in a wide range of contexts, in and out of school.

The changes were designed to affect how teachers prepared students for the examinations and, in particular, to encourage the teaching and acquisition of competencies that would be useful to the majority of pupils who would leave school after the examinations. Two types of information were provided to support these changes:

- incentive information, comprising the publication of a district and school order merit list based on performance on the examination (league tables);
- guidance information summarised in a newsletter based on an analysis of the performance of students nationally on individual questions, and suggestions for teaching topics and skills that students had problems with.

While the initial impact of the reforms was to widen achievement differences between districts, this trend was reversed after the system had been in operation for four years: nearly all districts in which performance had been relatively poor showed striking gains relative to performance in other districts.

National assessment activity spread through Africa during the 1990s. SAQMEC, PASEC and UNESCO's Monitoring Learning Assessment (MLA) have been highly instrumental in building national assessment capacity in more than 20 countries. The information obtained in a national assessment of strengths and weaknesses in the knowledge and skills students have acquired, and about how achievement is distributed, e.g. by gender and location, can play an important role in informing policy and decision making. Yet, information from assessments often remains within the research community and has not often contributed to the design and implementation of quality improvement strategies. International assessments provide comparative data on achievement in several countries. Few African countries have participated, so far. However, some of the national assessments that have been carried out allow international comparisons. These can provide important opportunities for learning from countries facing comparable constraints and challenges.

Although *classroom assessment* has attracted the least attention in proposals to use assessment to improve the quality of education, it would seem to have the greatest potential to enhance students' achievements. However, teachers' assessments are often of poor quality and do little to foster the development of higher-order and problem-solving competencies in students. Unfortunately, improving teachers' assessment practices is more difficult than improving or developing other forms of assessment.

The African experience to date suggests that assessment information *can* improve policy and the management of resources in education and can shape teachers' instructional practice, but that success is not assured. If assessment procedures are to contribute to the improvement of student learning, at least two conditions must be met. First, assessment policy should be integrated into a broader range of comprehensive and coordinated improvement measures, which assessment reforms are designed to reinforce. And secondly, since the success of educational reforms ultimately depends on their successful implementation in classrooms, resources should be provided to ensure that reform policy is understood, and acted on, in schools.

Teacher Development Practices are Changing

The classroom is where inputs are transformed into learning. Without a competent teacher no curriculum can be implemented effectively. In sub-Saharan Africa, improving teaching practice will require changes in the traditional rote learning methods that still dominate the vast majority of classrooms. Efforts to shift instructional practice towards open-ended approaches, such as child-centred, activity-oriented teaching, have been difficult to implement throughout the world. Given the reality of the African classroom with often very large student numbers or multi-grading, a shift towards instructional methods that are more direct and explicitly focused on learning appears as a more realistic starting point. Promising instructional methods for these situations do exist – they include the use of highly structured self-learning materials accompanied by explicit teaching of new content, as in Escuela Nueva (Colombia) and BRAC (Bangladesh).

Whatever instructional practices are adopted as desirable has implications for how teachers are prepared, at both the pre-service and in-service levels. In this respect, very significant changes are taking place in the way teachers are trained, hired, and remunerated. Some countries are recruiting teachers with more general education, shorter pre-service preparation, and more class room-based teaching practice experience (for instance, in Guinea). But in many others new teachers are hired as contract teachers, often by district authorities or communities, most with limited or no pre-service preparation. This places new demands on in-service training systems, which now must respond to the needs of an increasingly diverse teaching force. Uganda and Guinea have tackled this challenge with decentralised programmes aiming at continuous improvement of teaching practice instead of the traditional, centrally directed, occasional in-service events.

From 1992 until 1998, Guinea provided its prospective primary teachers with a three-year programme that was principally focused on content knowledge and provided only limited instruction in pedagogical knowledge and educational psychology. Student teaching was carried out in a demonstration school attached to each teacher training college. The student teachers/normal school teacher ratio was as low as 10:1 on average, which resulted in high unit costs and low outputs in terms of trained teachers. Faced with a projected shortage of 2000 teachers for the 1998-99 school year, Guinea decided to implement a reform in its teacher training programme that was designed to provide the country with 6000 contract teachers in three years and at lower unit costs while preserving quality (Diané et al, 2003).

The minimum entry level was set at grade 11. The first year of the programme consists of coursework at the teacher training college (focused on the teaching of the basic subjects such as French, mathematics, science and technology, and humanities, as well as on educational psychology and learning assessment). The year of coursework is interspersed with periods of student teaching in specially selected ordinary schools. Courses at the teacher training college are taught by the normal school teachers and periods of student teaching are supervised by pedagogical advisors in collaboration with the host/mentor teacher and school head. The second year is a school-year-long student teaching experience where the prospective teacher assumes full responsibility for a classroom. During this year, he or she still receives support from a pedagogical advisor as well as a mentor teacher. Several student teachers are placed in a given school so that they can support each other as well as engage in peer socialisation.

The quantitative objective was met beyond expectations as the programme delivered 7612 new teachers (37% of whom are women) by June 2003. Put differently, the programme delivered 1522 new teachers per year, compared with less than 200 previously. The unit cost is estimated to be 1,484,288 Guinean Francs, or approximately US$677. Beyond these figures, the graduates of the programme are reported to perform as well or sometimes even better than graduates of previous programmes. An evaluation conducted in 2002 by PASEC measured teacher effectiveness by the student scores on two written tests (a French test and a mathematics test) administered to a national sample of 2880 grade 2 and grade 5 students at the beginning and end of the school year. The results showed:

- students in grade 5 taught by the graduates of the new programme scored higher than students taught by graduates of former teacher education programmes;
- students in grade 2 taught by FIMG graduates scored lower than students taught by graduates of the previous teacher training college model, although the scores are very close;
- overall, students taught by FIMG graduates performed better than students taught by non-FIMG graduates.
- students taught by the second FIMG cohort scored higher than students taught not only by the first FIMG cohort but also by graduates of the previous programmes, which suggests that the new programme is gaining in effectiveness.

Reforms in in-service training programmes are often implemented in conjunction with reforms in pre-service programmes. The Teacher Development Management System (TDMS) is a primary teacher training delivery mechanism in Uganda (Eilor et al, 2003) centred on a reformed Primary Teachers' Training College called a Core Primary Teachers' College (Core-PTC). In terms of content, it is important to note that (i) the teacher education curriculum was revised to align it with the primary school study programmes and (ii) pre-service and in-service teacher education were integrated for uniformity and effectiveness. A total of 23 Core-PTCs were established, and each of them has two departments, namely, the Outreach department and the traditional pre-service department. The pre-service department runs the Primary Teacher Education (PTE) two-year residential course for prospective teachers recruited at O level and above, and a three-year, on-the-job training course intended to upgrade untrained and under-trained teachers. The pre-service course leads to the award of a PTE Grade III Certificate, a minimum requirement for teaching in primary schools in Uganda. The Outreach department employs a combination of distance education and short residential face-to-face sessions during the holidays to deliver in-service training and professional support for all serving teachers, head teachers, outreach tutors, education managers (particularly district inspectors of schools), school management committees, PTAs, and community mobilisers. Head teachers undergo a special one-year certificate course in basic management skills.

The outreach programmes are implemented through a network of coordinating centres, each of which coordinates a cluster of an average of 22 outreach schools. One school in each cluster is selected to serve as a coordinating centre school. The coordinating centre tutors are provided with motorcycles and/or bicycles to facilitate their mobility. They are expected to visit each outreach school for at least half a day each month. They also relate with their local communities through coordinating centre committee meetings and are in regular contact with their respective district education offices. The implementation of the Primary Education Reform Programme, especially the TDMS, is reported to have boosted teachers' morale, promoted equity in the distribution of qualified teachers across the country, and revitalised the primary teaching profession in Uganda by:

- restoring the status and integrity of teachers through training, continuous professional support, targeted incentives and better management of the teacher payroll;
- increasing the output and supply of qualified teachers (the percentage of unqualified teachers has decreased by half from about 50% in 1993 to 25% currently);
- ensuring a fairly equitable distribution of primary teachers across the country through implementation of the school staff ceiling formula – a system that has provided a framework for systematic staffing of primary schools and that has been used to determine the annual recurrent

budget for the primary teachers' wage bill and to detect 'ghost teachers';
- improving the welfare of teachers by upgrading the salaries of qualified teachers from Ug. Shs. 11,000/ in 1992/93 to Ug. Shs. 105,000/ presently, representing a tenfold increase in nominal terms over a period of 10 years; and,
- providing incentives for untrained and under-trained teachers to upgrade to Grade III Certificate.

Several lessons can be drawn from these and other experiences in the region:

(1) the curriculum and pedagogy of teacher education need to be informed by as well as inform curriculum and pedagogy in schools;
(2) the need to focus the pre-service training of prospective teachers with strong content knowledge and focus their preparation on the central tasks of teaching;
(3) guided practice in the field is critical at the pre-service phase of the learning-to-teach continuum;
(4) the classroom and the school are the best place for making progress toward improving teaching practice; and
(5) practising teachers learn effectively from each other, in the framework of school-based learning communities. At the same time external support is important to sustain the improvement process.

Some, if not all, of these messages are already reflected in teacher education policy and practice in several sub-Saharan Africa countries. The evidence reviewed clearly indicates that there are efforts to reform pre-service teacher education and to systematise continuous professional development for practising teachers in many countries. With respect to pre-service teacher education, the general tendency is towards shortening the length of training and making more space for the practical aspects through field experiences. As regards continuous professional development, there is a clear tendency to bring training closer to the teachers' workplace, and to involve them in decisions regarding the content and organisation of such training. However, there remain, unsurprisingly, formidable challenges and weaknesses of various kinds. These include, among others:

- limited attention to multi-grade teaching and teaching large classes: multi-grading is a promising strategy that needs more attention if quality UPE is to be achieved by 2015. It is a practice that can serve both large and 'normal' classes. Paying more attention to it should begin at the pre-service level.
- The absence of incentives for teachers in remote rural or difficult areas; given that attaining UPE will depend in large part on boosting enrolment in hard to reach areas, special attention needs to be accorded to teachers who are appointed to serve in those areas. This raises issues of both incentives and personnel management.

- Career planning for contract teachers: having a career plan stands as a critical motivational factor for contract teachers; as a matter of fact, in a context of relatively low salaries, it can be an effective strategy for making teaching an attractive career, sustaining the enthusiasm of prospective teachers, and retaining them in teaching upon graduating from their pre-service programme.

New Forms of Partnerships are Emerging

Following the 1990 Jomtien conference, bilateral and multilateral aid agencies increased their efforts to support basic education programmes and policy reform. But the dominant emphasis on the expansion of access, the relative neglect of the need to improve learning achievement, the pursuit of over-ambitious performance targets, the underestimation of capacity constraints, the absence of a sustainable financial framework and the fragmentation of external support often combined to thwart the anticipated outcomes, especially as regards quality improvement.

In response, a Sector-Wide Approach (SWAp) is emerging as a process that produces a comprehensive sector development programme providing coherence to the support of international funding agencies and increasingly also NGOs, and government funding priorities. Within this framework all significant funding for the sector supports a single sector policy and expenditure programme, linked to the government's budgeting process, under government leadership, adopting common approaches across the sector, and progressing towards reliance on government procedures to disburse and account for all funds. Of the 48 countries in sub-Saharan Africa, about 15 are currently active participants in SWAps. These countries have set national priorities for quality improvements in the context of the equitable distribution of sector funds. They are also taking the lead in partnerships with international agencies based on broadly accepted targets and strategies.

SWAps are helping to overcome the limitations of the project approach. The initial results are promising, although definitive outcomes remain uncertain. The analytical underpinnings of sector reforms have been strengthened, participation and consultation is becoming a part of the policy development process, and the link between policy and implementation has been strengthened. SWAPs have created an environment that allows explicit consideration of intra- and inter-sectoral trade-offs, channelling resources directly to schools (e.g. Tanzania, Uganda, Kenya and Guinea) and scaling-up of pilot programmes (Zambia, Guinea and Mali). Finally, as governments aim to reach people in remote areas, NGOs are being considered increasingly as effective operational partners.

The development of a SWAp in Uganda has been a major force in improving the quality of a primary education system that doubled in enrolments during one year. In 1993 Uganda began a series of quality-oriented reforms, including a gradual tenfold increase in teachers' salaries, liberalisation of the textbook market, revisions of the curriculum and examinations, and a teacher-development system. The Teacher Development and Management System provided in-service training to unqualified teachers, professional support to all teachers, and a rationalisation and changes in the pre-service network of teachers' colleges that brought them into synch with the other reforms. The TDMS also strengthened the capacity of district education offices and gave parents and communities an important role in monitoring and supporting schools.

These reforms were still progressing slowly from pilots in two districts when, in 1997, President Museveni effectively abolished school fees, resulting in an explosive growth in enrolment, from 2.6 million in 1993 to 5.2 million in 1997 (climbing to 7.2 million in 2003). The challenge facing the Government – and landing directly on the shoulders of the Ministry of Education and Sports – was to catch up in quality reforms with the huge leap in enrolments. Grade 1 and 2 classrooms holding 90 or 100 students were not uncommon; teachers were overwhelmed, and textbooks were in short supply. In addition, the HIV/AIDS scourge was peaking in Uganda, decimating the ranks of teachers and other ministry staff.

The international community responded to the crisis with increased funding. The US Agency for International Development and the World Bank, which had supported the quality reforms from 1993 on, were joined by British, Irish, Dutch, and other aid agencies. Perhaps more important than their funding pledges was the agreement among donors and lenders to collaborate in a SWAp to support the new Education Sector Investment Program (ESIP). The SWAp benefited from effective leadership within the Ministry, which, by 1998, was convening biannual sector programme reviews attended by representatives of all stakeholders, including NGOs. A key component of the SWAp was the active engagement of the ministries of finance and public service, which enabled participants in the process to develop a three-year annual rolling Medium Term Expenditure Framework (METF) that meshed with the Ministry of Finance's larger budget framework, and to recruit and pay many more teachers within the civil service structure. The ESIP and the MTEF thus provided everyone with a clear picture of priorities and trade-offs and paved the way for consensus on targets and a means for monitoring progress.

Had Uganda not instigated a SWAp, the TDMS might have been crushed by enrolment numbers overwhelming its still-fragile structure, and a bombardment of uncoordinated donor projects might have paralysed the Ministry. Instead, the Ministry took the lead in coordinating all players, prioritising problems and goals, and allocating resources. Since improvements in the country's macroeconomic situation and available funds, increases in foreign grants and loans, and proportionally larger allocations to primary education have helped the Government raise per-pupil expenditures from US$2.86 in 1993 to US$19.00 in 2001. Though quality 'inputs' are still unacceptably low, with pupil teacher ratios at 54:1 and textbooks at 5:1 in lower primary, the SWAp process provides assurance that the partnership of government and international agencies will continue to address problems collaboratively and within a sector-wide framework.

In many countries in the region the cooperation and coordination between countries and external partners has greatly improved. But important challenges remain. First, governments will need to extend the partnership beyond the major financing agencies and ensure opportunities for meaningful participation throughout the processes of programme design, review and implementation for all national and international stakeholders. Second, sector development programmes will need to make explicit provision to include mechanisms to support innovations and experimentation. Finally, financing arrangements will need to be flexible so that different legal and institutional constraints of major financial partners can be accommodated. SWAps vary considerably in the way they address these and other challenges. In fact, one of the strengths of the approach is the flexibility to take account in different ways of the ambitions and constraints of the partners.

The Challenges Ahead

The experiences reported above are encouraging and can help African policy analysts, planners and decision makers to tackle the challenge of quality improvement. But at the same time the study found important challenges that remain to be addressed. These are discussed below.

Reducing Disparities in the Opportunity to Learn

With the diverse patterns of living, gender imbalances and ranges of groups in difficult circumstances found in Africa, diverse patterns of educational provision will need to be the norm. Small rural and migratory communities need different arrangements from urban or larger rural groupings. Diversity, flexibility and openness to new ways of teaching must be features of an education system that aims to reach all children. This is not an argument for alternatives *to* formal education but instead for alternatives *within* the formal education system. It means that each government – doubtless in cooperation with appropriate partners – will need to develop and support a range of programmes to fit the needs of different communities and groups of learners.

This kind of diversity requires a 'paradigm shift' in thinking about educational provision. The current dominant paradigm is *'getting learners to come to school or class'*. The complementary paradigm is *'getting education to reach the learners'*. That would entail looking at where the learners actually are, negotiating with them or their families what they would accept as worthwhile education, and examining how best to arrange it within the possibilities of the learners' environment, means and commitments. This second paradigm already operates in adult education – REFLECT in

Burkina Faso is an example. It also operates here and there for children, for example, in the 'Save the Children' work in Mali, and in Nigeria's New Education Policy. Such a shift in approach would be likely to foster an openness to what has been called 'mutual learning' or 'non-formalising the formal while formalising the non-formal'.

It must be a matter of concern that few countries have a systematic approach to providing an equitable opportunity to learn to poor and rural children, in particular the girls, thus thwarting progress towards the EFA goals. Alternative learning systems remain marginalised, underfunded and often not equivalent in outcomes. The nomadic education in Nigeria programme may be an exception.

In 1989, some 3 million children of school age in Nigeria's nomadic and migratory fishing communities had no schools or education programmes that addressed their particular conditions. They had either to attend the traditional static schools or go without. Virtually all went without. In that year the authorities launched an initiative especially adapted for their way of life. Between 1989 and 2002, enrolments climbed by a factor of 12, from 18,831 to 229,944 pupils. Further, the gender parity ratio had improved from 0.54 to 0.85.

Relatively disappointing qualitative outcomes in the early years led in 1992 to several subsidiary initiatives. The first, 'Community Sensitization and Empowerment' (CSE), aimed to gain the active support of parents and communities. It deployed a range of media, including literacy classes, extension services and cooperative societies for the adults. The second thrust, 'Pedagogical Renewal and Teacher Development', aimed to orient mainstream teachers to the culture and values of the pastoral and fisher communities and to introduce more effective teaching methods and materials. Perhaps most important, it worked to recruit, train and retain teachers from the pastoral and fishing communities themselves. Alongside, 700 mobile collapsible classrooms were imported to move with the pastoral communities, while 25 motorised boat schools were introduced to follow and fetch the children of the migrant fisher communities. New incentives for the teachers comprised better housing, motorcycles and bicycles. The outcome was that the transition rate from primary to secondary school rose from 45% of 1274 pupils in 1992 (534 pupils) to 54.6% of 9120 pupils in 2002 (4976 pupils), an absolute increase of more than nine times.

The total development cost over the period 1990-2003 amounted to US$2,217,743, while the recurrent costs amounted to $4,156,607 or approximately $1.06 per pupil. The Federal Government of Nigeria bore all the recurrent costs and 96.3% of the overall development costs: these were apportioned 49% to curriculum and materials development, 45% to buildings and furniture and 6% to teacher development. The United Kingdom Department for International Development assisted with 27% of the teacher development costs.

It will clearly not be possible to reach all children in sub-Saharan Africa with traditional education delivery systems and programmes, let alone provide them with instruction that leads to equivalent opportunity to learn. A major challenge for government will be to form partnerships with NGOs and communities to develop alternative strategies that respond to local demand, take account of the local context and the economic constraints but at the same time deliver an education service that is of equivalent quality and allows students to pursue their education if they so wish.

Ensuring the Availability of Essential Inputs

Few schools have the inputs necessary for effective instruction, thus limiting the scope for improvements in classroom processes. In many instances attempts to improve the quality of education falter in the absence of even the most basic instructional materials and supplies. Several countries have defined the instructional materials that should be available. Table I provides an example of Kenya. The annual cost of the package is estimated at $10 per student per year. In Kenya schools are being provided with the funds necessary to purchase these materials as required. In many other countries most instructional materials are centrally procured, although increasingly schools have a choice between approved textbooks.

Basic pack o f school stationery	1 per student per year
Chalk	5 boxes per classroom per year
Teachers' preparation book	1 per teacher (to last for 4 years)
Enrolment and attendance registers	1 per class per year
6 core textbooks	1 textbook per 3 students for each subject and standard
8 core teachers' guides	1 per subject per grade for each teacher
Supplementary reading materials in English	1 reading book for each enrolled student
Supplementary reading books in Kiswahili	1readingbook for each enrolled student
Science kit for P1-P4	1 per school

Table I. Kenya – essential instructional materials (Primary 1-4).

In the mid-1980s, and as part of a broad sector reform programme, the Ministry of National Education of Benin initiated a participatory process that led to the definition and adoption of a set of 50 quality norms. A nationwide assessment of the conditions of teaching and learning using these norms as indicators revealed that on average schools were below one-third of the desired minimal level. As a result 10 priority norms were identified and used as a tool for designing three-year intervention and investment plans in priority zones to increase or maintain school characteristics at minimal level. This included the printing and provision of one French and one mathematics textbook for two pupils, one workbook per pupil, and 10,000 teachers' guides per subject for all subjects. The implementation of these plans is reported to have improved indicators such as gross enrolment ratio (GER) (68.84% to 88.49%), gender parity (0.61 to 0.69), grade repetition (25.11% to 19.84%), retention (41.8% to 49.2%), and completion (34.3% to 36.1%) between 1996 and 2001. However, these results are lower than expected. Explanatory factors include a 35.7% increase in the number of schools during the period, teacher shortage, a dysfunctional teacher development network, the presence of 40% unqualified teachers in the teaching force, and a lack of textbooks and limited use of those made available.

Improving Instructional Practice

Instructional practice in African classrooms often is poor. Assumptions that all teachers teach in a coherent and organised way (e.g. focusing on the instructional targets of the curriculum) and are capable of change, and that conditions in classrooms allow teachers to teach in a way that will meet the objectives of reform, may be based on an unrealistic perception of classrooms. How is one to expect adaptation in classrooms, Carron & Châu (1996) ask, in which 'one finds a chaotic reality: teachers and pupils are often absent, the teacher does not have the competence required to teach well, he/she does not follow a precise work plan, merely reads from the textbooks, does not use the blackboard' (p. 202). Lack of teacher competence has been observed by other commentators. Many teachers may have a poor command of the language that is the medium of instruction and poor knowledge of subject matter (especially science and agriculture). Close to half of South African mathematics teachers do not possess a formal qualification in mathematics. Pilot projects aiming to change teaching methods and classroom management practices have often reported positive results. But few – if any – have resulted in improvements in instruction beyond the pilot schools. There is a case for rethinking the traditional model. There are many successful small-scale experimental programmes that have tried to do this but they rarely move beyond the pilot stage.

Maybe there is a case to rethink the design requirements of pilot projects. Many pilot projects try to introduce teaching methods that deviate considerably from existing practice and anticipate teacher skills and instructional materials that are not likely to be available in many schools. Would it not be preferable to design innovations of a limited scope that do not deviate too far from existing practice, that can be adapted and applied by a large number of teachers without too much difficulty and support implementation over time of a series of those innovations? Gradually increasing the capacity of schools to change, and conceptualising improvement as a learning process for all involved is a strategy that may be more effective than the elusive search for the silver bullet of immediate change and improvement.

Developing Sustainable Early Childhood Programmes

The development of activities for very young children, and particularly pre-school education for children in the 4-5 year-old category, for the benefit of the most vulnerable populations, is the first objective covered in the Dakar Forum declaration on Education for All. There are a number of studies (for example Hyde & Kabiru, 2003) that highlight the benefits for the operation and quality of primary education (improved learning, reduced frequency of repetition and improved retention by students in the course of their primary education). Jaramillo & Mingat (2003) estimated that 50% coverage for two years of pre-school in a typical African country could reduce the frequency of grade repetition from 20 to 14% and increase the retention rate by 65-80%. However, pre-school education, as it is currently organised, is expensive: the estimated unit cost for traditional pre-school education, on average in African countries, is 40% higher than that of primary education. Public financing within the scope of a sector-based educational policy will therefore be difficult to justify economically and unlikely to be financially feasible in most sub-Saharan Africa countries.

On the other hand, it is possible to design a community-based form of organisation to develop such activities for young children, Comparative evaluations of the effects of formal and community-based pre-schooling conducted in Cape Verde and in Guinea showed that the benefits for children in terms of preparation for primary school were comparable (and even somewhat better for the community formula), but that the public costs for the community formula were significantly lower than those for traditional pre-schools. There clearly is an urgent need to further test, monitor and evaluate these models.

Implementing More Comprehensive Capacity Building Strategies

Evidence of weak capacity is abundant. Few countries are able to deliver an education service of acceptable quality to all children. Moreover, the fact that international agencies still play a critical role in setting the education agenda in many countries of the region indicates that ministries of education have not developed the capacity to take ownership of their policies and programmes. Ministries struggle to strengthen capacity, while the task becomes increasingly difficult as education systems become more extensive and complex.

As the circle of stakeholders involved in education has enlarged, capacity building is widely recognised as a critical priority. But not much progress has been made addressing it. Capacity building [6] has often been equated with off-site, one-shot training, the benefits of which are difficult to sustain in work environments that run counter to what trainees learn. Or it has been limited to introducing new functions, such as management information systems and performance monitoring systems. Most often these interventions have a narrow focus on skill development of analysts, planners, managers and policy makers. Or they are limited to introducing new functions, such as management information systems and performance monitoring systems.

International assistance packages thus often miss the mark. Management functions and structures are not adequately analysed. When a function falters, foreign technical assistants are brought in to keep things running, without the assurance that these foreigners will take the time to leave behind capable staff, people with the resources they need to do their job. Clearly, a broader perspective, focusing on improvement of *existing as well as new functions of the system* as well on the analysis of processes – the rules of the game – and incentives, is required.

Conclusions: towards a culture for quality improvement

The experiences documented in the country case studies commissioned by ADEA and the literature reviewed for this analysis suggest a framework for action on quality improvement, There are experiences that provide warnings and lessons about the obstacles to avoid. But also, and perhaps most importantly, there are promising experiences that offer lessons on the way forward. These experiences are summarised here in terms of a strategy for quality improvement that comprises at least seven components, which constitute the pillars of sustainable quality improvement:

- *create the opportunity to learn*: ensuring that essential inputs and supplies are in place and encouraging home support and school readiness;
- *improve instructional practice*: implementing a relevant curriculum, developing competent teachers, helping head teachers to become instructional leaders and paying special attention to effective instruction in the early years;
- *manage the challenge of equity*: reaching out to learners with an array of delivery mechanisms, ensuring equitable opportunities to learn for poor children, especially those in rural areas, addressing the gender challenge and recognising diversity and flexibility in design and provision as essential;
- *increase school autonomy and flexibility*: de-concentrating authority to regional and district offices, moving towards school-based management, supporting head teachers as transformational leaders, but recognising monitoring, supervision and support as an essential of school improvement;
- *nurture community support*: recognising that quality emerges from the interaction of parents, communities and schools, encouraging a broad community involvement and fostering communities as partners in school development;
- *ensure a realistic financial framework*, allocating US$10-15 per child/per year for non-salary expenditures, investing in those inputs that are known to have a strong positive impact on learning achievement,

carefully managing the salary bill, reducing the degree of random variation in the allocation of per student resources between schools, tapping community contributions and ensuring that no child is excluded from school for financial reasons.

Obviously the specific context and challenges in a country will determine the way the priority of these different elements of strategy combine into a coherent and effective programme of quality improvement.

Notes

[1] This chapter draws extensively on a study of the Association for the Development of Education in Africa for its December 2003 biennial meeting in Grand Baie, Mauritius. The discussion draft of the paper and the background studies that were presented and discussed at that meeting can be found on http://www.adeanet.org/biennial2003/papers/Discussion_ENG.pdf. A book length report on this work was published by ADEA in 2006.

[2] The difference between the gross and net enrolment reflects the fact that the net enrolment includes only children of the official school age.

[3] See the research carried out by UNICEF (Delamonica et al, 2001); UNESCO (Brossard & Gacougnolle, 2000) and World Bank (Mingat, 2002) to estimate the resources the countries will need to achieve UPE.

[4] In Madagascar, the 'dina' is an oral or written agreement made between community members (fokonolona) and is accepted by all the contracting parties as having the force of law, with sanctions (social or financial) for any breach.

[5] For instance, just keeping the same layout and illustrations generates significant cost savings.

[6] The ideas in this section draw very heavily on a paper prepared by Jeanne Moulton (2003).

References

Alidou, H. & Maman, M.G. (2003) Évaluation et enseignements des expériences d'utilisation des langues africaines comme langue d'enseignement. Background paper prepared for *The Challenge of Learning: improving the quality of education in sub-Saharan Africa*. Paris: Association for the Development of Education in Africa.

Barro, Robert J. & Jong-Wha Lee (2000) International Data on Educational Attainment Updates and Implications. NBER Working Paper 7911. Cambridge, MA: National Bureau of Economic Research.

Bennell, P. (2003) The Impact of the AIDS Epidemic on Schooling in Sub-Saharan Africa. Background paper prepared for *The Challenge of Learning: improving the quality of education in sub-Saharan Africa*. Paris: Association for the Development of Education in Africa.

41

Brossard, Mathieu & Gacougnolle, Luc Charles (2000) *Financing Primary Education For All: yesterday, today and tomorrow.* Paris: UNESCO.

Carnine, D. (1998) *The Metamorphosis of Education into a Mature Profession.* Sixth Annual Meeting, Park City, Utah. http://www.edexcellence.net/library/carnine.html

Carron, G. & Châu, T.N. (1996) *The Quality of Primary Schools in Different Development Contexts.* Paris: UNESCO/International Institute for Educational Planning.

Chapman, D.W & Adams, D. (2002). *The Quality of Education: dimensions and strategies.* Manila: Asian Development Bank.

Delamonica, Enrique, Mehrotra, Santosh & Vandemoortele, Jan (2001) *Is Education for All Affordable? Estimating the global minimum cost of education for all.* Florence: UNICEF.

Diané, B., Bah Elhadj, A.M, Fofana, M., et al (2003) La réforme de la formation initiale des maîtres en Guinée (FIMG): Étude-bilan de la mise en œuvre. Case study prepared for *The Challenge of Learning: improving the quality of education in sub-Saharan Africa.* Paris: Association for the Development of Education in Africa.

Eilor, J., Okurut, H.E, Martin, J., et al (2003) Impact of Primary Education Reform Programme (PERP) on the Quality of Basic Education in Uganda. Case study prepared for *The Challenge of Learning: improving the quality of education in sub-Saharan Africa.* Paris: Association for the Development of Education in Africa.

Hanson, R.A. & Farrell, D. (1995) The Long-Term Effects on High School Seniors of Learning to Read in Kindergarten, *Reading Research Quarterly*, 30(4), 908-933. http://dx.doi.org/10.2307/748204

Hyde, K.A.L. & Kabiru, M.N. (2003) Early Childhood Development as an Important Strategy to Improve Learning Outcomes. Background paper prepared for *The Challenge of Learning: improving the quality of education in sub-Saharan Africa.* Paris: Working Group on Early Childhood Development, Association for the Development of Education in Africa.

Jaramillo, A. & Mingat, A. (2003) *Early Childhood Care and Education in Sub-Saharan Africa: what would it take to meet the Millennium Development Goals?* Washington, DC: The World Bank.

Juel, C. (1991) *Beginning Reading. Handbook of Reading Research,* vol. 2, chapter 27. Harlow: Longman.

Mingat, Alain, Rakotomalala, Ramahatra & Tan, Jee-Peng (2002) *Financing Education for All by 2015: simulations for 33 African countries.* Africa Region Human Development Working Paper series no. 26. Washington, DC: The World Bank.

Mingat, A. (2004) *Combien d'années de scolarisation pour assurer la rétention de l'alphabétisation dans les pays d'Afrique sub-saharienne.* Washington, DC: The World Bank.

Moulton, J (2003) Capacity Building for the Improvement of the Quality of Basic Education in Africa. Background paper prepared for *The Challenge of Learning: improving the quality of education in sub-Saharan Africa.* Paris: Association for the Development of Education in Africa.

National Reading Panel (2000) *National Reading Panel Report*.
http://www.nationalreadingpanel.org

Niane, B. (2003) Décentralisation et diversification des systèmes: impliquer et responsabiliser pour une 'citoyenneté scolaire'. Background paper prepared for *The Challenge of Learning: improving the quality of education in sub-Saharan Africa*. Paris: Association for the Development of Education in Africa.

Sampa, F. (2003) Primary Reading Programme: improving access and quality in basic schools in Zambia. Case study prepared for *The Challenge of Learning: improving the quality of education in sub-Saharan Africa*. Paris: Association for the Development of Education in Africa.

United Nations Development Program (UNDP) (2002) *Human Development Report. Deepening Democracy in a Fragmented World*. New York: Oxford University Press.

United Nations Development Program (UNDP) (2003) *Human Development Report*. New York: UNDP.

United Nations Educational, Scientific and Cultural Organisation (UNESCO) (2002) *Education for All Global Monitoring Report. Is the World on Track?* Paris: UNESCO.

Watt, P. (2001) *Community Support for Basic Education in Sub-Saharan Africa*. Africa Region Human Development Working Paper Series. Washington, DC: The World Bank.

CHAPTER 2

Improving the Quality of Education in Nigeria: a comparative evaluation of recent policy imperatives

DAVID JOHNSON

Introduction

In the last few years, the Federal Government of Nigeria has launched a number of far-reaching policy imperatives aimed at improving the provision and quality of education. Education is seen by the Government as a central plank in a strategy for reducing poverty and accelerating economic growth. Indeed, Nigeria's own unique Poverty Reduction Strategic Paper (PRSP), the National Economic Empowerment and Development Strategy (NEEDS), expresses this broad commitment as follows:

> The goals of wealth creation, employment generation, poverty reduction, and value reorientations can be effectively pursued, attained, and sustained only through an efficient, relevant and functional education system. Education is critical to meeting the goals set by NEEDS. (Government of Nigeria, 2003)

But what is the starting point for turning this vision into reality? Although Nigeria has made some progress in the last 10 years in its efforts to achieve the goal of 'Education for All', major challenges remain. A report prepared by representatives of the seven international development partners (IDPs) working in the education sector in Nigeria (Zebroff et al, 2006) highlights the progress made towards policy reform and improvements in the education system during the last seven years.

Nigeria launched a Universal Basic Education (UBE) programme in 1989, demonstrating a political will to reform a poorly performing education system. The UBE Bill was passed into law by the National Assembly in May 2004, allowing for the disbursement of finances to all states.

A National Policy on Education was adopted in 2004, and recently, the Federal Ministry of Education has launched a participatory process for the development of a ten-year education sector plan. This is accompanied by an improved capacity for planning through the establishment of a National EFA Forum and State EFA Forums in each state. These mechanisms ensure a more open approach to educational policy and planning, including partnerships with civil society and non-governmental organisations (NGOs).

Importantly, a Child Rights Bill was passed by the National Assembly in June 2003, giving impetus to the campaign for the right of every child to quality basic education. The Child Rights Law includes, among others, the right of every child to free compulsory and universal basic education and compels the Government of Nigeria to fund such activities.

However, enrolment, completion and progression rates at all levels of education are low. A school census, carried out in March 2005, shows an increase in the number of students attending public primary schools (a total of 20.6 million children attending about 50,700 public primary schools) but it is a concern that of an estimated 23 million 'out-of-school' children in 112 countries, over 8 million of these, the highest reported number, live in Nigeria (United Nations Educational, Scientific and Cultural Organisation [UNESCO], 2007).

The educational system itself is poorly planned, resourced and managed, these functions undermined by weak systems of data collection, analysis and dissemination. Governance and management structures are 'over-bureaucratic' and too centralised, and lead to duplication and inadequate decision making and monitoring (Federal Ministry of Education [FME], 2006).

There are about 494,000 teachers, of whom only 297,000 are qualified teachers. Although Nigeria also boasts reasonable teacher–pupil ratios, a comparative survey conducted recently by UNESCO Institute for Statistics (UIS, 2005) shows that it needs an annual percentage increase of over 65,000 teachers to reach its universal primary education (UPE) targets. Further, capacity building and staff development for those teachers in the system is far from adequate.

Additionally, there are serious gender and geographical inequities in the education system – females are under-represented in both pupil and teacher numbers, and there is a sharp divide in educational participation between rural and urban areas and between the northern and southern states (UNICEF/UNESCO, 2004; FME, 2006). It is also telling that 33.6% of children in Nigeria are at least two years over age when they start school and that, of these, 44% are from the poorest fifth of households compared with 17% of children from the wealthiest fifth. The most marginalised groups according to a recent survey are children of indigenous and nomadic populations, children in Koranic school and disabled children (World Bank, 2006).

The quality of learning outcomes is poor and the curriculum is not appropriate for the needs of a modern society (United Nations, 2004; World Bank, 2007). A review of educational achievement in grades 4, 5 and 6 shows that in 1996 grade 4 students correctly answered only 25% of English test items, 32% of mathematics test items and 38% of test items in life skills. Seven years later, in 2003, there seemed to be very little improvement in the quality of learning (UNICEF/UNESCO, 2004). In tests of English language, mathematics, primary science and social studies, grade 4 scores range from 25 to 50% across the four subjects, grade 5 scores range from 25 to 39 and grade 6 scores range from 21 to 40 (UNICEF/UNESCO, 2004).

A more recent survey of children's attainments in numeracy in three states (Kano, Kaduna and Kwara) (Johnson et al, 2007) shows that the mean score of a sample of 1829 grade 4 children is 3.1 marks (of a total of 34 marks), and that a sample of 1915 grade 6 children achieved a mean of 2.3 marks (of a total of 33 marks). Reading literacy was also measured in the same survey and it was established that in a sample of 1873 grade 4 children, the mean number of words read accurately from a short, simple story containing 89 words was 19.1. In a sample of 1899 Grade 6 children, the mean correct response to reading comprehension questions was 4.9 out of a possible 29 marks.

The very low level of learning of primary school students is even starker when compared to international data on learning achievements. Verspoor (this volume) reports on a study in which learning achievements in 22 countries in sub-Saharan and North Africa are compared and finds that the learning achievements of students in Nigeria's primary schools were the lowest with national mean scores of 30% compared with 70% (the highest scores, Tunisia) and the median of 50.8 (Mali) (see Figure 1).

It is against this background that the Federal Ministry of Education has declared that 'the state of education in Nigeria is in crisis' (FME, 2006) and, with the support of its international development partners (the World Bank, the Department for International Development [DFIE, UK], the Japan International Cooperation Agency [JICA], USAID, UNESCO, and UNICEF) is spearheading a number of interesting, if in the context of Nigeria, untested, policy imperatives for strengthening the governance and efficiency of the educational system. This chapter discusses three such policy initiatives and assesses their viability in relation to similar policy imperatives in other developing countries. These are: the Community Accountability and Transparency Initiative (CATI), a policy imperative aimed at reducing corruption, and the wastage and leakage of educational funding by making local communities more aware of what funding is available and how it is managed and disbursed; Operation Reach all Primary Schools (ORAPS), a policy imperative which marks an attempt to re-mobilise a moribund school inspection system; and the Public–Private Partnership initiative aimed at securing more private money for the public sector and thereby extending the role of a wider range of stakeholders in shaping key elements of public policy.

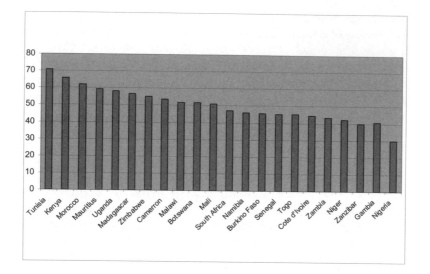

Figure 1. Comparison of learning achievements in 22 countries in sub-Saharan Africa (adapted from Verspoor, 2008 – this volume).

A Comparative Evaluation of Recent Policy Imperatives

The Community Accountability and Transparency Initiative (CATI)

In many parts of Nigeria, there is a strong and long-standing tradition of parental and community involvement in the construction and management of schools (Francis, 1998, cited in Zebroff et al, 2006). But the Federal Ministry of Education has seen that there are substantial opportunities in Nigeria for an increased role for civil society, including that the community takes certain responsibilities for ensuring that educational financing reaches schools. The Community Accountability and Transparency Initiative (CATI) is a policy initiative designed to provide information to the public about the funding available for education and schooling in their communities. The aim is to inform citizens about their entitlements and to encourage civil society groups and individuals to take a more active part in monitoring how money is spent, to get involved in the management and maintenance of schools, to hold officials to account, and to take ownership for raising academic achievement and the quality of education in general.

Recent examples from several developing countries show that public service delivery such as in Education can be drastically improved when citizens are better informed and more active in monitoring frontline services. Even though the neglect of schools is so visible in many communities, as are the frustrations of many parents and teachers, it is often the case that people simply do not know what rights they have as citizens and what demands they can legitimately make. Indeed, parents expect educational officials to take responsibility for their performance (serving the public interest in a fair and efficient manner) and their conduct (obeying the rules and not abusing their power), but traditional approaches to enforcing accountability are not always effective (Sirker, 2006). CATI is seen as a new approach to social accountability in Nigeria and one through which ordinary citizens and civil society organisations can hold public authorities accountable, as (Sirker, 2006) would put it, for their decisions, conduct, performance and actions

The Community Accountability and Transparency Initiative (CATI) is set against the background of the perennial problem of corruption in education in many countries in both the more-developed and less-developed world (Hallak & Poisson, 2007), especially the leakage and wastage of public funds. This problem has prompted studies into public expenditure in well over 35 countries in the developing world (see Table 1). These Public Expenditure Tracking Surveys (PETS) or Quantitative Service Delivery Surveys (QSDS) provide important data about the levels of public funding that reach schools (and other frontline social services). But CATI is not a PETS or a QSDS. It is an example of a campaign that puts the onus on communities to monitor educational finances and builds upon similar policy initiatives to minimise corruption and to stem the leakage of funds in countries such as Uganda, Brazil, India and Peru.

PETS	QSDS
Albania, Cambodia, Cameroon, Chad, Ghana, Honduras, Macedonia, Madagascar, Mozambique, Namibia, Nicaragua, Papua New Guinea, Peru, Rwanda, Senegal, Sierra Leone, Tanzania, Uganda, Yemen, Zambia	Algeria, Benin, Bolivia, Burkina Faso, Chad, Colombia, Ethiopia, Honduras, Laos, Macedonia, Madagascar, Mozambique, Nigeria, Pakistan, Papua New Guinea, Timor-Leste, Uganda, Zambia

Table I. Countries in which social sector Public Expenditure Tracking Surveys have been carried out between 1996 and 2004. Adapted from Winkler (2005).

When a PETS revealed that there was a high degree of financial leakage in Uganda, the central government broadcasted information on the monthly transfers of public funds to districts on the radio and published these figures in newspapers. They also asked primary schools to display on their notice boards and other accessible spaces, information on the inflow of funds to the school. The objective of this campaign was to promote transparency and increase public sector accountability by giving citizens access to information which allowed them to understand and examine the workings of capital grants to primary schools (Reinikka & Svensson, 2004). The Ugandan case is an example of a cost-effective policy that helped to demystify the process by which money was made available to local schools. Because primary schools and district authorities were compelled to post notices on all inflows of funds, schools and parents had access to information they needed to understand and monitor any grants to their schools. The commitment of the Ugandan authorities to transparency and the flow of information to local communities served to empower communities to take action. As a result of the media campaign, primary school enrolment rose from 3.6 million to 6.9 million students between 1996 and 2001 and the share of funds reaching schools increased from 20% in 1995 to 80% in 2001.

In Tanzania, PETS in 1999 and 2001 showed that leakage of funds in education was about 57%. The problem of ghost teachers and delays in pay were identified as the main causes. The response of the Tanzanian Government was similar to that of the Government of Uganda. The treasury initiated regular dissemination of local government budgets to members of parliament and regular publication of budget allocations in both Swahili and English language newspapers. This, however, did not produce as strong a catalytic effect as it did in Uganda.

In Ghana a PETS showed that only 50% of non-wage education expenditure reached the frontline facilities and that most of the wastage occurred between line ministries. Like Uganda, the Government of Ghana has not been able to initiate a strong response to reduce leakage.

We have seen from the above that while studies into the leakage of public funds are extremely important, especially where they reveal factors that constrain educational progress, the key to meaningful change is a government's commitment to do something about it. The adoption of CATI in Nigeria reflects a strong commitment by the educational authorities to involve communities in playing a more active role in monitoring how money is spent and to take ownership for the improvement of education, but establishing this kind of social accountability will not be an easy process. That the policy imperative is an important one is not in doubt. Developing within local communities the will and the momentum to turn it into a 'movement' for social change is, however, a bigger challenge. Examples from other developing countries show that the emergence of grass roots organisations and advocacy groups plays a significant part in building social movements with clear goals and a commitment to act. I return to this issue later in this chapter.

Operation Reach all Primary Schools (ORAPS) and Operation Reach all Secondary Schools (ORASS)

The supervision, monitoring, and evaluation of the day-to-day functioning of an educational system are important elements in improving its quality. The school inspectorate especially has a critical role to play in establishing and monitoring standards and in identifying how these can be raised. Although a large number of people work for the inspectorate services at federal and state levels and many others work as supervisors at the local government authority (LGA) level, in many states these officers are under-utilised, weakly equipped and often immobile due to inadequate funding and training. There is also frequently a duplication of function between the inspectorate and various 'universal basic education monitoring units', as well as between the federal, state and LGA tiers of the inspectorate.

In an attempt to revitalise what was largely seen as a moribund inspection service, the Federal Ministry of Education launched two linked initiatives, Operation Reach all Primary Schools (ORAPS) and Operation Reach all Secondary Schools (ORASS) aimed at inspecting all secondary and primary schools in Nigeria. It identified five important reasons for so doing: first, to investigate first hand some of the factors underlying the poor and declining quality of education in Nigerian schools; second, to document and publish the findings as part of the Federal Ministry's drive for an honest and transparent assessment of the state of education in Nigeria; third, to establish the principle that schools must be accountable for their performance and that information about their performance must be open to public scrutiny; fourth, to test whether there is capacity in the system, and the tools necessary, to carry out regular inspections of schools; and fifth, to support pockets of educational quality, through giving authority and legitimacy to those schools which have a strong desire to improve standards.

If one were asked to write a slogan for the policy campaign, 'Reach all, Reach for, Reach out' is probably a good way to capture its underlying aims. The desire to 'reach all' schools signalled the concern of the Federal Ministry that in the last inspection period only 3.5% of Nigerian secondary schools were inspected and, consequently, very little qualitative information about the physical conditions of schools and the teaching and learning environment was made available to the Federal Ministry and indeed to other stakeholders. 'Reaching for' gave expression to the Federal Ministry's desire to reach for the highest possible standards in education. This is an important part of Nigeria's long-term vision to become one of the top 20 economies in the world (see FME, 2006). Finally, 'reaching out' indicated that the emphasis on performance monitoring was mediated by a sensitivity to the conditions that exist in many schools and the fact that many teachers and head teachers are in need of professional support.

With this, the Federal Ministry of Education, together with various stake holders, such as School-Based Management Committees, moved swiftly to launch a nationwide visit of schools. But what did the initiative achieve and what are the prospects of meeting the longer term goals of improving educational quality through monitoring and supervision? We know from examples elsewhere that strengthening the school inspection service has been linked to the achievement of higher standards, more often than not because evidence of the performance of schools was made available to parents. Indeed, the converse is also true. In Denmark, for example, there was no formal intervention in underperforming schools and no performance information such as league tables or inspection reports were published for parents. The Organisation for Economic Cooperation and Development

(OECD) highlighted this lack of accountability as a key factor explaining underperformance in Danish schools. The Danish authorities have since responded to this concern by introducing a wide range of reforms including that all schools have to publish a detailed website of information about the school, including performance information.

However, the evidence of the effects of school inspection on improving standards in education is mixed. There are two dominant views about what inspection is designed to achieve. On the one hand, there are those who argue that supervision is central to achieving a basic level of educational quality. In this view, inspectors are seen as 'critical friends', providing guidance and supervision to heads and teachers. In Burkina Faso, for example, using *chefs de circonscription* (district officers) for supervising and supporting the process of 'whole school development' and the creation of pedagogical advisors for supporting individual teachers in their classrooms appears to have had a positive impact on the quality of schooling (Samoff et al. 2001). In Senegal, the development of job performance specifications was used to provide a clearer guide to inspectors as to what to focus on, particularly when addressing concerns about the quality of instructional practice. As a result of the programme, pupils' results improved but there were many difficulties in implementing the programme, including teachers' conservatism and inadequate logistics. Despite this, the results were telling: School organisation improved with the introduction of new managerial instruments and a results-based approach (Niane, 2003).

The second view is that inspection is about ensuring accountability. Certain standards are set and schools are required to meet them. In this view accountability will lead to improvement because being accountable implies that if a school underperforms, actions to correct this will follow. Dalin (1992), for example, shows that in the case of Bangladesh, tight inspection and control were crucial to the success of improving schools.

But there is little evidence that inspection per se brings about improvement to the quality of teaching and learning within schools (Shaw et al, 2003) and indeed some research has shown that it could even reduce levels of student achievement in the year of the inspection (Rosenthal, 2004). There is, however, some evidence that inspection can lead to some improvement amongst the weakest institutions (Matthews & Sammons, 2004) and that it can act as an important catalyst for change (Gray & Gardner, 1999). Further, the British Office for Standards in Education (Ofsted, 2004) – 'Improvement through inspection' – recognises that inspectorates have no direct control over all the factors that might lead to schools improving but that direct interventions such as the feedback provided to the school and the publication of school reports are highly likely to lead to improvement.

Although strong empirical evidence on the effects of school inspections on school improvement is still lacking, we do know that where there is an absence of a strong monitoring framework, accountability and performance is undermined (Dalin, 1992), as the examples of Burkina Faso, Senegal and Bangladesh show.

There are thus a number of issues for Nigeria to consider. I shall return to a discussion of these later in the chapter.

Public–Private Partnerships in Education

The private sector plays an important role in the provision of education in Nigeria, although there is insufficient data to determine with any form of exactness the number of privately operated schools.

Apart from fee-paying private schools that are run by individuals or consortia, there are many other examples of public–private partnerships in education in Nigeria. Some international development partners, like UNICEF, have private sector partnerships for school improvement with British Airways, DHL, Lever, and MTN, and there is scope for further expansion in this area (Zebroff et al, 2006). According to the IDPs (Zebroff et al, 2006), the oil companies have made substantial investments in classroom construction in the Delta area. There are also plans for the old mission schools, once common especially in the South, and long since taken over by the Government, to be returned to the churches. Similar proposals are being considered in the North where there are large numbers of Islamiyya schools. If they were successful in their attempts to combine more traditional forms of Islamic education with the modern secular curriculum, such schools could have a particularly significant impact on the recruitment and retention of girls, who are dramatically under-represented in these areas.

It is against this background that the Federal Ministry of Education has launched the Public–Private Partnership (PPP) initiative as a way of securing more private money for the public sector and thereby engaging a wider range of stakeholders in the shaping of public policy to provide a higher quality of service.

Whilst there appears to be strong support for CATI and ORASS/ORAPS discussed above, the policy imperative to establish public–private partnerships been less warmly received – the fear being that the Government is seeking to sell off national assets. In discussion with the Minister of Education in post at the time, the FME claims that it remains committed to a public service ethos and the initiative is not an attempt to 'sell off' or privatise the running of schools. Rather, it believes the following:

- that the primary purpose of all PPP activity should be to benefit learning and increase the opportunities of learners;
- that democratic accountability must be maintained; and
- that schools and school principals must receive full and appropriate support in and training for dealing with PPP activity (private communication, 2006).

In spite of potentially deep policy divisions around the issue of privatisation, falling standards in education and schools that fail to deliver a good quality service are a big concern for Nigeria. Those against the idea of private investment would argue that the answer lies in increasing expenditure in education; but increasing public funding is not an entirely adequate strategy to deal with the long-term erosion of the quality of education. There is growing agreement in many parts of the world that where the responsibility for the delivery of education is devolved to a wider range of stakeholders, the quality of education, good governance and a better application of public funds can be achieved.

The United Nations-sponsored Financing for Development conference in Monterrey in 2002 identified development-driven partnerships between public and private actors as one of the most important solutions to improving the quality of education in developing countries. As a follow-up to the Monterrey conference, the World Economic Forum's Financing for Development Initiative and the United Nations Department for Economic and Social Affairs organised a series of multi-stakeholder meetings to examine the effectiveness of PPPs in three areas of development including education. The first of two meetings on PPPs in Basic Education was held in Brazil in 2004, and the second in Paris in 2005. These gatherings examined the question of what works and what does not in the formulation and management of development-driven PPPs and concluded that engaging other industry sectors in planning and developing school infrastructure, sustaining and scaling up strategic social investments in basic education, and establishing strong business coalitions to improve basic education were key considerations.

It seems likely that the incoming government in Nigeria, with the support of its international development partners, will seek to push ahead with increasing the number and types of PPPs. Here again it would be helpful to review briefly examples of the various approaches to establishing PPPs.

There are three broad approaches to establishing a PPP. These are delegation (where a government retains responsibility for the function of schooling while delegating the actual activity of managing schools to the private sector), divestment (handing over government schools to private companies who mange them for a fee) and displacement (a process that leads to government being displaced gradually by the private sector).

Whatever option the Government of Nigeria adopts, it would do well to be guided by the increasingly common practice to establish PPP units, either as new government agencies, or as special cells within a cross-sectoral ministry such as finance or planning. In South Africa the PPP unit has been established within a ministry but relies on long-term consultants. Some countries have opted to set up PPP units as autonomous entities to create greater independence. These units are attached to but not fully part of the bureaucracy. Examples here include the Philippines and Pakistan. A third approach has been adopted in Canada where the PPP unit is a government-owned company. Overseen by a government–private board, it offers higher salaries than that offered by the civil services to attract people with key financial skills. A fourth way is the joint venture company which is owned in part by private shareholders. Such units receive performance-based pay and examples here include Partnerships UK. This model is being replicated in various states in India such as Karnataka and Rajasthan (World Bank, 2006).

Discussion

Broadening the Basis for Social Accountability

Nigeria, like many other developing countries, has increased spending on basic education in recent years. However, like many other countries, it has been disappointed with the results of its additional investments and has begun to ask questions about the relatively small gains it has made in improving access to and the quality of education. The poor state of Nigerian schools reflects in part a huge wastage of public funds and there is a strong emerging consensus that something must be done about this. As discussed above, the Government of Nigeria has announced a policy on social accountability and transparency. But we must consider whether the policy in itself is a sufficient driver of social and behavioural change. In other developing countries the success of social accountability strategies seems to have had deep grass roots support and organisation, this often facilitated by advocacy groups who have supported the development of community-based social accountability strategies including participatory budgeting, participatory budget analysis, and performance monitoring (see Sirker, 2006). Some such examples are briefly discussed below.

The best example of citizens getting involved in participatory budgeting is in Porte Alegre in Brazil. Participatory Budget Councils have been formed and are composed of delegates from civil society groups such as neighbourhood associations. These Participatory Budget Councils work in collaboration with municipal councils and government representatives to formulate and monitor local budgets. As a result, between 1989 and 1996 the number of children in schools doubled. Over 80 Brazilian cities are now following the Porte Alegre model.

Participatory Budget Analysis is a process whereby the technical language of budgets and resource allocation is made more accessible to ordinary people. Increasingly, advocacy groups and other stakeholders in civil society in many developing countries have been researching, deconstructing and monitoring budgets and disseminating information about public expenditure and investments to local communities in a way that they can understand it. A good example is where the Government of India promised to allocate money for social programmes for tribal groups in Gujarat. An NGO, the 'People's Budget Information and Analysis Service', found, on close inspection of the budget, that these allocations had not been included.

It published the findings, and the response of ordinary people was swift. National budgets are now routinely scrutinised by the People's Budget Information and Analysis Service and this has resulted in the correction of numerous numeric discrepancies and other errors and a better flow of information between ministries. The Gujarat model is now being replicated by 12 other Indian states.

A good example of performance monitoring is the use of 'score cards' through which citizens judge the performance of public servants. Such scorecards can be produced at both community and more macro levels. The first example of citizen report cards was found in Bangalore in India. These stimulated civil society activism and many more groups became involved in monitoring public agencies. Formerly apathetic public institutions have begun to react to citizens' concerns and many have reviewed their service delivery mechanisms. At the same time, public awareness on the issue of service quality has been significantly increased (Sirker, 2006). Report cards as a form of civil society performance monitoring have been replicated in many other Indian cities and are routinely used in other countries such as the Philippines, Kenya and South Africa.

In Nigeria the social accountability initiative appears to be driven from the top down. The Federal Ministry of Education has published information of educational disbursements on its website as well as information about the conditions by which the various states can gain access to matching grants. Further, detailed breakdowns of disbursements to all 36 states in Nigeria are given in specially prepared CATI booklets. These booklets are to be made available to all primary and junior schools, parent teacher associations, civil society groups, NGOs, international development organisations, faith-based organisations, and other institutions and individuals. It is not clear how accessible this information campaign is and whether the published booklets are clear enough and simple enough to be interpreted and acted upon by local communities. Accordingly, it remains to be seen whether various community groups will use the policy as a lever in holding local administrators, contractors and various line ministries accountable for the disbursement of public funds, to get involved in the management and maintenance of quality and minimum standards, and to take responsibility for the falling standards of academic achievement in schools.

We turn now to the question 'what promise does CATI hold for Nigeria?' CATI builds on examples of social accountability and transparency that have achieved dramatic results in the improvement of public service delivery in education in other developing countries. It contains elements of providing necessary information to communities and civil society about their entitlements but it also invites communities to act and to take responsibility for the management and improvement of education. The Federal Ministry of Education, together with various partners, has put in place a number of important building blocks to ensure the success of community accountability and transparency, including School-Based Management Committees.

Judging from other examples of social accountability discussed in this chapter, the chances of CATI being a successful stimulus to mobilising citizenship participation and accountability and transparency in public spending are high, but the question remains whether communities themselves are ready to rise to the challenge.

Building a System of Monitoring and Inspection

We have seen that the current system of inspection in Nigeria is weak. The ORASS and ORAPS policy imperative is an important first step in testing the capacity of the inspectorate to reach all its schools, reach for the highest standards through a strong sense of accountability and transparency, and to reach out to support those schools in the most desperate conditions of disrepair and where standards are weakest. But the policy initiative opens up an important area of debate about the role of inspection and the feasibility of regular inspections in a country the size of Nigeria and lays the basis for a wider discussion of policy alternatives for reforming the inspection system.

There would seem to be three fundamental issues for Nigeria to grapple with. First, it needs to find a way of establishing a system of regular inspection and school supervision. This in itself is a difficult task in a large country and problems such as transport, funding and, more crucially, clearly defined roles for the inspectorate, are as evident here as in many other developing countries. Second, even if these physical constraints were overcome and a clarity of purpose established, building a system of monitoring and supervision that gives schools a stake in finding solutions, and in this way, making them more accountable, is extremely difficult. The problem is that in traditional systems of inspection, schools have very little input into establishing performance indicators and in interpreting how far their efforts in the delivery of education go towards meeting these targets. Whilst it is important that measuring performance has a degree of objectivity, in some African countries like South Africa, school inspections work side by side with a system of self-evaluation. Third, a critical problem in many African countries and in the developing world in general is the conceptual clarity about how information about school performance can be used as a catalyst to improving educational quality. Such information that can be gathered often ends up in the in-files of the professionals (because improving quality is seen to be the job of professionals) and rarely, if ever, are parents informed about the performance of schools. This is where so many initiatives in the developing world falter. The overall trend towards social accountability in Nigeria, such as we have seen through the CATI initiative discussed above, could have important consequences for bringing parents and communities more firmly into the sphere of monitoring educational quality.

Only time will tell what effects a revitalised inspection system might have on improving educational quality in Nigeria, but for now, the ORASS/ORAPS imperative should be applauded as a determined initiative by the Federal Ministry of Education to learn about and deal with some of the factors underlying the decline of education in Nigerian schools, to document and publish the findings as part of its drive for an honest and transparent assessment of the state of education in Nigeria, and to establish the principle that schools must be accountable for their performance and that information about their performance must be open to public scrutiny.

Increasing the Number and Scope of Public–Private Partnerships

As pointed out above, the issue of integrating private sector expertise and services into the system of public sector schooling is an issue of debate and controversy. In Nigeria, as is often the case in many developing countries, the standards of education in public schools are not high; schools are generally characterised as having high drop-out rates and poor quality of teaching. Such conditions in many countries have led to the rapid growth of low-cost private schools and an increasing tendency for even some of the poorest parents to buy out of public schools in favour of private education. An example of this is found in the slums in Hyderabad, India, where poor parents prefer to send their children to effective private schools for want of good quality public schools. Public schools in developing countries that cater to the economically backward strata of society often have better facilities than private schools but in some countries it is the private schools that perform better. In Kenya, for example, children went to public schools when education was made free; however, most returned to private schools as they offered better quality. In addition, this did not allow more children access to basic education; it simply allowed those already in an educational system to have it for free. In India, however, public schools in the poorest communities tend to achieve better results than low-cost private schools (Srivastava & Walford, 2007) so the picture is mixed.

It would be beneficial for the education system as a whole, including the total volume of resources going into education, for the private sector to play a much larger role than it does now, especially at the secondary and tertiary levels. Private schools could alleviate some of the burden on state systems, but they should be screened, registered and monitored to ensure quality of provision.

Meanwhile, we have seen also that there is a trend towards public–private-partnerships and that a variety of multinational corporations are involved in various forms of this practice. The Federal Government has made clear its intention to increase the range and extent of such partnerships and should perhaps consider, and try to avoid, some of the difficulties that other developing countries have experienced. These include difficulties in negotiating and reaching agreement between non-traditional parties; a lack of political will and public support for the participation of the private sector and the business community in providing basic education; a lack of awareness and communication between public and private actors; a lack of an 'institutionalised voice' to represent the private sector; an agreement on key performance targets; and transparency and accountability within the PPP (World Economic Forum, 2005).

The question of scaling up and sustaining strategic social investments in basic education is clearly a difficult one but there are examples of approaches that are being used to effect in a number of countries. Again, it would be useful for the Nigerian Government to be aware of these.

One excellent example of cooperation between national and international businesses in supporting education can be seen in the Jordan Education Initiative. Here the national government makes an upfront financial commitment to local funding initiatives, which is in turn matched by international business. The Jordan Education Initiative has become a benchmark for replication and scaling up in other regions of the world. It is already being replicated in the state of Rajasthan in India.

The experiences of other countries with the establishment of PPPs suggest that there is much work to be done in Nigeria if this policy initiative is to succeed. The consensus of participants at the Paris roundtable meeting on PPPs was that ministers of education review existing regulatory environments with the aim to removing barriers to private education. Further, deregulation is also seen as one of the solutions to facilitate the PPP process. However, deregulation is not necessarily a panacea for all problems, but at very least, there is a need to improve the dialogue between national governments, donors, international and national businesses and local community initiatives around some of the policy options highlighted in this chapter and around regulatory reform.

Conclusions

This chapter has reviewed and evaluated three policy imperatives under consideration by the Nigerian Government and supported by its international development partners (the World Bank, DFID, JICA, USAID, UNESCO, and UNICEF). Using examples from other developing countries to assess whether these policy initiatives are likely to impact upon the quality of education in Nigeria, it reaches the conclusion that the policy imperatives discussed here have much promise. The movement towards more community and private involvement in the governance of education, transparency in the way in which educational finances are managed, and accountability for what is taught and how it is learned is very encouraging and sets the tone for a change in the landscape of education in Africa.

References

Dalin, P. (1992) *How Schools Improve: an international study*. Oxford: Blackwell.

Federal Ministry of Education (FME) (2006) *Vision Statement of the Federal Ministry of Education Nigeria*. Abuja: FME.

Government of Nigeria (2003) *National Economic Empowerment and Development Strategy (NEEDs)*. Abuja: Government of Nigeria.

Gray, C. & Gardner, J. (1999) The Impact of School Inspections, *Oxford Review of Education*, 25(4), 455-469.

Hallack, J. & Poisson, M. (2007) *Governance in Education: transparency and accountability*. Paris: International Institute for Educational Planning.

Johnson, D., Hsieh, J. & Oniborn, F. (2007) *A Baseline Study of Children's Learning in Nigeria*. Nigeria: Department for International Development.

Matthews, P. & Sammons, P. (2004) *Improvement through Inspection*. London. Office for Standards in Education.

Niane, B. (2003) Improving the Quality of Education in Sub-Saharan Africa by Decentralising and Diversifying: involvement and empowerment for school citizenship, Association for the Development of Education in Africa. Working Paper.

Office for Standards in Education (2004) *Office for Standards in Education Handbook: Guidance on the Inspection of Schools*. London. The Stationery Office.

Reinikka, R. & Svensson, J. (2004) *Information and Voice in Public Spending*. World Bank Development Research Group. Washington, DC: World Bank.

Rosenthal, L. (2004) Do School Inspections Improve School Quality? Ofsted Inspections and School Examination Results in the UK, *Economics of Education Review*, 23(1), 143-151.

Samoff, J., Sebatane, E. & Dembele, M. (2001) Scaling up by Focussing Down. Creating Space to Expand Educational Reform. Association for the Development of Education in Africa Working Paper. Paris: Association for the Development of Education in Africa.

Shaw, I., Newton, D.P., Aitkin, M. & Darnell, R. (2003) Do Ofsted Inspections of Secondary Education Make a Difference to GCSE Results? *British Educational Research Journal*, 29(1), 63-75.

Sirker, K. (2006) *General Social Accountability Concepts and Tools*. Washington, DC: World Bank.

Srivastava, P. & Walford, G. (2007) *Private Schooling in Less Economically Developed Countries: Asian and African perspectives*. Oxford: Symposium Books.

UNESCO Institute for Statistics (UIS) (2005) *Statistical Data for Sub-Saharan Africa*. Montreal: UIS.

United Nations (2004) *Demographic and Health Survey (2004): Nigeria*. New York: United Nations Development Programme.

United Nations Educational, Scientific and Cultural Organisation (UNESCO) (2007) *Strong Foundations: early childhood care and education*. EFA Global Monitoring Report. Paris: UNESCO.

UNICEF/UNESCO (2004) *Monitoring Learning Achievements*. Paris: UNESCO.

Winkler, D. (2005) Public Expenditure Tracking in Education. EQUIP2 Policy Brief. Washington: USAID.

World Bank (2006) Public Policy for the Private Sector. Note 311. Washington, DC: World Bank.

World Bank (2007) *World Development Report. Development and the Next Generation.* Washington, DC: World Bank.

World Economic Forum (2005) *Development-Driven Public–Private Partnerships in Basic Education: emerging priorities from the second roundtable discussion.* Washington, DC: World Bank.

Zebroff, T., Ojikutu, S. & Ackers, J. (2006) Discussion on Education Sector Development in Nigeria: perspectives from the international development partners. Unpublished Paper.

CHAPTER 3

Education and Democracy in The Gambia: reflections on the position of development projects in a small African state

MICHELE SCHWEISFURTH

In studying the changing landscape of education in Africa, The Gambia makes an interesting case study in a number of ways. The Gambia shares many characteristics with other sub-Saharan African states. Among these common traits are: high levels of poverty and underdevelopment; a colonial history; a notable urban–rural divide; a population consisting of several different ethnic and linguistic groups; traditional values co-existing with modern influences; and a drive within the education sector for higher levels of participation and quality. On the other hand, some of its more unique characteristics also generate interest: it is one of the continent's smallest states, and also one of its most stable politically.

This chapter examines the relationship between education and democracy in this context, through reflections on two small-scale development projects on this theme. By analysing factors which have affected the projects' processes and outcomes, the aim is to highlight context-specific issues, and to note where these intersect with wider forces which are impacting upon education in a more global way. This 'dialectic of the global and the local' (Arnove & Torres 1999) is seen to be particularly acute in a small developing state.

The chapter begins by unpacking some assumptions about democracy and its relationship to development and education. A brief description of key aspects of The Gambian context follows, and an outline of the projects, including aims, methods and outcomes. Finally, some of the local, 'small state' and global factors at play are considered.

Assumptions

This discussion, and the projects in question, are underpinned by five key assumptions regarding democracy, development and education. Firstly, democracy is not only an inherently good thing from an ethical point of view: it is both a means and an end to development. As Sen (1999) has argued, democratic freedoms and rights are conducive to development of all kinds in a country, including economic development; however, to focus on how democracy leads to development is to miss the crucial point that:

> substantive freedoms (that is, the liberty of political participation or the opportunity to receive basic education or health care) are among the *constitutive components* of development. Their relevance for development does not have to be freshly established through their indirect contribution to the growth of GNP or to the promotion of industrialisation. As it happens, these freedoms and rights are also very effective in contributing to economic progress ... But while the causal relation is indeed significant, the vindications of freedoms and rights provided by this causal linkage is over and above the directly constitutive role of these freedoms in development. (p. 5)

In other words, to paraphrase the title of Sen's book, development *is* freedom. On the one hand, the freedoms associated with democracy can, for example, prevent famine. This link is to a large degree because of the accountability of elected governments to the people: many economic disasters are preventable, but dictators have little incentive to do much to protect the poor of their countries or to be transparent in their workings. Similarly, Harber (2002) has used a variety of examples to show how the prevalence of authoritarian governments in sub-Saharan Africa has directly contributed to the persistence of poverty, violent civil unrest and conflict, fiscal crisis linked to large military expenditure, and the loss of educated citizens ('brain drain'). Sierra Leone is a classic example. On the other hand, freedom and democracy are so important that in themselves they need to be seen as constituent elements and indicators of development, regardless of their links to more traditional measures.

The second assumption is that democratic political structures need support. As Julius Nyerere, former president of Tanzania, put it: 'Democracy means much more than voting on the basis of adult suffrage every few years' (Nyerere, 1998, p. 27). To quote Harber (2002):

> If democratic institutions are to survive and prosper they must be embedded in a society composed of individuals and organisations which are permeated by the values and practices which are supportive of democracy. (p. 271)

This includes the organisations of civil society, which must be active and strong to underpin democratic institutions at the national level.

The third assumption is that the political culture conducive to the development of a strong civil society and therefore democratic government is based on the presence of a set of skills, knowledge and values in the population. Examples generated from a brainstorming activity in The Gambia include the skills of listening and interacting with diverse other people; knowledge about rights and current affairs; and such values as tolerance and respect for others (in Davies et al, 2002, p. 12) Sen (1999) argues that one such prerequisite is socially responsible reasoning which goes beyond self-interest. People are not born with these predilections; however,

> Space does not have to be artificially created in the human mind
> for the idea of justice or fairness – through moral bombardment or
> ethical haranguing. That space already exists, and it is a question
> of making systematic, cogent and effective use of the general
> concerns that people do have. (Sen, 1999, p. 262)

Without these, and the behaviours that stem from them, democracy cannot thrive. The fourth assumption is that education has the potential to play a role in inculcating these skills, knowledge and values – although preferably without, as Sen would put it, 'moral bombardment or ethical haranguing'. Education, and schooling in particular, can have a direct effect on their development, through subjects such as Civics or Citizenship Education, which aim explicitly to impact on learners' repertoires of democratic potential. Less directly, schooling also creates possibilities for the modelling of democratic behaviours, for example, through structures such as school councils which provide a forum for the representation of different stakeholder voices, or through transparent and fair interactions between teachers, school managers, and learners. Schooling therefore can be a necessary, but not sufficient, means to develop capabilities in individuals that help to sustain a democratic political culture.

The fifth assumption is that schooling as it currently exists does not live up to this potential. International evidence suggests that, far from creating democrats and nurturing equitable and peaceful relationships, it equally has the potential to nurture conflict (e.g. Davies, 2004); encourage gender violence (e.g. Leach, 2003); reinforce racial prejudice (e.g. Vally & Dalamba, 1999); sustain class inequalities (e.g. Bowles & Gintis, 1976); and perpetrate all of the above (Harber, 2004). In The Gambia, the most frequently mentioned aspect of schooling that year 4 pupils dislike is 'the fighting' (Department of State for Education [DOSE], 2000). In order for schooling to better fulfil its positive potential, interventions and changes are necessary. This is the starting point for the two projects in The Gambia being examined here – one working with teacher educators and trainees, and one with school inspectors and advisors.

The Gambian Context

The Gambia is a former British colony, which gained independence in 1965. Along with other West African states, it is underdeveloped using a wide range of indices. The UNDP Human Development Index ranks it at 155th out of 174 countries (United Nations Development Programme [UNDP], 2004), and it has a particularly vulnerable economy relying heavily on the export of groundnuts, and, more recently, the import of sun-seeking European tourists. The World Bank has classified it as a low-income country (World Bank, 2006). There have been notable improvements in recent years in such areas as infant mortality, life expectancy, and education enrolment (UNDP, 2004).

The Gambia is a small state using the most common measures: population and physical size. It is also the smallest state in Africa in terms of land area (The Gambia, 2001). Physically, it is a sliver of a country with the River Gambia as its spine; it is completely surrounded by the former French colony Senegal, except for the small Atlantic coastal area around the capital, Banjul. Using the Commonwealth Secretariat's definition of small states as having less than 1.5 million population, at 1.4 million (UNDP, 2004), The Gambia can be classified as such. At 3.4%, however, it has a high population growth rate, attributable largely to a high birth rate. Despite its small scale, the population is diverse, with five major ethnic groups and several minor ones, each with its own language and cultural traditions (The Gambia, 2001). Estimates vary, but at least 85% of the population are Muslims, with the Christian minority concentrated in the capital.

Unlike the experiences of other nations, African and other, this diversity has not necessarily led to conflict.

> many Gambians point out and emphasise that today their society is, in reality, relatively harmonious ... Intermarriage between members of different ethnic groups is common and relationships between Muslims and Christians are generally regarded as being harmonious. Many people speak, almost without any visible hesitation, ethnic languages other than their own mother tongue. (Okumu-Nyström, 2003, p. 73)

In personal conversations, Gambians have noted the sense of humour with which people from different ethnic groups tease each other, helping to maintain a sense of distinct identity while defraying possible conflict.

However, as Okumu-Nyström (2003) goes on to point out, 'there is one issue that does divide Gambians, namely politics' (p. 73). Despite this, politically, compared to other states in this turbulent continent, The Gambia can be, and often is, described as 'relatively' stable. In recent years, one bloodless coup d'état in 1994 saw the overthrow of President Jawara's long-standing government, with the coup leader, President Jammeh, eventually elected democratically in 1996 and re-elected in 2001. The mood is often tense at election time, but the most recent election was held without notable incidence of violence.

Along with other government sectors, education is being decentralised, with greater responsibility and powers devolved to the six regions. As in many countries, as one gets further from the capital, the regions become more rural and less developed, and schools less well equipped in terms of human and physical resources. The national education policy sets out six years of primary/lower basic, three years of junior secondary/upper basic, and three years of senior secondary schooling. The first two phases are gradually being universalised towards nine years of uninterrupted basic education (DOSE, 2000). The first six years are technically free, but, as in other developing countries, the incidental fees such as for uniforms and books, and the opportunity costs of sending children to school instead of benefiting from their economic contribution to the household, mean that for poor families, especially in rural areas, schooling is an economic burden. Despite this, impressive gains have been made towards achieving education for all (EFA). The net primary enrolment ratio stands at 73%, higher than most countries of similarly low human development. Many teachers are untrained but this too is improving. The Gambia College School of Education is the sole provider of teacher education in the country, and has programmes which cater for pre-service teachers, in-service teachers, and unqualified teachers who wish to qualify.

Along with enrolment and teacher supply, a major concern of the DOSE has been the quality of education. It is within this remit for improving quality that the two projects on education for democracy have been placed, and supported by the Standards and Quality Assurance Directorate (SQAD) within DOSE. There is also explicit policy support for schooling's role in educating democratic citizens; one of the 10 basic aims of education policy for the past 15 years has been

> to create an awareness of the importance of peace, democracy and
> human rights and the responsibility of the individual in fostering
> these qualities. (DOSE, 1988)

The Projects

Since 2000, the Centre for International Education and Research [1], University of Birmingham, United Kingdom has planned and implemented two projects, funded by the Centre for British Teachers (CfBT), for the promotion of education for democracy in The Gambia. The first project, based on a feasibility study, was a collaborative effort with The Gambia College, and the participants were lecturers and trainee teachers. It aimed to foster greater understanding and skills in democratic education through a series of two-day workshops on this theme. The workshop materials were consolidated into a published guidebook (Davies et al, 2002), which was widely distributed and is also being tested in other countries.

During the course of this project, as our understanding of the local educational situation grew, the project team became aware of the importance of reinforcing these principles once teachers were in schools. It was not enough to create skills and preferences for democratic practice, if these were not supported once the newly qualified teachers were placed in schools. It became evident that the role of inspectors and advisors was crucial to this process. We were strongly encouraged to conduct a second project in collaboration with SQAD within DOSE and in the regions. The second project consisted of two-day workshops with inspectors, advisors and education officers in the six regions of the country. These were tailored for the quality assurance role of this group, and focused on the relationship between democracy and quality in education, and how the processes of inspecting and advising teachers can be conducted based on democratic principles. Decentralisation processes within DOSE and SQAD made it particularly important that the workshops be run through the regional offices. Additionally, the widely different conditions in terms of resources and capacities between the metropolitan regions (1 and 2) and the more rural and remote (regions 3-6) reinforced this necessity.

As part of the second project, a network of interested organisations and individuals has been established: the Alliance for Education for Democracy in The Gambia. The alliance includes governmental, non-governmental and Pan-African organisations with an interest in education for democracy and human rights. This was facilitated at a national invitational workshop, where representatives from these organisations had the opportunity to share information and assess needs. The second project also generated a second guidebook, this one on the democratic supervision of teachers for professional development (Davies et al, 2005).

During both projects, in addition to the training component, action research was conducted to evaluate the impact of the project and its resonance with local needs. Qualitative and quantitative data were gathered, including: surveys of Gambia College staff and students on attitudes to democratic practice; follow-up visits to participants in their workplaces, incorporating observations and interviews; longitudinal case studies of a small number of individuals; workshop feedback forms; and a survey of attitudes of participants at a final dissemination seminar.

As interventionist projects, these aimed to change educational practice through a collaborative effort. Literature on educational change teaches us that such impact is highly problematic, particularly where the innovations advocated demand attitudinal changes and where cultural values are involved. As has been discussed elsewhere (Schweisfurth, 2002; Harber, 2006), evidence from action research has suggested that the impact of the projects has been variable but significant. Participants were enthusiastic about the theme of the project and the workshops themselves, and many of them incorporated methods from the workshops into their own practice, often mediating them in order to accommodate their own ideas about what would work in their contexts. Examples included teachers encouraging greater democracy in schools through negotiation of classroom rules, more open classroom discussion and greater responsibilities for elected student representatives, and inspectors using indicators of democratic practice in their supervision of teachers, and being more transparent in their judgements. There was evidence that local understandings of what constitutes democracy varied slightly from our own 'cosmopolitan' version, and such factors as Islamic and traditional Gambian values played key roles. However, the most obvious finding was that participants – including 100% of the final seminar participants – agreed that further democratisation was both desirable and inevitable in The Gambia and in Gambian schools and classrooms.[2] A number of factors, some specific to the Gambian context and some more global in nature, were likely to have affected the degree and nature of modifications to attitude and practice among participants.

Small State Factors

Among the contextual factors are a number of issues related to the scale of The Gambia. A body of literature on the special circumstances of small states (e.g. Bacchus & Brock, 1987; Bray & Packer, 1993; Lillis, 1993; Schweisfurth, 1995; Crossley & Holmes 1999; Holmes & Crossley, 2004) has pointed to shared characteristics, challenges and strengths in small states, many of which affect education. Several of these are significant in The Gambia and in the context of these projects. One is the impact of key individuals, which can facilitate system-wide change. Both centrally and regionally, DOSE and SQAD is a network of a relatively small number of people. Therefore, each of them has the potential to make a significant impact on their own constituencies, and, compared to their counterparts in larger states, on the whole system. Even a single teacher can gain the attention of a wide audience more easily than in a more populated system with more bureaucratic layers. For example, one trainee teacher who was impassioned by ideas generated at workshops was placed at a school where the head teacher and deputy were impressed by him and by the potential of democratisation. The teacher went on to do regional teacher workshops on Education for Democracy, and to establish a national network of students.

In The Gambia, who these key individuals are has also facilitated the projects' impact. Local contacts and collaborators play a crucial role in any situation where projects are brought in to any context by outsiders. There is also evidence that the meeting of local and outsider agendas in projects is not necessarily based on shared understandings, and this can limit the possibilities of impact (e.g. Leach, 2001; Delens, 2001; Lacey & Jacklin, 2001). In The Gambia, the Director and Deputy Director of SQAD, the Principal Education Officers in four out of six of the regional offices, and several other powerful individuals have all studied at the University of Birmingham, with members of the project team, and had therefore previously been attuned to the ideas that underpinned the projects' aims and approaches. The same professional development process undergone during their study period also served to raise capacity for research and for critical understanding of the interface between global trends and agendas, and local needs. They were therefore supportive of the projects from the outset, and have been collaborators and promoters throughout. As well as being powerful by virtue of their positions, the small state context, where a large proportion of the population knows each other personally, tends to make most relationships interpersonal, creating further layers of accountability and loyalty around those with influence.

In The Gambia, as in other small states, the polyvalence of individuals is demanded, due to the small numbers of trained people, and economies of scale in terms of specialisation (Bacchus & Brock, 1987). For example, head teachers often function additionally as inspectors and advisors. This means that one person attending a workshop could potentially have a dual impact, both within their own schools and more widely. Because of the shortage of such individuals within the system, combined with the small physical scale of the country, key people are often moved between roles and regions. This again facilitated the spread of ideas, and also created situations where individuals attended similar workshops more than once in different places, and professed to get more out of them the second time.

As with other states of a similar scale, the provision of tertiary-level education is limited. The Gambia College is the sole provider of pre-service teacher education, and a primary provider of in-service teacher education in the country. By concentrating the first project in this institution, there was the possibility of impact on a significant number – in an ideal world, all – of the trainees undertaking studies. This ambition is not realistic of course, given the scale of the project, and the complexities of educational change. However, the potential for national impact through work with one institution is a small state phenomenon.

A final aspect which is crucial here is the fact that, despite its small scale, The Gambia is an autonomous state with the right to make its own national policy. Small states may be small, but they are states. This may seem like an obvious point, but, as with many other small states (Lillis, 1993), at various points in its history The Gambia could easily have become part of larger unit, in this case, Senegal. Its existence is an accident of colonial history during which French and British powers carved up West Africa, and, as recently as the 1980s, there were discussions about a union between The Gambia and Senegal (Jeng, 1995). The creation and preservation of nationhood has allowed The Gambia to choose a direction in terms of politics and education that may not have been possible as marginalised regions of a larger country, and the direction has been the sustaining of democracy. The projects would not have been possible under other priorities.

Global Discourses and Pressures

Globalisation trends mean that hegemonic global discourses are increasingly influential. Arguably, small states are even more vulnerable to global influences and pressures than larger nations. Their identities are more fragile, and more likely to be subject to external cultural influences for a number of reasons: the prevalence of imported goods and media, since diseconomies of scale make local production difficult; the dominance of larger countries in regional cooperation schemes; the presence in numbers of foreign tourists; dependence on aid and expertise from elsewhere; and the lack of availability of higher-level local education, again because of economies of scale, necessitating overseas training of high-level local personnel (Schweisfurth, 1995). Cross-national projects aligned with global movements – such as Education for All, and democratisation – may be particularly influential, as their inputs are in cumulation with others.

In most developing countries, regardless of scale, their own commitment to the millennium development goals (MDGs), including Education for All, has been reinforced by donor agencies' emphasis on the MDG agenda. The most heavily-indebted countries, such as The Gambia, are by nature more dependent on aid and therefore more likely to be vulnerable to pressures exerted during the negotiation of priorities and strategies. The Gambia is one of 18 'fast-track' countries receiving extra support in meeting these goals (United Nations Educational, Scientific and Cultural Organisation [UNESCO], 2002), and the quest for higher enrolment, particularly among girls, is a major focus of Gambian education policy. The sixth goal set by the Dakar World Education Forum in 2000 also called for:

> Improving all of the quality of education and ensuring excellence
> of all so that recognized and measurable learning outcomes are
> achieved by all, especially in literacy, numeracy and essential life
> skills. (UNESCO, 2000, para. 7)

The project objectives resonate with this emphasis beyond enrolment ratios to the quality of education, and beyond literacy and numeracy to life skills.

Global movements such as these are perceived at the local level to be an inevitable part of 'progress'. There was a strong sense among many Gambian respondents that times are moving on, and that if The Gambia wanted to keep up, things needed to change. Democratisation was seen as part of a movement bigger than local values. For example, The Gambia is a signatory to the UN Declaration of the Rights of the Child, and the national legal framework is currently being revised in order to bring laws into harmony with the requirements of the convention. Additionally, multilateral and bilateral development assistance agencies have in recent years emphasised 'good governance' as a prerequisite for aid. In The Gambia, international pressures played a role in the transition from military to democratic government following the coup (Okuma-Nyström, 2003).

However, these pressures have not effected anything like a complete transition at the grass roots level. As in many developing countries, local traditional values co-exist with more 'modern' values, largely cosmopolitan in nature. As Riggs (1964) and Harber & Davies (1997) have argued, it is not a question of modernity replacing tradition: the two live side by side, with individuals daily playing out the contradictions. Gambian respondents indicated that members of their communities, and sometimes they themselves, had mixed feelings about the empowerment of young people. The workshop participants, by virtue of their level of education and their positions, are more likely to be aware of western perspectives, and perhaps open to them, but they reported that communities were less enthusiastic. In response to the statement: 'The majority of people in my community are concerned that democracy in schools could lead to a lack of discipline', 17 out of 45 respondents at the final seminar strongly agreed, and only 15 disagreed or strongly disagreed. While traditional relationships between elders (including teachers) and children were seen as unsustainable in the modern world, this was perceived as a mixed blessing at best.

Corporal punishment was a recurrent theme that illustrates some of these tensions. National policy has recently restricted who can administer corporal punishment in schools, and under what circumstances, and puts limits on the instruments and severity of caning. However, even restricted use contravenes democratic and human and child rights principles. Nevertheless, as in many countries, its use is widespread in The Gambia, and workshop debates revealed that many participants saw it as a manifestation of cultural realities, and a necessary tool in discipline. Participants argued that their communities would not tolerate what would be perceived as 'softening' of school discipline. Of the participants in the final workshop, likely to be more democratic in their attitudes than the wider population, 11 out of 45 disagreed or strongly disagreed that 'Corporal punishment should be completely abolished'. In workshops, as facilitators we tried to get around this potential impasse by concentrating on alternatives to beating, acknowledging that the sudden removal of all forms of control is likely to lead to chaos. Additionally, materials from other African countries making the transition from corporal punishment to more democratic forms of discipline were used as examples, in order to avoid setting up a 'North' vs. 'South' dichotomisation in the debate. Interestingly, during the most recent workshop the tension around issues of corporal punishment seemed markedly less pronounced than it had in other regions. It transpired that recent workshops run by a Gambian non-governmental organisation, linked to the harmonisation of local laws and practices with the Convention on the Rights of the Child, had already sensitised a number of the participants to the issues – highlighting once again how these powerful global forces are converging to challenge discordant beliefs and practices.

Conclusion

There is reason to believe that factors of scale in The Gambia may contribute to the potential of a small-scale project to impact on educational practice in relation to democracy. In a small state, a small project appears more substantial: the 'big fish in a small pond' syndrome. The influence of sympathetic individuals and single institutions can facilitate this, where project goals and implementation are in harmony with local aspirations and national policy.

However, these projects are only one of many factors that may impact on – or thwart – processes of democratisation in education. Cultural factors are of critical importance. It is also necessary to bear in mind that in countries like The Gambia, all projects, individuals, institutions and movements are operating in the same small state context, and have similar potential for influence. Thus, movements that are anti-democratic might also find allies and have equal opportunities to affect practice.

One key to the long-term sustainability of whatever project impact exists may be the intersection of its aims with global forces at work in this small state. The Gambia's place in international networks, such as the Commonwealth and the United Nations, its signed commitment to UN Human and Child Rights Conventions and Education for All agreements, and its relationships with donor agencies help to shape and reinforce national goals related to education and democracy. Projects situated at these intersections are likely to have a more robust chance of making a difference.

Acknowledgements

CfBT Research and Development has generously funded both of the projects discussed. The opinions expressed in this article are those of the author, and not necessarily those of CfBT.

The contribution of all those involved in The Gambia is gratefully acknowledged, including central SQAD personnel (especially Fatou Njie and Momodou Jeng), Gambia College staff, regional office staff, and all workshop participants.

Notes

[1] In addition to the author, CIER staff involved in both projects were Lynn Davies and Clive Harber.

[2] For a more detailed discussion of the first project in particular, including processes, evidence of impact and local interpretations of democracy, see Schweisfurth (2002). For further elaboration on the findings of the survey undertaken at the final dissemination workshop at the end of the second project, see Harber (2006).

References

Arnove, R. & Torres, C. (Eds) (1999) *Comparative Education: the dialectic of the global and the local*. Lanham: Rowman & Littlefield.

Bacchus, K. & Brock, C. (Eds) (1987) *The Challenge of Scale: educational development in the small states of the Commonwealth*. London: Commonwealth Secretariat.

Bowles, S. & Gintis, H. (1976) *Schooling in Capitalist America: education reform and the contradictions of economic life*. New York: Basic Books.

Bray, M. & Packer, S. (1993) *Education in Small States: concepts, challenges and strategies*. Oxford: Pergamon Press.

Crossley, M. & Holmes, K. (1999) *Educational Development in the Small States of the Commonwealth: retrospect and prospect*. London: Commonwealth Secretariat.

Davies, L., Harber, C. & Schweisfurth, M. (2002) *Democracy through Teacher Education: a guidebook for use with student teachers*. Birmingham: Centre for International Education and Research/CfBT..

Davies, L., Harber, C. & Schweisfurth, M. (2005) *Democratic Professional Development: a guidebook for supervisors and inspectors of teachers*. Birmingham: Centre for International Education and Research/CfBT.

Davies, L. (2004) *Education and Conflict: complexity and chaos*. London: Routledge.

Delens, M. (2001) Whose Rules Apply? Educational Project Management in Less Developed Countries: cultural considerations, in L. Leach & A. Little (Eds) *Education, Culture and Economics*, 347-370. London: Falmer Press.

Department of State for Education (DOSE), The Gambia (1988) *Revised Education Policy*. Banjul: Government of The Gambia.

Department of State for Education (DOSE), The Gambia (2000) *Monitoring of Learning Achievements Project: National Report*. Banjul: Government of The Gambia.

Gambia, Republic of The (2001) *Fact Sheet: The Gambia at a glance*. http://www.gambia.com

Harber, C. (2002) Education, Democracy and Poverty Reduction in Africa, *Comparative Education*, 38(3), 267-276.

Harber, C. (2004) *Schooling as Violence: how schools harm pupils and societies*. London: Routledge.

Harber, C. (2006) Democracy, Development and Education: working with the Gambian inspectorate, *International Journal for Educational Development*, 26(6), 618-630. http://dx.doi.org/10.1016/j.ijedudev.2006.02.004

Harber, C. & Davies, L. (1997) *School Management and Effectiveness in Developing Countries: the post-bureaucratic school*. London: Cassell.

Holmes, K. & Crossley, C. (2004) Whose Knowledge, Whose Values? The Contribution of Local Knowledge to Education Policy Processes: a case study of research development initiatives in the small state of Saint Lucia, *Compare*, 34(2), 197-214.

Jeng, P. (1995) *Modern Gambia: a catalogue of errors*. Stockholm: Oxford University Press.

Lacey, C. & Jacklin, A. (2001) The Evaluation of Education Development Projects and Bureaucratic Cultures: prospects for the education sector within the context created by the White Paper on International Development, in K. Watson (Ed.) *Doing Comparative Education Research*, 295-330. Oxford: Symposium Books.

Leach, F. (2001) Dilemmas between Economics and Culture in Educational Aid, in F. Leach & A. Little (Eds) *Education, Culture and Economics*, 371-394. London: Falmer Press.

Leach, F. (2003) Learning to be Violent: the role of the school in developing adolescent gendered behaviour, *Compare*, 33(3), 385-400.

Lillis, K. (Ed.) (1993) *Policy, Planning and Management of Education in Small States.* Paris: International Institute for Educational Planning.

Nyerere, J. (1998) Governance in Africa, *Southern African Political and Economic Monthly*, 11(6), 26-28.

Okuma-Nyström, M. (2003) God Turns the Chapter and Everything Changes: children's socialisation in two Gambian villages. PhD thesis, Institute of International Education, Stockholm University.

Riggs, F. (1964) *Administration in Developing Countries: the theory of prismatic society.* Boston: Houghton Mifflin.

Schweisfurth, M. (1995) Quality and Quantity in Education in a Micro-State: a case study of the Turks and Caicos Islands. Unpublished MSc thesis, Department of Educational Studies, University of Oxford.

Schweisfurth, M. (2002) Democracy and Teacher Education: negotiating practice in The Gambia, *Comparative Education*, 38(3), 303-314.

Sen, A. (1999) *Development as Freedom.* Oxford: Oxford University Press.

United Nations Development Programme (UNDP) (2004) *Human Development Report: cultural liberty in today's diverse world.* http://www.ireland.com/newspaper/special/2004/unreport/index.pdf

United Nations Educational, Scientific and Cultural Organisation (UNESCO) (2000) *The Dakar Framework for Action, Education for All: meeting our collective commitments* (adopted by the World Education Forum, Dakar, Senegal, 26-28 April 2000). Paris: UNESCO.

United Nations Educational, Scientific and Cultural Organisation (UNESCO) (2002) *EFA Global Monitoring Report – Education for All: is the world on track?* Paris: UNESCO.

Vally, S. & Dalamba, Y. (1999) *Racism, 'Racial Integration' and Desegregation in South African Public Secondary Schools.* Johannesburg: South African Human Rights Commission.

World Bank (2006) *World Development Report.* Washington: World Bank.

CHAPTER 4

International and Comparative Research and the Quality of Education: learning from the Primary School Management Project in Kenya

MICHAEL CROSSLEY

Introduction

This chapter reflects upon recent developments in the field of international and comparative education, in the light of the experience of collaborative research and evaluation relating to the Primary School Management Project (PRISM) in Kenya, East Africa. This is followed by an account of the origins and rationale for PRISM, and a brief analysis of its implementation strategy and impact in practice. The main focus of the chapter is, however, upon the nature and influence of the PRISM research and evaluation strategy, and its contribution towards ongoing project development. Ways in which this Kenyan research and evaluation experience relates to wider trends in contemporary international and comparative research and development cooperation are then explored in drawing conclusions.

Developments in International and Comparative Research in Education

The last decade has seen a major revitalisation of interest in international and comparative research in education. A widened constituency, including policy makers, planners and practitioners, has joined increased numbers of researchers in exploring the potential to be gained from international and comparative experience and insights. In the United Kingdom, for example, the Department for Education and Skills (DfES) is currently taking increasing interest in comparative experience as a way of informing ongoing policy developments. It has also recently introduced an annual International Education Week as a way of promoting the benefits of international dimensions throughout all sectors of UK education. New specialist research centres are being established worldwide and this is reflected in the renewed growth of collective organisations such as the British Association for International and Comparative Education (BAICE) (see http://www.baice.ac.uk) and the World Council of Comparative Education Societies (WCCES) (http://www.hku.hk/cerc/wcces). Moreover, bodies such as the United Kingdom's Economic and Social Research Council (ESRC) are also paying increased attention to the methodological lessons to be learned from international and comparative research across all fields and disciplines.

The stimulus for these developments has come from a combination of factors that include: changing geopolitical relations that have reshaped global politics and challenged dominant world views; the intensification of globalisation that has transformed priorities and perspectives worldwide; advances in information and communications technologies (ICT); and paradigmatic developments that draw increased attention to the importance of cultural and contextual differences in both research and development processes. A more detailed consideration of these trends is given elsewhere (Crossley & Watson, 2003), where it is also argued that the revitalisation of international and comparative research must be accompanied by a fundamental 'reconceptualisation' in terms of theory, methodology, substantive issues and organisation. In this article, ways in which such thinking was reflected in the PRISM research and evaluation process form the main focus of attention. First, however, it is necessary to consider the origins and nature of the project itself.

The Primary School Management Project (PRISM)

PRISM was a Kenyan Ministry of Education, Science and Technology (MoEST) project, funded by the United Kingdom Department for International Development (DFID). Project implementation ran from 1996 to the year 2000 and was managed by the Centre for British Teachers (CfBT) through their office based in Nairobi. The core aims of PRISM emphasised increased access to primary education, the reduction of 'wastage' (a combination of low enrolments, repetition and drop-outs), and improvements to the quality of teaching and learning. These were to be achieved primarily through the strengthening of primary school leadership and management. This, it was argued, would help head teachers to provide more effective professional leadership, manage the mobilisation and accountability of community funds, improve school and community linkages, and assume increased responsibility for whole-school development in an increasingly decentralised system. A key element of the PRISM rationale assumed that such training would improve head teachers' understanding of the needs of disadvantaged and marginalised children – notably the poor, girls, and those with special educational needs – so increasing enrolments, enhancing equity, helping to reduce wastage and improving school performance. Broader social goals emphasised the potential for the project to contribute to improved gender equity and poverty alleviation.

Reflecting the above priorities, PRISM initially targeted the training of 9000 head teachers chosen from 42 of the more disadvantaged districts in Kenya – mainly arid and semi-arid lands – and a further 3000 working in identified pockets of poverty in non-targeted districts. In addition, project planners envisaged that more prosperous districts would recognise the potential benefits of PRISM training for their staff, and that they would voluntarily pay for their participation on a district/community funded cost-sharing basis. With this in mind, a further 4700 head teachers were initially catered for, bringing the overall target to a total of 16,700 head teachers.

The design of PRISM was influenced by a combination of national and international factors. At the national level, a needs analysis, conducted for the Ministry of Education in 1994, highlighted the importance of improved practical management training for head teachers (Aitken & Brown, 1994). This was seen as essential if earlier efforts to strengthen the quality of teaching and learning through, for example, the Strengthening of Primary Education (SPRED) project, were to be consolidated. At that time, few primary school head teachers received any management training, and appointments tended to be based upon seniority, rather than proven leadership skills and successful experience. Furthermore, Kenyan schools were seen to demand a higher level of management skills from head teachers, if they were to deal effectively with the greater degree of devolution of responsibility envisaged for the system as a whole.

At the international level, the influence of the 1990 Jomtien Declaration was significant, with its impact upon: international development cooperation agendas and priorities and emphasis upon basic education for all; universal access and improved equity; enhanced learning environments for improved quality; strengthened partnerships; the development of supportive policy contexts; and the mobilisation of increased resources for education (Little et al, 1994). The application of western research on school effectiveness was also significant in the international development arena, and this played a further part in shaping the PRISM rationale and its key characteristics. To this we should add the impact of powerful neo-liberal values and assumptions that promoted cost-sharing and marketisation principles within the global development discourse, and through the work of many government ministries and international development agencies such as DFID.

The origins of PRISM thus stemmed from a combination of national and international factors. In-country studies had revealed an urgent need for improved primary school management and leadership training, but this was consistent with international development trends and priorities at that time.

Not surprisingly, PRISM emerged as a model that would have been familiar to those engaged in educational development in a wide range of contexts elsewhere within sub-Saharan Africa and beyond.

The PRISM Implementation Strategy

For many of the same reasons articulated above, the PRISM implementation strategy also developed along somewhat familiar lines. Reflecting the widespread commitment to decentralisation processes, and to whole-school planning, the implementation strategy was based upon a cascade model for nationwide management training. In brief, this consisted of a national lead team of 13 senior and experienced educationalists. This group was established to maintain leadership, develop materials and train 88 regional trainers of trainers. These regional trainers were subsequently to be responsible for training 1500 zonal inspectors. The regional trainers and zonal inspectors were then intended to provide training for the 12,000 primary school head teachers initially targeted by PRISM. The potential weaknesses of cascade training systems were acknowledged from the outset, and efforts were, therefore, made to devise ways of strengthening the PRISM model by combining formal training with on-the-job mentoring and community-based head teacher support groups. Details of this can be found in an earlier article focused upon the role and impact of head teacher support groups (Juma et al, 2002).

The Lead Team worked with local and external consultants to develop five home-grown management training self-study modules, and to develop three related training courses for the different levels of the cascade system. The five training modules provided the core content material for the training courses, and each focused upon one distinctive theme in the light of suggestions made in the 1994 Needs Analysis. These modules were titled:

Module 1: School Development Planning
Module 2: Management of the Curriculum
Module 3: Management of People
Module 4: Management of Resources
Module 5: Training of Trainers and Training Skills

Although these materials were specifically written and developed for PRISM, paying close attention to the Kenyan context, they were informed by more general management literature and principles, including the *Better Schools* series published by the Commonwealth Secretariat (1994).

The training that was provided for head teachers was carried out at 10 training centres (pre-service teacher training colleges) distributed throughout the country. The training itself consisted of a split-site model, with a core three-week residential component based at a teacher training college. This was followed by a six-month, school-based period during which the production of a three-year school development plan formed the basis of the

PRISM training course assignment. A recall week followed the school-based component during which progress was reviewed, new assignments were carried out and further planning was undertaken to help maintain momentum for the implementation of development plans at the school level. Approximately 100 head teachers were trained every three weeks, in each of the training centres, during this phase of PRISM. One or two regional trainers were responsible for each course and a member of the Lead Team would attend to monitor quality and obtain feedback as part of an integrated quality assurance strategy.

Strategies for Institutionalisation and Sustainability

From the outset of project design, ways of facilitating the ongoing sustainability and eventual institutionalisation of PRISM were considered. With this in mind, the following strategies were seen to be key components.

Firstly, neo-liberal, cost-sharing principles were again evoked and it was envisaged that, once PRISM systems and materials had proved their worth, districts and school communities nationwide would be willing to buy into the initiative and contribute to ongoing costs. Indeed, it was hoped that the new management skills promoted by PRISM training would inspire head teachers to re-invest in further training with new funds that they could generate through improved finance and community initiatives. Secondly, as the initial project drew to a close, it was planned that the PRISM training system would be integrated into the work of a new MoEST In-service Training Unit – thereby ensuring institutionalisation and the sustainability of ongoing provision for continuing professional development for new cohorts of head teachers. Materials revision was also undertaken towards the end of the project phase, with revised versions of the five training modules (and other materials) being made available for nationwide dissemination.

At the local level, the continued functioning of head teacher support groups (networks of up to six nearby primary schools) would provide a foundation for ongoing mutual support and creativity. Towards the end of the project phase, a training and promotional PRISM video was also produced to further disseminate experience and examples of good practice, and to support their sustainability. Finally, the integral research and evaluation strategy was, in itself, seen as a vehicle for contributing to formative project evaluation, helping to inform ongoing modifications that would enhance institutionalisation and sustainability. It is to this dimension that we now turn.

The PRISM Research and Evaluation Strategy

Research and evaluation was initiated from the outset of PRISM, and designed to have both formative and summative dimensions. This was planned and carried out by a team that incorporated personnel drawn from the Kenyan MoEST, CfBT Education Services, Kenyatta University and the University of Bristol, Graduate School of Education, in the United Kingdom. The core members of the research and evaluation team thus developed a collaborative partnership that was sustained throughout the project life-span (1996-2000). In addition, at different times, many of the Lead Team members and regional trainers were involved as field researchers – contributing to a diverse team of around 80 people; insiders and outsiders, with varying levels of professional and/or research experience or expertise. This gave some of the specific studies characteristics of action and participatory research and evaluation – where those involved in the innovation were brought into systematic and critical reflection upon ongoing progress. In such ways, the research and evaluation process began to contribute directly, and simultaneously, to the dissemination of fieldwork findings to the Ministry personnel who most needed to improve their own awareness and understanding of emerging implementation issues.

The involvement of personnel with little research experience or expertise also increased the need for the incorporation of appropriate methodological training – so emphasising research capacity building/process goals, in a way that came to characterise the PRISM research and evaluation design overall.

The initial operational goals focused upon the generation of a quantitative database and ongoing feedback that would contribute to the refinement of head teacher training programmes, strategies and materials, and provide evidence of project impact in achieving desired outputs. This was to be achieved by the generation of a quantitative baseline study, conducted at the start of implementation, documentary evidence and perceptions of existing head teacher management and leadership skills prior to PRISM training. Subsequent surveys would then record changes against this baseline, supplemented by findings from related in-depth qualitative case studies of schools and their communities. It was further envisaged that this feedback would contribute to the formulation of indicators that could be used for the ongoing monitoring and evaluation of progress at the school level. This initial sequence of proposed studies was essentially applied and operational in nature – and directly focused upon these specific aspects of educational policy and practice in Kenya.

As the implementation of PRISM progressed, later components of the research and evaluation strategy built upon this foundation and incorporated a wider range of qualitative studies designed to, for example, document emerging and unanticipated issues and management needs, and to generate more theoretically informed and locally grounded analyses of PRISM policy and practice (Crossley & Vulliamy, 1997). This helped to stimulate increased critical reflection and to focus greater attention on the role of the project in dealing with the broader social goals relating to gender equity and poverty alleviation.

In practice, PRISM research and evaluation generated one of the most sustained and comprehensive sequences of studies on primary education carried out in Kenya. Three nationwide qualitative surveys were conducted, covering five groups of respondents (head teachers, deputy heads, teachers, school committee chairs and zonal inspectors) from a sample of 1200 schools. The first of these, the Baseline Study, was carried out in 1996, followed by two impact studies, in 1998 and 2000, that adopted the same basic framework and sequence of questions. In addition, a number of qualitative studies were conducted, involving detailed field observations, focus group discussions, open-ended interviews, and the collation and analysis of documentary evidence. These included school/community studies consisting of in-depth field visits designed to assess stakeholder perceptions of the nature and extent of school/community interaction; a critical analysis of school action plans; an enquiry into the extent, and functioning, of head teacher support groups; and detailed school case studies in 24 contrasting districts designed to complement the final year 2000 survey.

In total, over 17 separate research and evaluation studies were carried out between 1995 and 2000, producing substantial sets of data on primary schooling in Kenya, helpful findings for formative evaluation, robust evidence of project impact, and broader theoretical insights relating to processes of educational reform and international development cooperation. A list of key reports is provided in the Appendix.

Operationally, these studies revealed considerable success relating to PRISM implementation. By the year 2000, for example, 19,056 head teachers (or deputies) had received management training (exceeding the overall target); the strengthened cascade model had worked with strong support from the participants; PRISM materials had proved accessible, helpful and popular – being successfully revised and disseminated nationwide in the light of initial feedback; head teacher support groups were reported to be widely active; and there was evidence that systematic school budgeting was in operation in 68% of schools. Evidence of the impact of these achievements upon a reduction of wastage, or in terms of the wider social goals of poverty reduction was, however, more mixed and less conclusive.

Numerous problems were also revealed in the research and evaluation findings, especially relating to the questionable appropriateness of cost-sharing assumptions and strategies in contexts of poverty, and to the formalistic limitations of top-down/cascade training inspired by school effectiveness principles. Moreover, as dramatic political changes followed the concluding of the project phase, the policy context for any ongoing institutionalisation of PRISM activities also changed significantly. At the start of 2003, for example, the new government rapidly introduced free primary education, which led to sudden increases in the numbers of primary school pupils (estimated at more than 1 million in early 2003), changed the nature and focus of the 'wastage' phenomena, and generated new educational challenges and priorities. To a great extent, this vividly demonstrated the significance of financial considerations in previously inhibiting primary school enrolments – factors that PRISM research itself highlighted throughout the studies reported here. Changes of this magnitude – along with shifts away from project modalities towards broader sector-wide approaches to development cooperation – also demonstrate how changing contextual factors not only affect the potential for continuity and consistency in policy implementation, but also the complexities involved in making productive use of lessons learned from prior experience. We will return to these broader issues later in drawing conclusions relating to the nature of international and comparative research and processes of development cooperation.

For its time, PRISM was, nevertheless, widely regarded as one of the most successful educational interventions in sub-Saharan Africa, and those engaged in similar work elsewhere took a keen interest in learning from this experience. Moreover, the part played by the collaborative research and evaluation component was seen to have brought added benefits of increased local ownership, greater flexibility and direct feedback to practitioners, that contributed significantly to the documented successes of PRISM (Republic of Kenya, 2000). It is to the lessons to be learned from this experience that we now return.

Research and Evaluation for Educational Development: learning from the Primary School Management Project

While the achievements and problems encountered by PRISM are important in their own right, in this section we turn primarily to the lessons that can be learned from PRISM relating to the processes of research and evaluation for educational development.

The fact that PRISM studies were simultaneously begun at the outset of the project, initially prioritising the establishment of the Baseline Study, helped to overcome reference point problems that were then seen to have limited the systematic monitoring and evaluation of similar development initiatives elsewhere. As indicated above, however, elements of case-study and action research soon began to be incorporated, helping to move the overall design beyond the rather quantitative and positivistic emphases that characterised its origins. Increased recognition of the potential of in-depth fieldwork further strengthened efforts to improve the context sensitivity of the collective studies, taking team members directly into a diversity of school and community contexts nationwide. In paradigmatic terms, this drew upon the strengths of interpretive and hermeneutic traditions that prioritise the influence of context and culture, and take greater cognisance of historical antecedents in research (Habermas, 1972; Kazamias, 2001). An original combination of methodological orientations and data collection methods thus came to characterise PRISM research and evaluation, in ways that connected well with broader epistemological and theoretical debates that were increasingly recognising the potential of participatory approaches, partnerships and collaboration (Gibbons et al, 1994; Penny et al, 2000; Crossley & Holmes, 2001). Increased stakeholder involvement in PRISM research and evaluation, therefore, engaged with elements of Gibbons et al's influential 'Mode Two' reconceptualisation of research, while the strengthening of qualitative components increased the team's ability to identify and understand unanticipated project effects and implications. In such ways, the responsiveness and flexibility of the project were considerably enhanced, at the same time as the process goals of research and evaluation capacity building were extended to a wider range of Kenyan personnel.

The limitations of the research and evaluation can also be more effectively understood in the light of this reflective analysis. While the applied and operational strengths should not be underestimated, this strong operational focus had a down-side in creating little intellectual space for important theoretical considerations. In a more general sense, it is this type of danger that leads writers, such as Pring (1998), to challenge the advocates of policy-oriented studies. The PRISM experience thus underscores the argument that when little space and minimal resources exist for independently funded research – as is often the case in sub-Saharan Africa – the case for internationally supported initiatives to find better ways of bridging theoretical and applied research perspectives is especially compelling. In the case of PRISM, the operational parameters that guided the initial studies focused little attention upon any potential flaws embedded within the project conceptualisation and design itself. In practice, however, the flexibility that later came to characterise the overall research and evaluation strategy eventually opened up such forms of enquiry, helping to, for example, document the limitations of PRISM cost-sharing principles, particularly in the less advantaged contexts that comprised the priority target districts. Indeed, some of the most consistent and coherent evidence to emerge from the research and evaluation studies demonstrates how, despite their commitment to PRISM, the ability of the poorer communities to support further cost-sharing and more income-generating initiatives, in partnership with their schools and head teachers, was seriously constrained in practice. Stronger links with related comparative research could also have proved helpful in project design and development, for studies by Bray (1996, 1999), in East Asia, for example, demonstrate the complexities and dangers of policies that rely too uncritically upon the parental and community financing of education in contexts of austerity. Bray's work, along with that of other scholars working in, for example, Nicaragua (Fuller & Rivarola, 1998), Tanzania (Penrose, 1998) and Malawi (Rose, 2003), also draws attention to ways in which the uncritical international transfer of decentralisation policies can increase, rather than reduce, the disparities between schools and their communities – especially in low-income countries – at the great expense of the poor. With regard to PRISM's parallel concern to redress gender inequalities, there is also much international and comparative evidence, including that generated within Kenya, to suggest that the damaging effects of cost-sharing policies reflect even more forcefully upon poor girls (Lloyd et al, 2000; Vavrus, 2002).

Perhaps most pertinently for the present discussion, it is argued that in times when global research and development agendas are becoming increasingly influential worldwide, the importance of strengthened local research and policy analysis capacity is heightened throughout the South. This is demonstrated in the PRISM experience and reflected in the rationale that was established for the African Capacity Building Initiative (World Bank, 1998, p. 1) that aims to:

> build, over the long term, a critical mass of African policy analysts
> and economic managers and to ensure the more effective use of
> those already trained. The ultimate objective is substantially
> improved indigenous analysis and management of Africa's
> economic and development processes.

With regard to educational development, it is argued that it is increasingly important for less economically developed countries to provide research and evaluation training that will help local personnel to play a more active role in understanding, mediating and, where appropriate, challenging externally inspired development agendas. This points to the need for more critical and theoretically informed analyses of the relationships established between all engaged in international development cooperation, if new partnership modalities are to have a realistic chance of greater success than those that have preceded them.

The relevance of such issues for the research and evaluation capacity debate are significant since they help to highlight the political dimension of global and local knowledge tensions, they draw attention to the implications of the imbalances of power that continue to characterise many international research partnerships (Levesque, 2001), and they help to strengthen the rationale for future research and development strategies that are both more critically and theoretically informed, and more sensitive to a diversity of cultural, cross-cultural and profession perspectives.

Conclusions

In drawing conclusions, it is argued that the PRISM experience helps to demonstrate the potential of a number of contemporary developments relating to the advancement of international and comparative research in education and to the future of international development cooperation. Together, for example, many of the arguments presented above highlight the importance of a broadening of paradigmatic and methodological orientations as an integral part of reconceptualising research and evaluation capacity for development. There is also much to support the forging of stronger linkage between the literatures and discourses of theory and those of policy and practice. Such a 'bridging of cultures and traditions' (Crossley, 2000), it is argued, holds potential benefits for the formulation of more context-sensitive policy, for the generation of more realistically grounded theory, and for the future of comparative and international research in education. By way of illustration, the PRISM experience relates well to the methodological and ethnographic work of post-colonial researchers such as Tuhiwai-Smith (1999) and Hickling-Hudson (1998), who help to open the way for innovative qualitative studies, applying methods and processes, such as case study, critical ethnography, narrative research and life history, that can bring indigenous knowledge and grass-roots voices more firmly into the deliberations of educational and development policy makers. Indeed, in matters of implementation and sustainability, it is perhaps increasingly to such local and often marginalised voices that we should look – as the perspectives and priorities of national elites throughout the South are increasingly seen to align with those of the global elite elsewhere (Illon, 1998).

On a broader level, many of the arguments presented here accord closely with proposals for a fundamental reconceptualisation of international and comparative research in education (Crossley, 1999). Theoretical work of this nature, and the current reflections on the PRISM experience, highlight the benefits to be gained from collaborative research partnerships and from a more effective bridging of cultures and traditions, as noted above, be it between the North and South, theoretical and applied studies, policy and practice, insiders and outsiders, different paradigmatic orientations, or micro and macro level studies. Such multidisciplinary perspectives, it is argued, have theoretical, methodological, substantive and organisational implications for the nature of future research. They can also do much to improve our understanding of the significance of culture and context in educational research, and educational development worldwide. In doing so, the complexities of learning from elsewhere are highlighted along with increased awareness of the dangers of the uncritical international transfer of policy and practice. Commenting on research and policy analysis carried out in South Africa, Chisholm (2005), for example, notes that:

> the sharing of knowledge, expertise and lessons learnt amongst
> countries in the region are an important activity, but the direct
> transfer of ideas developed in one context to another, is likely to
> be a more unpredictable and possibly hazardous activity given
> their orientation within very specific contexts and their mutability
> within different contexts. (p. 82)

It is in this qualified spirit that lessons can best be learned from the PRISM experience – and from the wider international and comparative experience. The benefits to be gained from international research collaborations, nevertheless, emerge strongly from this line of thinking, as does the importance of research and evaluation capacity building throughout the South.

Finally, with regard to modalities of development cooperation that increasingly prioritise policy advice, knowledge sharing and integrated strategies for sectoral reform, the case for increased attention to improved dialogue between all involved is also heightened. To cite Samoff (1998, p. 24): 'what is required is genuine dialogue among partners who not only talk, but also listen and hear'. The analysis presented here thus raises important questions about whose knowledge should guide and inform development, and whose research and evaluation findings should provide the evidence base for future policy. In concluding, it is, therefore, argued that better ways must be found to mediate increased sensitivity to contextually and culturally specific realities, with the influence of more internationally inspired goals and agendas. In acknowledging what Arnove & Torres (1999) call the 'dialectic of the global and the local', the present analysis, therefore, adds renewed support for ongoing efforts to strengthen multidisciplinary research and evaluation partnerships and collaborations at all levels, within and between systems.

Acknowledgements

Thanks are extended to all colleagues in Kenya who participated in the studies reported here, to DFID for supporting the research and to CfBT for facilitating and encouraging creative and sustained collaboration. The views expressed are those of the author, though some of the material presented draws, with much gratitude, upon collaborative research and the jointly authored book *Research and Evaluation for Educational Development: learning from the PRISM experience in Kenya*, by M. Crossley, A. Herriot, J. Waudo, M. Mwirotsi, K. Holmes & M. Juma (2005).

References

Aitken, W. & Brown, M. (1994) *Management Needs Analysis for Primary School Headteachers in Kenya*. Report to the Ministry of Education, Republic of Kenya.

Arnove, R.F. & Torres, C.A. (1999) *Comparative Education: the dialectic of the global and the local*. Lanham: Rowman & Littlefield.

Bray, M. (1996) *Counting the Full Cost: parental and community financing of education in East Asia*. Washington, DC: World Bank.

Bray, M. (1999) *The Private Costs of Public Schooling: household and community financing of primary education in Cambodia*. Paris: UNESCO/IIEP.

Chisholm, L. (2005) The Politics of Curriculum Review and Revision in South Africa in a Regional Context, *Compare*, 35(1), 79-100.

Commonwealth Secretariat (1994) *Better Schools Series*. Management Training Booklets. London: Commonwealth Secretariat.

Crossley, M. (1999) Reconceptualising Comparative and International Education, *Compare*, 29(3), 249-267.

Crossley, M. (2000) Bridging Cultures and Traditions in the Reconceptualisation of Comparative and International Education, *Comparative Education*, 36(3), 319-332.

Crossley, M. & Holmes, K. (2001) Challenges for Educational Research: international development, partnerships and capacity building in small states, *Oxford Review of Education*, 27(3), 395-409.

Crossley, M. & Vulliamy, G. (Eds) (1997) *Qualitative Educational Research in Developing Countries*. New York: Garland.

Crossley, M. & Watson, K. (2003) *Comparative and International Research in Education: globalisation, context and difference*. London: Routledge.

Crossley, M., Herriot, A., Waudo, J., Mwirotsi, M., Holmes, K. & Juma, M. (2005) *Research and Evaluation for Educational Development: learning from the PRISM experience in Kenya*. Oxford: Symposium Books.

Fuller, B. & Rivarola, M. (1998) *Nicaragua's Experiment to Decentralise Schools: views of parents, teachers and directors*. Washington, DC: World Bank.

Gibbons, M., Nowotny, H., Limoges, C., Schwartzman, S., Scott, P. & Trow, M. (1994) *The New Production of Knowledge: the dynamics of science and research in contemporary societies*. London: Sage.

Habermas, J. (1972) *Knowledge and Human Interests*. Cambridge: Policy Press.

Hickling-Hudson, A. (1998) When Marxist Post-modern Theories Won't Work: the potential of post-colonial theory for educational analysis, *Discourse*, 19(3), 327-329.

Illon, L. (1998) The Effects of International Economic Trends on Gender Equity and Schooling, *International Journal of Educational Development*, 44(4), 335-356.

Juma, M., Herriot, A., Waudo, J., Mwirotsi, M. & Crossley, M. (2002) The Development and Operation of Head Teacher Support Groups in Kenya: a mechanism to create pockets of excellence, improve the provision of quality education and target positive changes in the community, *International Journal of Educational Development*, 22(5), 509-526.

Kazamias, A.K. (2001) Re-inventing the Historical in Comparative Education: reflections on a protean episteme by a contemporary player, *Comparative Education*, 37(4), 439-449. http://dx.doi.org/10.1080/03050060120091247

Levesque, D. (2001) Whose Money? Whose Education System? Improving Aid Effectiveness by Examining Paradigm, Policy and Implementation Perception Gaps in Pakistan's Donor Funded Primary Education Development Programme 1991-2000, doctoral dissertation, University of Reading.

Little, A.W., Hoppers, W. & Gardner, R. (1994) *Beyond Jomtien. Implementing Primary Education for All*. London: Macmillan.

Lloyd, C.B., Mensch, B.S. & Clark, W.H. (2000) The Effects of Primary School Quality on School Drop-Outs among Kenyan Girls and Boys, *Comparative Education Review*, 44(2), 113-147.

Penny, A.J., Mehru, A.A., Farah, I., Ostberg, S. & Smith, R.L. (2000) A Study of Cross-national Collaborative Research: reflecting on experience in pakistan, *International Journal of Educational Development*, 20(6), 443-455.

Penrose, P. (1998) *Cost-Sharing in Education*. London: Department for International Development.

Pring, R. (1998) Woodhead under Fire, *The Guardian*, 15 December.

Republic of Kenya, Ministry of Education, Science and Technology (2000) *PRISM. An Evaluation of the Kenyan Primary School Management Project 1995-2000*. Nairobi: Republic of Kenya, Ministry of Education.

Rose, P.M. (2003) Community Participation in School Policy and Practice in Malawi: balancing local knowledge, national policies and international agency priorities, *Compare*, 33(1), 47-64.

Samoff, J. (1998) Education Sector Analysis in Africa: limited national control and even less national ownership. Paper presented to the 10th World Congress of Comparative Education Societies, Cape Town, South Africa.

Tuhiwai-Smith, L. (1999) *Decolonising Methodologies: research and indigenous peoples*. London: Zed Books.

Vavrus, F. (2002) Making Distinctions: privatisation and the (un)educated girl on Mount Kilimanjaro, Tanzania, *International Journal of Education Development*, 22(5), 527-547.

World Bank (1998) *World Development Report 1998/99: knowledge for development*. Washington, DC: World Bank.

APPENDIX
PRISM Research and Evaluation Reports

Baseline Survey 1996

Cost-sharing Study 1996

School-Community Report 1997

Cascade Systems and Learning Organisations – a research paper presented to the 1997 Oxford International Conference on Education and Development

Impact Study 1998

Analysis of Action Plans 1998

Follow-up Research on Action Plans 1999

School Action Plan Impact Study 1999

Evaluation of Rating Averages of PRISM Training Courses 1999

Head Teacher Support Group Enquiry 1999

Head Teacher Support Group Enquiry – a research paper presented to the 1999 Oxford International Conference on Education and Development

Quantitative Impact Study 2000 – Final Executive Report 2000

Qualitative Impact Study 2000 – Final Executive Report 2000

Qualitative Study in Twenty Four Schools – Final Report 2000

PRISM Research and Evaluation – Synthesis Report 1996-2000, 2000

PRISM – An Evaluation of the Kenya Primary School Management Project: 1995-2000 (Barasa, Harley & Kaabwe, October 2000)

Voices for Change – a research paper presented to the Year 2000, University of Cambridge, Voices for Change Conference

Participatory Research, Local Knowledge and Educational Policy: the PRISM research and evaluation process in Kenya – a research paper presented to the 2001 Oxford International Conference on Education and Development.

CHAPTER 5

Remaking the Nation: changing masculinities and education in South Africa[1]

ELAINE UNTERHALTER

Since the first democratic elections of 1994 South Africa has experienced enormous political, economic and social change. Much of the scholarship on this assesses the state of the nation and the extent to which the aspirations of the early 1990s have or have not been met (Marais, 2001; Nattrass & Seekings, 2005). A significant part of the writing on education is explicitly concerned with these issues (Motala & Pampallis, 2001; Chisholm, 2004). An important body of literature on gender in politics and society considers the same themes, mapping both achievements and difficulties (Gouws, 2005; Morrell, 2005; Hasim, 2006). This chapter draws ideas from assessments of uneven changes in the political economy, the persistence of inequalities in education, and the complex forms in which gender justice has been achieved. It attempts to sketch different formations of masculinity, their location within different parts of the education sector, and some of their implications for a project regarding gender equality in education. Because this chapter is largely conceptual it has not addressed methodological issues with any rigour. It is thus rather eclectic, using some approaches from cultural studies and illustrating the discussion with examples from published work on schools. The discussion is presented in three sections. The first outlines different ways of viewing the changed nation in South Africa. The second gives instances of how the different forms of the remade nation can be linked with different forms of changing masculinity. The third section considers the performance of changing masculinities and their link with different education sites. In conclusion, I consider the implications of these forms of masculinity for assessing gender equality, education and the remaking of the nation.

Changing the Nation

The form of a nation is always mutable. Nation formation has been linked with complex processes that attempt to meld a single identity across social and geographical divisions often holding contradictory ideas in tension (Anderson, 1991; Anthias & Yuval Davis, 1992). The borders of a nation can be drawn and redrawn, not only on maps, but in minds and on bodies. Over the last one hundred years the bearers of South African national identity have shifted from groups defined by a single race and language to those defined by their diversity and intermingling. A number of authors have analysed this process of border demarcation and nation formation and their connections to gender identity in nineteenth and twentieth century South Africa (Gaitskell & Unterhalter, 1989; McClintock, 1995; Morrell, 2001).This process of forming and reforming the nation has not ended with the construction of 'a rainbow nation'. It has just become more complex to disentangle.

As part of this process I want to identify four forms of changes in the nation since 1994. The first form of change I have termed *reconstitution*. This form signals the ways in which the nation was given a new legal and institutional basis. This took place through an inclusive process of constitution making from 1992 to 1996 and culminated in the adoption of the new Constitution in 1996 which placed stress on democratic processes and human rights for all. The new Constitution signalled a radical remaking of political power and a visioning of political processes oriented towards realising the rights of the majority, rather than the interests of small white minorities. Substantial reconstitution is also evident in other areas linked to the forms of the state. For example, one national Department of Education was formed in 1994 out of the 14 racially and ethnically segregated departments of the previous era. New fiscal and welfare regimes have emerged, and the use of protectionist state machinery to bolster segments of the economy linked to the constituency of the former rulers has been replaced with a more market-oriented policy based on competition, which argues that growth secured through greater global competitiveness will secure the economic basis for redistribution and development (Marais, 2001; Nattrass & Seekings, 2005).

The second form of change in the nation I have termed *repositioning*. In the apartheid era South Africa was politically, economically and culturally isolated, subjected to sanctions, academic and cultural boycotts and excluded from major international bodies, like the Commonwealth, the United Nations (UN) organisations, and major regional organisations such as the Organisation of African Unity and the Southern African Development Community. Since 1994 South Africa has repositioned itself, both in relation to the region and the global international community. It has formally rejoined all the international organisations from which it was excluded and has gone even further in taking a new leadership role and helping envisage new forms of international collaboration. South Africa has played a leading role in the establishment of the New Partnership for Africa's Development and has seen itself as a bridge builder between the rich countries, who are insiders to the World Trade Organisation (WTO), and poorer countries who are excluded because of the restrictive terms of the WTO dispensation. Other dimensions of repositioning have been the very high profile of South Africa as a setting for major UN conferences – the World Conference against Racism of 2001 and the Earth Summit of 2002. South Africa took a seat in the Security Council of the UN in 2006.

Repositioning is also evident in the changing forms of migration to and from South Africa since 1994. Under apartheid South Africa was positioned as a place behind a curtain of oppression, from which political exiles and other non-participants in racism and oppression moved away. Professionals (who stressed a depoliticised identity) were imported into the country to make up for a lack of local skills. In the changed global order since 1994, South Africa's relation to global migration has shifted. It has received many thousands of immigrants from other African countries, Europe and North America. It has also exported skilled professionals (for example doctors, nurses, teachers), generally to Organisation for Economic Cooperation and Development (OECD) countries, either on short-term negotiated contracts or through emigration. A feature of these changed forms of migration is the repositioning of South African higher education, a source of coveted professional training both for students from other countries in Africa and for countries like the United Kingdom, which is experiencing labour shortages of teachers, nurses and doctors.

Remaking the nation takes a third form I have termed *recognition*. What I want to signal with this is a form of the nation looking not so much outward as inward into its history and knowing this again (re-cognising) in a new form . The aspiration in this process is to recognise pain, exploitation, and violence – both material and emotional – that are all a feature of the past. On the basis of this knowledge, the argument claims, it is possible for all the members of the nation to formulate in the present some new ways of living together. The most well-known example of this form of recognition is the Truth and Reconciliation Commission (TRC), which undertook an extensive and very public documentation of gross violations of human rights in apartheid South Africa between 1995 and 1998. The TRC was a key enterprise of the first government of national unity, reflecting its important aspirations for uniting a divided country. Another example of recognition has been legislation to promote black empowerment with regard to the ownership of enterprises and the hiring practices in firms. A third has been the process of developing a new curriculum approach for schools that seeks to give children the skills to understand and criticise forms of discrimination and exploitation.

The last process in this analysis of remaking the nation I have termed *re-semblance*. With this term I want to signal some of the ambiguities entailed in remaking the nation; that is, that despite processes of reconstitution, repositioning and recognition, the formal level at which these political, economic and cultural processes take place masks a deeper level at which change is slower and less profound, and where the new nation looks a great deal like the old. There is thus both an element of dissembling with regard to the newness of democratic relations in South Africa and ways in which the new society feels in some ways much like the old, hence re-semblance. Some examples of re-semblance are how the distribution of wealth remains extremely unequal, and still maintains old contours relating to race, class and gender despite some small shifts. Thus, a study using data from household and labour force surveys between 1995 and 2003 found that the earnings of unskilled men and women declined and the earnings gap widened between workers with lower and higher levels of skill and between low skilled workers and managers. Although there was a narrowing of the pay gap for men and women senior managers of all races, the differentials on the basis of race and gender for all other categories of workers had remained or had widened (Woolard & Woolard, 2007). High levels of economic growth not matched with expanding work opportunities has seen unemployment rise. While official figures put this at 25% of the labour force, wider measures indicate a much higher rate, which has actually grown for some population groups since 1997 (Bannerjee et al, 2006). The high levels of sexual violence, primarily against women, are deeply shocking and have not changed substantially from the pre-1991 situation (Jewkes & Abraham, 2002; Unterhalter, 2003). The inadequacies and vacillations of the political leadership with regard to the HIV and AIDS epidemic has been one very visible and tragic instance of failures to engage with equality in gender relations or the distribution of treatment, so that levels of infection and death indicate high levels of inequality with regard to race, gender and class. Features of re-semblance are also evident in the racialised dimensions of who passes the school leaving examinations. Between 1994 and 2005 the pass rate in the school-leaving examination increased from 58% to 68.3% (South Africa, 2007, p. 3); however, the aggregated increase masked how the highest grades were achieved in historically white schools (Fiske & Ladd, 2004; Nattrass & Seekings, 2005).

In my view the four forms of the reformed nation I have identified link with four different modalities of education. Education has been reconstituted with regard to the institutional form of national governance. South African education has been repositioned in relation to an international nexus through which people and ideas flow. It has moved from an outer periphery to a place close to the centre. The education system, and particularly the outcomes-based curriculum, seeks to structure knowledge in such a way that children can look again, and recognise ideas and the ways they are utilised to develop skills in communication and evaluation. But in many ways, with regard to the everyday experience of schools and classrooms, relations are changing much more slowly and the present often uncomfortably resembles the past (Karlsson, 2003; Chisholm, 2004).

These different formations of the nation and their links with modalities of education are also associated with changing formations of masculinity, to which I now turn.

Changing Masculinity

The study of masculinity has opened up new terrain in social science, history and cultural studies. Writers on masculinity have been concerned to show how there is not a single timeless form of masculinity, but how masculinity shifts and is constructed and reconfigured in different times, linked to different social processes (Connell, 1998; Adams & Savran, 2002; Beynon, 2002; Ouzgane & Morrell, 2005). Judith Butler has noted how femininity comes to be performed in ways that reproduce the social order and the ethos of the times ((Butler, 1999). Her work has been used to develop a very rich literature on shifting forms of masculinity. In different periods some forms of masculinity are celebrated and linked to national and cultural icons, such as sportsmen or political and military leaders, while others are marginalised, ostracised or criminalised. There is not a single form of masculinity, and shifting subject positions might mean that a single individual performs different masculinities in different settings. However, in some social formations some forms of masculinity become hegemonic, legitimating a patriarchal order of inequality (Connell, 1998).

A different performance of masculinity is associated with each of the four forms of the remade nation I outlined in the previous section. The processes of reconstitution appear to link with a recontextualised form of the heroic masculinity I identified in an earlier article on the South African anti-apartheid struggle (Unterhalter, 2001). I defined heroic masculinity as the performance of a form of masculinity concerned with putting the demands of the struggle and commitment to creating and new and more just society above the needs of family or self. This entailed both a distancing from violent forms of masculinity, but also a marginalisation of women engaged in political activism. In the period since the end of apartheid many of the leaders of the anti-apartheid struggle, who engaged a form of heroic masculinity, have come to occupy important positions in government. In times of peace and reconstitution they bring to their new roles many of the same assumptions, forms of organising and metaphors for work of the previous period. For example, Kader Asmal, Minister of Education from 1999, in introducing his corporate plan for the new education system entitled his speech 'Call to Action: mobilising citizens to build an education and training system for the 21st century'. He spoke about 'revolutionary change' in thinking about education and the necessity of aligning South Africa with global challenges (Asmal, 1999). In another speech Asmal prepared for a conference in London at the end of 2003 oriented to celebrating 10 years of democracy in South Africa he wrote:

> Let us acknowledge the generations who are growing up in non-racial schools, and who no longer attach any special significance to the racial attributes of their friends. We applaud their non-racialism, but we will continue reminding them of *what happened in our country and what must never happen again*. The achievements are spread across a wide front. …We have been able to *defend and advance* the interests of public education, with the vast majority of schools in the public sector. (Asmal, 2003, p. 2; emphasis added)

The metaphors of battle, the idea of government as struggle for the common good to 'make history' are all aspects of heroic masculinity I identified earlier in the writings of the anti-apartheid movement. In the reconstitution of the nation this form of heroic masculinity is recontextualised. The struggle has moved from the street or the prison cell to parliament, the cabinet, or the board room. But the tropes of heroic masculinity, the stress on battle, history and collective undertaking, formulated in the previous era, remain the same.

The reformation of the nation I have identified as repositioning is associated with a different form of masculinity. It is a form where South African men carry a double-sided identity that links them at once powerfully with their past, their place in South Africa, but also makes them take new global identities, as new kinds of men, who mix with world leaders, remake global relations, but are nonetheless rooted in family, home and South Africanness. This is the image Nelson Mandela projects of himself. He combines the local – rooted in South Africa and in the relations of father of the nation – with the international – routed through world capitals and international gatherings. We are thus simultaneously reminded that he is a father, grandfather, husband, owner of a garden, smiling patron of every South African child and an international actor with regard to the HIV and AIDS epidemic, or the peace process in Burundi or the war in Iraq. Another less familiar example of this repositioned masculinity rooted in South Africa, but routed through the world – and beyond – is the South African spaceman, Mark Shuttleworth, who, having made a fortune on the Internet, took a journey in space to fulfil a lifetime ambition. The family ties to South Africa are crucial to Mandela's identity. In newspaper photographs of Shuttleworth, who was living in London at the time, these links are represented in more emblematic form as a flag. In both cases it is roots and connections to a notion of the 'land' that is part of the performance of masculinity, as these notable figures move through the international and interplanetary superhighways.

The third form of new masculinity I want to comment on links with the processes of national re-cognition. In this form the old macho masculinity of the soldier, the tyrannical farmer, the callous rugby player is remade in a new form of care and compassion, but interestingly not the care of a father, but that of a teacher, someone who reveals and who comforts through the pain of learning new truth. Archbishop Tutu exemplified this new masculinity when he led the TRC and often publicly wept with people at the hearings as they revealed appalling experiences of loss, humiliation and hopelessness. Research with learners and teachers in a Durban school since 2000 indicates how the HIV and AIDS epidemic has forced some young men to take seriously responsibility for cooking, the care of siblings and peers at school. Some are open about events when they can do nothing but cry (Unterhalter et al, forthcoming 2008). Elsewhere in the country there are accounts of men in rural districts rejecting violence, engaging in gender rights and undertaking what is traditionally regarded as women's work (Walker, 2005). The young Nkosi Johnson, suffering from AIDS, also seemed to embody this new form of masculinity, using childhood not to play and be carefree, but to teach. This new form of masculinity entails using bodies differently – crying, caring, dressing a child in an adult's suit. It also entails using knowledge not only of the world of 'history' and public affairs, but making public the private world of personal and painful relationships, the form of the body that can sicken and die.

The last form of masculinity I want to discuss links with the form of the nation I have termed re-sembling. This form of masculinity, like the persistent forms of inequality, has not changed from the previous era. It is still a form of masculinity concerned with violence, assumptions of male dominance and female subordination, and compulsory heterosexuality. It is evident in the casual sexism of advertisement hoardings, assumptions by some men that they can push in front in a queue and not be challenged, the ways in which the views of a woman in a meeting might be overlooked.

What does the performance of these different forms of masculinity tell us about education? A key feature of the heroic masculinity, articulated in the autobiographical texts of the anti-apartheid struggle, was the need to make a mark not so much on the body, but on time, on history (Unterhalter, 2001). This distinguished these masculinities from the violent South African masculinities many have commented on where bodies are often invoked to signal toughness or power (Morrell, 2001). Thus the site of the performance of a form of masculinity reveals important dimensions of its significance. Judith Butler writes about gender as performance without ontology, a status or identity that is constructed and embodied in tension with what cannot be performed (Butler, 1990, 1993). It seems to me that education presents two different kinds of sites for the performance of gendered identities. The first is as a place, that is, an institution that is bound by particular rules and particular social boundaries, a 'container' for distinctively designated pedagogic and managerial practices – the school, the curriculum, the terms of service of teachers, the education department would all be examples of education as a boundaried place (Lefebvre, 1991; Karlsson, 2003). Education, however, is not simply bounded by place and institutional regulation; it is an intermingling of ideas, processes, experiences in particular settings which merge with the forms in which those experiences are narrated. Karlsson (2003) draws on the work of Soja (1996) to consider some of these aspects of 'space' in thinking about schools. I think this notion of space, more than place, distinguishes where certain forms of masculinity are performed.

Table I attempts to summarise some of the connections and distinctions I am making.

Re-formation of the nation	Associated form of masculinity	Major site of performance	The excluded other dimension of performance
Reconstitution	Recontextualised heroic masculinity	In government, corporations, leadership of trade unions or large NGOs. Sites of political and economic leadership. Education as a place	The past of racism, discrimination, lack of political representation
Repositioning	Masculinity as roots + routes	International settings; conferences, meetings, media presentations. Education as a space.	Physical and spiritual dimensions of prison South Africa
Recognition	Masculinity as its reverse	The TRC, the media. Also families; the private realm. Education as a space.	Violent masculinities of the past
Re-semblance	Compulsory heterosexuality Tough love	'Local', unofficial settings – schools, families, workplaces. Education as a place.	Gender equality as policy text and lived experience

Table I. Re-formations of the nation associated with forms of masculinity, sites of performance, and excluded terms.

The analysis suggests that while for the heroic masculinities of the anti-apartheid struggle there was only one major site of performance – the struggle – which was continued in and out of prison, in and out of family life, in and out of schools, the new masculinities are performed in a range of different sites and invoke understandings of a range of different forms of education.

Recontextualised heroic masculinity, which links with reconstitution of the nation, is performed in official places, where government leaders and other key figures in blue chip non-governmental organisations (NGOs) or civil society organisations meet. Schools, universities, education departments and other education *places* are one such site. This form of masculinity is performed in relation to a past of racism, discrimination and oppression. These are its excluded discourses. Speeches or policy texts stress the importance of the border that divides then and now.

Repositioned masculinity is performed for national and international audiences and a major site of performance is new information technologies, television and the Internet. Learning materials used in and outside of schools draw on these sources. What is excluded in this performance is the past positioning of South Africa as a prison or a fortress (physical or spiritual). Thus the confinement of the past is excluded by the breadth of the current range of new positions.

Masculinity engaged in recognition is performed in many of the same spaces as repositioned masculinity, and uses education (in its widest sense) as a space through which important ideas of public memory can be articulated. However, there are some empirical studies of this recognition/reflective masculinity also being performed within families, in private spaces and in conversations that respond to reflection and consideration (Parkes, 2005; Sideris, 2005). For this form of masculinity what is excluded are violent formations of masculinity associated with brutality and coercion.

Re-sembling masculinity is a disqualified discourse for each of the three other forms of masculinity. It is not performed on an international stage, but in local sites – families, schools and workplaces. Sometimes in its most brutal forms it hits the headlines, but generally it is a quotidian patter of unexamined assumption. Schools situated at some distance from the policy declarations and the management regimes of reconstituted masculinity are one site where this form of masculinity continues to be perfomed. The discourse it excludes – and mocks – is that of the policy statements on equality, and most notoriously gender equality. This form of masculinity is subversive of many official declarations, such as those which promote gender equality or criticise gender-based violence.

The extent to which the three changed forms of masculinity and the one form that remains the same have or have not impacted on local settings, particularly education settings, requires empirical research. It must also be stressed that different individuals might at different times exhibit features of all four forms of masculinity. The overlapping and ambiguous identities of some South African sportsmen or writers or chief executives can be analysed, seeing how at different moments and for different audiences they take on different forms of masculinity.

What are the implications of these different formations of masculinity for gender equality and particularly gender equality in education? I have taken time to separate out the different modes of articulating masculinity but I want to stress that in thinking about gender equality we need to think across all the levels and formations I have distinguished. Although the remaking of the nation has been linked with some reformations of masculinity, these have not been accompanied by sufficient attention to gender equality. Thus the recontextualised heroic masculinity of the political leadership is quite comfortable with a few references to gender equality in key policy documents, but very little attention to making this work on the ground. A persistent comment of South African women in parliament and in key NGOs has been how difficult it is to give substance to the formal rights or representation and presence women have won (Gouws, 2005; Hasim, 2006). Repositioned masculinity has not used its access to global forums to demand greater levels of gender equality. The new forms of masculinity associated with care and compassion are clearly considerably better than older forms that ignored or actively set out to harm others, and I have argued elsewhere that recognising new ways of understanding the society is an important precursor to acting to change it, redistribute power, and take equality seriously (Unterhalter, 2007). However, there is a danger that care and compassion, which is a minimum achievement on the road towards gender equality, becomes a maximal achievement, occluding concerns with redistribution and gender equality. Needless to say, the fourth form of dissembling 'new' masculinity has little concern with gender equality, except in so far as the meaning of the term is twisted.

Thus, despite new formations of the nation and of masculinity, I have sketched some very old formations that persist with continued gender inequality and scant attention to justice. Is there thus little cause for optimism? I do not feel pessimistic with regard to changes in South Africa and in closing I want to try to identify what some of the important countervailing forces are that will help promote gender equality in education and more widely in the society. Firstly, South African girls and women are well educated, with a majority completing secondary school and significant numbers in higher education. This is in striking contrast to girls and women in East, West and North Africa. While there are many difficulties with their experiences of education, and discrimination in workplaces and families continues to be documented, the effects of these higher levels of education over a generation are much more likely to sustain demands for greater gender equality than undermine it. They are also likely to have some impact on changing masculinities, although the evidence from societies with very high levels of women's education, such as the USA or the United Kingdom, shows that this is not an easy or straightforward process.

Secondly, although the significant numbers of women in parliament have not been able to secure their maximum agenda, laws have changed, and very important achievements concerning inheritance, social welfare payments, reproductive rights, and levels of pay for domestic workers (a majority of whom are women) have been won through sustained work by Members of Parliament (many of them women) concerned to foreground gender equality.

Thirdly, the not for profit sector in South Africa is large, employing many people, and engaged in a wide range of social development activities. Here women are in a majority in leadership positions. They find rapid promotion and an important site to articulate ideas. Because of the ethos of this sector, many men who work in not-for-profit organisations learn about gender equality and become gender advocates.

This chapter has looked at different configurations of the new nation in South Africa and associated forms of masculinity. In seeking to analyse different education sites for the performance of a range of masculinities it has distinguished those that are bounded by institutional regulation which sometimes means that policy change does not fully address gender equality and changed relations between men and women. By contrast, education sites which are more fluid may be more open to transformational ideas, but also allow for resistance and subversion of notions of gender equality. Remaking the nation requires attention not only to building improved cultures of learning and teaching in South African schools but also different formations of masculinity that can help sustain gender equality.

Note

[1] Earlier versions of this chapter were delivered at seminars in Cambridge (November 2002), Warwick (March 2003), London (June 2003) and Oxford (February 2004). I am grateful for comments received at all presentations, for suggestions from Andrew Parker and for continued discussion with Robert Morrell over a number of years on this theme.

References

Adams, R. & Savran, D. (Eds) (2002) *The Masculinity Studies Reader.* Oxford: Blackwell.

Anderson, B. (1991) *Imagined Communities: reflections on the origin and spread of nationalism.* New York: Verso.

Anthias, F. & Yuval Davis, N. (1992) *Racialised Boundaries: race, nation, gender, colour and class and the anti-racist struggle.* London: Routledge.

Asmal, K. (1999) Call to Action: mobilising citizens to build an education and training system for the 21st century. Statement by the Minister of Education. http://www.capegateway.gov.za/Text/2004/5/tirisanocalltoaction.pdf (accessed December 2004).

Asmal, K. (2003) Introductory Comments to the Commission on Education. Speech delivered to the London Solidarity Conference, South Africa House, 1 November.

Bannerjee, A., Galiani, S., Levinsohn, J. & Woolard, I. (2006) Why Has Unemployment Risen in the New South Africa?' Paper prepared for research forum, University of Michigan.

http://www-personal.umich.edu/~jamesl/Treasury_10_06_labor.pdf (accessed September 2007).

Beynon, J. (2002) *Masculinities and Culture*. Buckingham: Open University Press.

Butler, J.P. (1990) *Gender Trouble: feminism and the subversion of identity*. London: Routledge.

Butler, J.P. (1993) *Bodies that Matter: on the discursive limits of 'sex'*. London: Routledge.

Butler, J. (1999) *Gender Trouble: feminism and the subversion of identity* (2nd edn). New York: Routledge.

Chisholm, L. (Ed.) (2004) *Changing Class – education and social change in post-apartheid South Africa*. Cape Town: HSRC Press and London: Zed Books.

Connell, R.W. (1998) *Masculinities and Globalization*. London: Sage.

Daniel, J., Habib, A. & Southall, R. (Eds) (2003) *State of the Nation. South Africa 2003-2004*. Cape Town: HSRC Press.

Fiske, E. & Ladd, H. (2004) Balancing Public and Private Resources for Basic Education: school fees in post-apartheid South Africa, in L. Chisholm (Ed.) *Changing Class – education and social change in post-apartheid South Africa*, 57-88. Cape Town: HSRC Press and London: Zed Books.

Gaitskell, D. & Unterhalter, E. (1989) Mothers of the Nation: a comparative analysis of nation, race and motherhood in Afrikaner nationalism and the African National Congress, in N. Yuval-Davis & F. Anthias (Eds) *Woman-Nation-State*, 58-78. London: Macmillan.

Gouws, A. (Ed.) (2005) *Unthinking Citizenship: feminist debates in contemporary South Africa*. Burlington: Ashgate.

Hasim, S. (2006) *Women's Organizations and Democracy in South Africa – contesting authority*. Durban: University of Kwazulu Natal Press.

Jewkes, R. & Abraham, N. (2002) The Epidemiology of Rape and Sexual Coercion in South Africa, *Social Science and Medicine*, 55(7), 1231-1244.

Karlsson, J. (2003) Apartheid and Post-apartheid Discourses in School Space: a study of Durban. PhD thesis, Institute of Education, University of London.

Lefebvre, H. (1991) *The Production of Space*. Oxford: Blackwell.

Marais, H. (2001) *South Africa: limits to change: the political economy of transition*. London: Zed Books.

McClintock, A. (1995) *Imperial Leather: race, gender and sexuality in the colonial contest*. London: Routledge.

Morrell, R. (2001) *Changing Men in Southern Africa*. London: Zed Books.

Morrell, R. (2005) Men, Movements, and Gender Transformation in South Africa, in L. Ouzgane & R. Morrell (Eds) *African Masculinities*, 271-288. New York: Palgrave.

Motala, E. & Pampallis, J. (2001) *Education and Equity: the impact of state policies on South African education*. Johannesburg: Heinemann.

Nattrass, N. & Seekings, J. (2005) *Class, Race, and Inequality in South Africa*. Yale: Yale University Press.

Ouzgane, L. & Morrell, R. (Eds) (2005) *African Masculinities – men in Africa from the late nineteenth century to the present*. New York: Palgrave Macmillan.

Parkes, J. (2005) Children's Engagement with Violence: a study in a South African school. PhD thesis, Institute of Education, University of London.

Sideris, T. (2005) 'You have to Change and You Don't Know How!': contesting what it means to be a man in a rural area of South Africa, in G. Reid & L. Walker (Eds) *Men Behaving Differently – South African men since 1994*. Cape Town: Double Storey Books.

Soja, E.W. (1996) *Thirdspace: journeys to Los Angeles and other real-and-imagined places*. Oxford: Blackwell.

South Africa (2007) *Key Development Indicators: Education*. Pretoria: Department of Education.
http://www.info.gov.za/otherdocs/2007/developmentindicator/education.pdf (accessed September 2007).

Unterhalter, E. (2001) The Work of the Nation: heroic masculinity in South African Autobiographical Writing of the Anti-Apartheid Struggle, in C. Jackson (Ed.) *Men at Work: labour, masculinities, development*, 157-178. London: Frank Cass.

Unterhalter, E. (2003) The Capabilities Approach and Gendered Education. An Examination of South African Complexities, *Theory and Research in Education*, 1(1), 7-22.

Unterhalter, E. (2007) Truth Rather Than Justice: historical narratives, gender and public education in South Africa, in H.E. Stolten (Ed.) *History Making and Present Day Politics: the meaning of collective memory in South Africa*, 98-113. Copenhagen: Nordic Africa Institute.

Unterhalter, E., Morrell, R., North, A. & Bhana, D. (forthcoming 2008) Mobilizing the Gender of Care: accounts of gender equality, schooling and the HIV epidemic in Durban, South Africa, in S. Aikman, E. Unterhalter & T. Boler (Eds) *Gender Equality and HIV and AIDS: challenges for the education sector*. Oxford: Oxfam.

Walker, L. (2005) Negotiating the Boundaries of Masculinity in Post-apartheid South Africa, in G. Reid & L. Walker (Eds) *Men Behaving Differently – South African men since 1994*. Cape Town: Double Storey Books.

Woolard, I. & Woolard, C. (2007) *Earnings Inequality in South Africa, 1995-2003*. Pretoria: Human Sciences Research Council.

Yuval Davis, N. (1994) *Gender and Nation*. London: Sage.

CHAPTER 6

Redressing School Inequalities in the Eastern Cape, South Africa[1]

ANTHONY LEMON

Introduction

Edgar Brookes, a prominent white South African liberal, memorably described apartheid education as 'the only education system in the world designed to restrict the productivity of its pupils in the national economy to lowly and subservient tasks, to render them non-competitive in that economy, to fix them mentally in a tribal world'.[2] Notwithstanding late-apartheid reforms, education remains a critical element of post-apartheid restructuring in South Africa, albeit a sector in which improvements will inevitably take time to bear fruit.

In 1994 the African National Congress (ANC)-led government of national unity inherited a racially divided and highly discriminatory education system described by Nelson Mandela (1990) as 'a crime against humanity'. Apartheid reforms in the 1980s led to major increases in expenditure on African education, and also, through funding of so-called 'own affairs' under the 1984 constitution, in educational spending on coloured and Indian South Africans.[3] The average white pupil nevertheless benefited from educational expenditure nearly four times as great as the average African pupil in 1994. Elements of a market-driven system were introduced in historically white schools in the early 1990s, ceding control to governing bodies of 'model C' schools to which the physical assets (and maintenance costs) were transferred, leading to the admission of small numbers of black pupils but at fee levels affordable only by middle-class parents. Nothing was done at that stage to address either the accumulated inequality of generations of unequal funding or the demand from black groups for a unitary education system for all South Africans.

A comprehensive survey of needs in the country's 28,000 schools revealed not only deep inequality but also the conditions of deprivation and extreme neglect in which the great majority of children continue to be

107

educated.[4] Education as a whole received over 20% of all budgetary expenditure in the closing years of apartheid, a proportion which could not realistically be expected to rise significantly.[5] Redistribution within the new, unitary system is therefore critical to attempts to implement the principles of equity and redress which were first enunciated by the reports of the independent National Education Policy Investigation in 1990-92 [6] and have been central to policy implementation since 1994. Initially the ANC's Reconstruction and Development Programme did infuse significant new money into education, but since the introduction of the Growth, Employment and Redistribution strategy (GEAR) in 1996, the macroeconomic environment has inhibited the kinds of redistributive educational policies which the government still claims to promote.[7]

In the absence of fiscal capacity to enact new policy, Jansen argues that the state has no alternative to 'playing up the symbolic value of policy'.[8] In these circumstances, he argues:

> the making of education policy in South Africa is best described as
> a struggle for the achievement of a broad political symbolism to
> mark the shift from apartheid to post-apartheid society. We search
> in vain for a logic in policy-making connected to any serious
> intention to change the practice of education 'on the ground'.[9]

It is not the intention of this chapter to focus on the policy-making process or to critique national education policies, topics that have received a great deal of attention already.[10] Rather, attention is focused firmly on the realities of the situation in schools themselves, bearing in mind the observation of Chisholm & Fuller that 'the effectiveness of local schools will not magically increase if the policy agenda remains centred on symbols of opportunity'.[11] Particular attention will be paid to geographical issues, in the recognition that apartheid, as an inherently spatial policy framework, created a very distinctive geography whose restructuring poses equally geographical challenges.[12]

The next section of the chapter focuses on national policies concerning the funding of schools and those elements of South Africa's quasi-federal system which influence the delivery of education. The focus then shifts to the Eastern Cape Province, beginning with a short description of key features of the geographical context in which the province seeks to apply national education policies. Problems and policies for educational delivery in the province are then addressed, drawing on extended discussions with the Deputy Permanent Secretary of the Eastern Cape Education Department (ECED) and the District Manager for the Grahamstown District. Two key indicators of the apartheid educational inheritance are then briefly considered. The final part of this section investigates the geography of examination performance, using raw data supplied by the provincial examinations centre in King William's Town and mapped on the basis of school districts for the years 1999 and 2001.

Research in specific schools is reported in the next and most substantial part of the chapter. It was decided to focus on the secondary sector because of the opportunity to study schools still very much in post-apartheid transition: many students in these schools, especially in the older age cohorts, had experienced racially segregated primary education, perhaps with limited desegregation of white schools in the closing years of apartheid. The secondary sector also enables ready comparison of outcomes in terms of examination performance. Research on the primary sector is equally crucial, given its formative influence both academically and socially and hence its critical impact on the life chances of the poor.

The location chosen was the Grahamstown District, one of four districts in the ECED's Western Region.[13] The District Manager, Mr Mgolodela, offered helpful advice in choosing a representative range of schools. The 15 schools visited include private schools, former model C (white) schools, a former coloured school, African township schools in Grahamstown itself and the small coastal town of Port Alfred, and rural schools in Bathurst and Riebeeck East. The discussion continues with an analysis of the most important evidence emerging from the survey. The chapter concludes by making some practical suggestions for more effective progress in widening opportunities for those currently disadvantaged so as to bring the delivery of education closer to realising the goals of equity and redress.

National Education Policies

Whilst South Africa retains a small but significant private school sector, the vast majority of schools administered by the various apartheid education departments have been recast as public schools with school-based governance structures and a financing system increasingly orientated towards site-based management.[14] Personnel costs are publicly funded according to a standard formula based on learner–teacher ratios (LTRs). Disbursement of public funding for non-personnel costs is based on criteria that attempt to redress inequalities in existing levels of infrastructure and in relation to the economic capacity of the parent community. Critically, the South African Schools Act of 1996 enables schools to set user fees at a level acceptable to the school's parent community and encourages governing bodies to supplement public funding through school-based funding initiatives. Notions of equity and public right are thus reduced to basic provision rather than to comparability of quality across the whole system.

Legally, no child can be excluded from a state school because his or her parents are unable to pay the fees. Parents qualify for a reduction if the household income is less than thirty times the annual fee. Sayed criticises the assumption of middle-class benevolence as naïve: most parents do not want to 'subsidise' children of poorer families, and schools themselves are inclined to minimise the number of families paying reduced or no fees.[15] They do this by delineating geographical feeder areas to the school and otherwise controlling the admissions process. Whilst there is an obligation to admit children for whom the school is the closest to their home, the widening of the school's feeder area tends to increase the number of applicants from whom it can choose. Language or other admissions tests are prohibited in terms of the Schools Act, but the onus for determining who is exempt from fees is placed on governing bodies and the absence of any monitoring system permits schools to 'screen out' those who are unable to pay. Some schools require proof of living in an area, such as electricity bills or rent statements, which can exclude children of domestic workers or sub-tenants. Insistence on dealing with biological parents may also exclude many African children who are cared for by grandparents or other relatives.[16]

The playing field from which schools start in the competition for the most 'desirable' learners is not remotely level: schools bring to the process reputations based on previous performance, facilities and staffs inherited from the apartheid period, and their geographical location. Parents naturally seek access for their children to what they consider to be the best schools they can afford within the bounds of cost and geographical distance. The outcome is described by Soudien et al as 'the commodification of provision' in which 'consumer choice thus eclipses social redress and reconstruction'.[17]

The Role of the Provinces

South Africa's post-apartheid constitutional dispensation devolves considerable responsibilities to the nine provinces created in 1994, of which the Eastern Cape is one. In education, policy development and coordination remain central government responsibilities, but the management and financing of school education is devolved to the provinces. This has led to a situation where central policy aspirations come into conflict with the administrative and resource constraints of provincial governments, with many 'unfunded mandates' – policy commitments embedded in national legislation that provinces lack the financial or human capacity to implement – such as the reduction of learner–teacher ratios without any concurrent increase in resources to pay teachers' salaries.[18] The central government is often unable to change the speed and direction of policy implementation in the provinces, since this would require stepping over the fine line between national powers and provincial competences.

The problem of administrative capacity is partly derived from the apartheid inheritance and the nature of administrative restructuring after 1994. Devolution of functions and staff from the centre to the new provincial governments would in itself not have been unproblematic, but in South Africa the situation was complicated by the existence of both the 'own affairs' structures of the tricameral parliament and the 10 former black 'homelands', four of which were supposedly independent states and the other six self-governing in many respects, including education. The Eastern Cape has a particularly complicated inheritance, as its new provincial administration was faced with taking over functions and staff from all the following units of apartheid government: the Cape Province (white education), the Department of Education and Training (African education outside the homelands), Ciskei and Transkei (both formerly 'independent' homelands: Figure 1), the House of Representatives and the House of Delegates (coloured and Indian education respectively, responsible for 7% and less than 1% respectively of the Eastern Cape population). This complex administrative restructuring was not helped by the low calibre of some of the staff involved, especially in the former homelands.

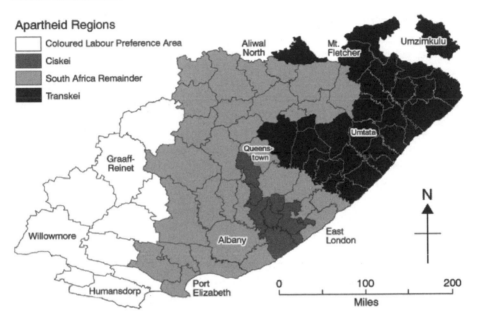

Figure 1. Apartheid political divisions in the Eastern Cape, 1994.

In 1997 the director general of public service and administration published a report on provincial governance which revealed that three provinces – the Eastern Cape, KwaZulu-Natal and the Northern Province – were on the verge of collapse. The national government threatened to impose section 100 of the constitution, which gives it power to take over devolved functions from a province if these are not being carried out competently. In the event the Eastern Cape was rescued with a one-off grant, subject to the implementation of mechanisms to improve financial control and management. The problems identified included grossly inadequate financial, information and human resource management systems, chronic shortages of skilled staff, a lack of discipline and the prevalence of fraud and theft in many departments.[19] National departments were asked to formulate proposals to assist their provincial counterparts in overcoming these problems. In budgetary terms provincial education departments have typically experienced 'a full cycle of expansion, over-expenditure, curtailment and restoration of fiscal balance', leading to organisational disarray, poor services and depressed morale.[20]

Schools have, as a result, suffered setbacks in personnel management, curriculum reform, the construction and maintenance of buildings and the provision of learning materials. One episode will serve to illustrate the uncertain environment in which schools have to function. In late 1999 the Eastern Cape Education Department (ECED) was given an additional R200m. emergency payment by the central government, but early in 2000 the provincial MEC (Minister) of education said that his department would exceed its 2000 budget by at least R600m. He said this to explain his announcement of the closure of the province's farm schools only a few days after he had promised the Human Rights Commission that he would provide these impoverished schools with a R14m. subsidy.[21]

Teacher allocation and redeployment is an important provincial responsibility which is critical to the achievement of greater equity in the school system. Each province has its own formula for calculating the quota of teachers to which each school is entitled, and teachers above that quota are placed on a redeployment list. In the Eastern Cape, learners in grades 1-3 are weighted above 1, those in grades 4-7 at 1, and learners in grades 8-12 according to subject. The formula is then based on the school's share of all weighted learners in the province multiplied by the number of available posts in the province. Schools with excess teachers may decide which teachers should be placed on the redeployment register. This offers some opportunity for manipulation, as schools may designate teachers who offer subjects unlikely to be in demand at deficit schools.

In August 2000 the Eastern Cape had 68,863 'educator posts', of which 3161 were vacant. The 10,289 teachers initially declared in excess represented a higher proportion of the teaching force than in any other province apart from the North West Province; thus the redeployment challenge was formidable. By August 2000 7730 (75%) had been redeployed and 2559 (25%) remained on the redeployment register (ECED, 2000). Initially teachers in excess were expected to apply for other posts, but not all of them did so. Now that the province has reached what it regards as the 'mopping up' stage of the redeployment process, excess teachers no longer have a choice: they are matched to suitable vacancies and receive 'placement letters' informing them of their allocation to these posts. Some resign rather than move, others appeal on grounds of marriage, health or other reasons. In some cases their school governing bodies reappoint them and pay their salaries out of school funds.

The Eastern Cape: a poor province

With a population of 6.8 million in 2000, the Eastern Cape had 15.4% of South Africa's population, but its share of the country's gross domestic product (GDP) was only 7.2%. Its per capita GDP was less than half the national average, lower than all other provinces apart from the Northern Province.[22] The province's 'equitable share' of nationally raised revenue, based on a formula which takes into account such factors as the magnitude of the province's infrastructural backlog and number of schoolchildren, was 17.5%.[23] This matches its share of enrolled school learners, which was 17.95% in 2000 [24], but any allowance for the massive backlog in educational infrastructure must presumably have been cancelled out by other factors in the funding formula.

The poverty of the Eastern Cape is clearly linked statistically to the low proportion of whites in the population (5.6%), just under half the national average (11.6%) in 2001.[25] Only the Northern Province had a lower proportion of whites. The relatively low level of urbanisation – 42.9% compared with a national average of 56.1% in 2000 [26] – is also significant, given the extent of rural–urban inequality in South Africa as a whole. Unemployment, a major cause of poverty, is above the national average: 32.0% (strict rate) and 48.4% (expanded rate) in the Eastern Cape in 2001, compared with 29.5% and 41.5% respectively for South Africa as a whole.[27] The widening of the gap in the case of the expanded rate suggests that many of the unemployed have ceased to look for work, probably because they see no prospect of finding it.

Among many educational indicators that might be cited, the proportion of underqualified teachers (26%) was above the national average of 22% in 2000 [28]; the LTR of 35.7 in 1999 compared with an average of 32.7 [29] and the computer–learner ratio of 1:558 was less than half the national average of 1:254 in 1996.[30] Examination results in the Eastern Cape were well below the national average in 2001: 46% passed Senior Certificate (school leaving) examinations, compared with 62% nationally, and only 7% qualified for matriculation exemption (university entrance), the lowest figure in South Africa and less than half the national average of 15%.[31] This gap between provincial and national performance has widened markedly since the late 1990s.

Spatial Patterns of Educational Provision and Outcomes in the Eastern Cape

Data on examination performance in 1999, 2000 and 2001 were obtained from the provincial Examination Department. The latter consisted of lists of all schools in the province in descending order of performance on a spreadsheet, but rearrangement of the schools into their respective school districts made it possible to calculate district performance in the Senior

Certificate examination and Matriculation Exemption. These data have been mapped for 1999 and 2001.

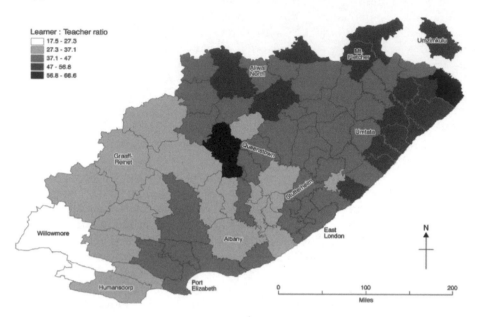

Figure 2. Learner–teacher ratios in Eastern Cape Magisterial Districts, 1991.

LTRs in 1991 (Figure 2) illustrate clearly the more favoured status of whites and coloureds in the former Coloured Labour Preference Area (CLPA) (Figure 1). This was an area which covered all the present Western Cape province as well as smaller parts of the Eastern and Northern Cape, in which the predominance of coloured people led the previous government to give preference to coloureds over Africans in employment, in an attempt to minimise African immigration and maintain the coloured and white character of the region. In the Willowmore District, for example, there were a mere 35 African pupils, and in the neighbouring Aberdeen and Jansenville Districts 257 and 765 respectively.[32] Of those districts with an average of more than 47 learners per teacher, 14 out of 17 fall within the former Transkei homeland but none are within the former boundaries of Ciskei. This may reflect the major contrast in functional urbanisation levels between the two homelands: 11.7% in Transkei in 1989 and 84.7% in Ciskei, which includes East London's huge satellite township of Mdantsane.[33] In the province as a whole, urban areas have average rather than exceptionally good teacher provision. This probably reflects the increased ratio of Africans to whites among younger age groups – the pupils on which the LTR is based, together with the impact of African urbanisation which leaves many older people behind in rural areas.

The two maps of examination results across the province reveal a striking east–west contrast (Figures 3 and 4). They are based on school districts, which in the more sparsely populated west of the province tend to be much larger in area than the Magisterial Districts in Figure 2, but the 50% pass rate in the Senior Certificate is clearly confined to seven districts comprising the western part of the province together with the city of East London in 1999 (Figure 3). The two most successful school districts, Humansdorp and Graaff Reinet, correspond closely to the former CLPA. Areas with pass rates of below 40% coincide equally closely with Ciskei and Transkei, with the former Transkeian capital, Umtata, the single island of slightly greater success. Six districts have average pass rates below 25%, all of them in Transkei.

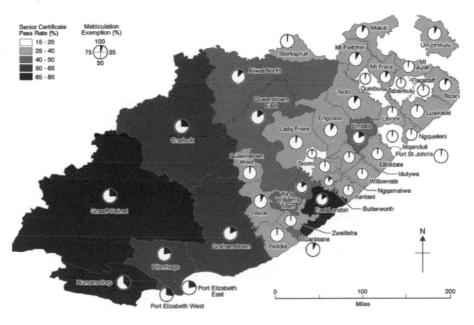

Figure 3. Examination results in school districts of the Eastern Cape, 1999.

Levels of matriculation exemption show similar patterns of variation. In Transkei only Umtata (17.9) and Butterworth (10.5), the main industrial growth point, managed rates of over 10% in 1999; no district in Ciskei achieved this. Most areas outside the former homelands had matriculation exemption rates of over 15%, rising to 28.1% in Port Elizabeth West and 37.8% further west in Humansdorp.

Comparison of Figures 3 and 4 requires awareness of overall variation between 1999 and 2001. There was a significant increase in the Senior Certificate pass rate in South Africa from 49% in 1999 to 62% in 2001. In the Eastern Cape, however, the improvement was much less impressive: from 40% in 1999 to 46% in 2001. Likewise the Eastern Cape failed to participate

115

in the national improvement in the rate of matriculation exemption, from 12 to 15%; the Eastern Cape figure remained unchanged at 7%. Allowing for the improved overall Senior Certificate pass rate, the geographical variations in Figure 4 repeat the broad pattern of 1999, as would be expected only two years later. Analysis of the raw data reveals, however, that regional inequalities may have widened slightly. Of 24 school districts falling within the former Transkei, one-third experienced a decrease in their Senior Certificate pass rate, compared with only 2 districts out of 13 in non-homeland areas. Only one district out of five had a lower pass rate in the former Ciskei, but this district, Mdantsane, was by far the largest in terms of population. This widening inequality is even more marked in terms of matriculation exemptions, with 21 districts out of 24 in the former Transkei achieving worse results in 2001. Thus, not only is the Eastern Cape falling further behind the national average, but within the province the poorest areas appear to be making least progress.

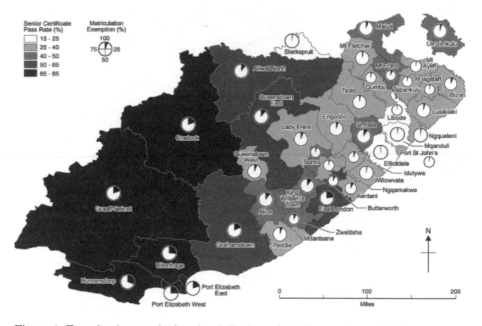

Figure 4. Examination results in school districts of the Eastern Cape, 2001.

The region chosen for fieldwork, the Grahamstown District, is not one of the poorest areas, and it is important to bear this in mind in relation to the resources, conditions and examination results of the African schools visited. It falls within former 'white' South Africa and includes no former homeland or CLPA areas. It did, however, offer the opportunity to visit a wide range of schools, including wealthy private sector schools, English- and Afrikaans-medium formerly white, ex-model C state schools, a formerly coloured school, African township schools and rural schools, including one where the coloured/African divide had been blurred even in the apartheid years.

Grahamstown: profile of a small apartheid city

The city of Grahamstown, the location of 11 of the schools visited, lies some 80 miles north-east of Port Elizabeth. It was bisected by the national road to East London until the apartheid authorities decided to build an expensive bypass to avoid the African townships during a politically turbulent period in the 1980s. The Settlers' Monument, a massive hilltop memorial to the 5000 British settlers of 1820-21, embodies Grahamstown's claim to be the capital of 'settler country' in the Eastern Cape. The Anglican Cathedral and English-medium Rhodes University, at opposite ends of the High Street, symbolise both the 'Englishness' of Grahamstown and its function as an educational and cultural centre, relying heavily on its university and schools for employment.

Grahamstown's physical location in a basin, and its relatively small size, make it possible to view the whole city at once from the Settlers' Monument. Unusually for an apartheid city, the African townships were and are a prominent feature of the landscape visible from many white parts of the city. Distances within Grahamstown are small, and thus a much less significant obstacle to school desegregation than in larger cities. The apartheid legacy could hardly be plainer. Former all-white suburbs in the west are well treed and relatively spacious. The major schools, several with extensive boarding facilities, are prominent features in the landscape. A small Indian area can be identified by the prominence of its modern Hindu mandir. The coloured area forms a transitional belt before the African townships are reached. Much of the open land which formed a 'buffer strip' in apartheid days – criss-crossed with the paths trodden by Africans walking to shops and jobs in the white town – is now covered with African people's homes. Beyond the older townships – the Fingo Village, Tantyi, Makana's Kop – more recent formal and informal African housing stretches for two or three miles up the eastern slopes: a dense mass of buildings and shacks with few trees or open spaces, but a few schools, a sports stadium, small churches and the towering floodlights which provide economic if intrusive street lighting in most of South Africa's African urban areas. This part of the town is obviously poor, though with islands of relative affluence and some signs of improving infrastructure including electricity, more tarred roads and telephones.

Despite Grahamstown's limited employment base, large numbers of Africans have been moving there since the 1990s either to escape the rural poverty of much of the former Ciskei homeland or when forced to leave commercial farms as they shed labour. The latter process has accelerated since 1994 as farmers anticipated new laws giving Africans greater rights to stay on white farms by evicting many of them while they could legally do so.[34] The city's population was recorded as 62,640 in the 1996 census, but five years later the real figure was estimated to be about 100,000, including some 15,000 whites, a few thousand coloureds and 300 Indians.[35] The result of this growth, in the absence of significant economic growth, is an estimated unemployment rate of 60-70%. Survival, for many families, depends upon old age pensions (often supporting younger members of the family as well as their recipients) and informal employment.

This experience of population growth without parallel economic growth, with ensuing unemployment and widespread poverty, is common to many small and medium-sized towns in the Eastern Cape. Rapid growth of the school-age population is a challenge to the ECED, while the poverty of most Africans in both urban and rural areas severely limits any parental contribution to school costs.

Private Schools in Grahamstown

It was important to include private schools in this study, given their prominence in Grahamstown and their disproportionate share of educational resources in the city and region. Kingswood, St Andrew's and the Diocesan School for Girls (DSG) had only 1400 pupils between them, and only 1000 at the secondary level (grades 8-12) which is the focus of this chapter (Table I). Numerically, therefore, they jointly equate to just one of the larger township schools. Most pupils board – two-thirds of seniors at Kingswood, 85% at St Andrew's and 80% at DSG. Significant numbers come from outside South Africa: over 15% at Kingswood, and about 10% at St Andrew's and DSG. Kingswood draws particularly from Botswana, and to a lesser extent Zambia and Lesotho, in all of which the school actively markets itself. Currency restrictions have made it impossible for most Zimbabweans to afford the fees since the 1970s. One-third of the school's South African students come from outside the Eastern Cape, principally Gauteng and the Free State. St Andrew's and DSG have small numbers of pupils from many countries in southern and eastern Africa, Europe, Hong Kong, Australia and elsewhere. Often these are children of company executives who move around, and want their children's education to be anchored in one place.

School	Students/% by race (1)	Teachers: ECED (2)	Extra Teachers	LTR	Fees p.a. (Rands)
GRAHAMSTOWN *Private*					
Diocesan S for Girls	350 grades 4-12 210 grades 8-12 85-90 W, 10-15 B	0	35	10:1	23,000; boarders 44,000
Kingswood College	600 grades 1-12 350 grades 8-12 80 W, 17 B, 3 I/C	0	49 grades 8-12: 35	10:1 (grades 8-12)	25,000; boarders 50,000

St Andrew's College	440 86 W, 11B, 3 I/C	0	42	10.5:1	30,900; boarders 48,800
Ex-Model C Victoria Girls High	360 42 W, 8 I/C, 50B	16 (3)	4	17:1	2,400; boarders 6,000
Graeme College	612 grades 1-12 303 grades 8-12 65 W, 20 B, 12 C, 2 I	23 (2)	6	20:1	3,260; boarders 10,660
Hoërskool P J Olivier	354 grades 1-12 34W, 33C, 33B	12	8	17:1	2,200
Ex-Coloured Mary Waters School	857 65 C, 35 B	27 (4)	0	31:1	200
Township schools Benjamin Mhalalesa	653 100 B	30 (5)	0	21:1	50
Khulitso Daniels	492 100 B	15	0	31:1	50
Nathaniel Nyaluza	695 100 B	25	0	27:1	80
Nombulelo	1,330 100 B	41 (3)	0	32:1	60
PORT ALFRED Port Alfred High	792 grades 1-12 67 W, 6 C, 27 B	23	11.5	22:1	2,460
Nomzamo Secondary	668 100B	29 (7)	0	22:1	30 2001: 50
RURAL Shaw Park Combined	213 grades 1-12 163 grades 8-12 100 B	9	0	24:1	40
Riebeeck East	235 grades 1-12 c.70 B, 30 C but no clear divide	13 (3)	0	17:1	60

Notes
1. W = White, B = Black, C = Coloured, I = Indian
2. Numbers in parenthesis indicate teachers on the redeployment list.

Table I. Selected interview data for the schools visited.

These schools no longer receive any state subsidies, and fee levels exclude all but the most affluent, with the consequence that the racial composition of all three schools is dominantly white (Table I), although as private schools with

119

a relatively 'liberal' tradition they have been admitting pupils of other races since this became legally possible in 1972. Kingswood commented on increasing difficulties of recruitment in the face of a white emigration process that is selective of those with money and skills. Grahamstown's image as a relatively safe place helps competition within a shrinking pool of affluent whites, but the black upper middle class is small in the Eastern Cape. St Andrew's sometimes has a waiting list, but seldom a large one. DSG had a waiting list at all grades except one, perhaps because of its small size and because it is the only girls' private school in the area. Even for those parents who can afford it, the high quality of Grahamstown's former white state schools, which also offer boarding facilities, offers a vastly cheaper alternative (see below). What, then, are parents buying at private schools?

Academic results are predictably excellent – 100% is the norm in the Senior Certificate and almost all pupils also gain matriculation exemption – but this is not significantly different from former white state schools (Table II). The possibility of a post-matriculation year is attractive to some. Very low LTRs guaranteeing personal attention are important, and the low proportion of African children is perceived to be an advantage by parents who believe that a higher proportion would lower standards, or who are 'culturally conservative' [36], as is the case with many Eastern Cape farmers. The same factor also attracts some African parents who want their children to be educated in a white/European/Western environment, with the standards they associate with this. Spiritual values are also important to some parents – all three schools are church foundations with a strong Christian ethos.

School	Senior Cert. 1999	Senior Cert. 2000	Senior Cert. 2001
GRAHAMSTOWN			
Ex-Model C			
Victoria Girls High	100.00	100.00	100.00
Graeme College	100.00	100.00	93.62
Hoerskool P J Olivier	96.30	100.00	96.55
Ex-Coloured			
Mary Waters School	52.11	54.88	60.00
Township schools			
Benjamin Mhalalesa	37.62	16.84	31.65
Khulitso Daniels	29.85	36.17	29.79
Nathaniel Nyaluza	61.97	54.76	35.58
Nombulelo	89.91	86.26	76.53
PORT ALFRED			
Port Alfred High	89.13	100.00	100.00
Nomzamo Secondary	39.00	50.89	90.48
RURAL			
Shaw Park Combined	33.33	no data	no data
Riebeeck East Comb.	6.25	38.89	27.27

School	Matriculation 1999	Matriculation 2000	Matriculation 2001
GRAHAMSTOWN			
Ex-Model C			
Victoria Girls High	80.00	84.85	92.73
Graeme College	76.32	85.18	70.21
Hoerskool P J Olivier	29.63	25.92	27.59
Ex-Coloured			
Mary Waters School	7.04	9.76	10.67
Township schools			
Benjamin Mhalalesa	0.99	17.89	3.80
Khulitso Daniels	2.99	6.38	2.13
Nathaniel Nyaluza	12.68	11.90	13.46
Nombulelo	26.13	25.19	19.39
PORT ALFRED			
Port Alfred High	56.52	58.33	43.64
Nomzamo Secondary	7.00	9.82	42.86
RURAL			
Shaw Park Combined	5.55	no data	no data
Riebeeck East Comb.	0.00	0.00	0.00

Table II. Percentage pass rates in Senior Certificate and Matriculation Exemption for 1999, 2000 and 2001 in the state schools visited.

Another obvious attraction is the outstanding facilities of all three schools. DSG and St Andrew's, which share some resources, have nearly 200 computers between them. They offer an unusually wide range of sports and DSG alone boasts two full-time drama teachers and five full-time and 10 part-time music teachers, many of them from Rhodes University, offering tuition on every instrument. They share a multimillion rand design and technology centre on the St Andrew's campus. St Andrew's has eight rugby fields, nine tennis courts and five squash courts, three swimming pools (one of Olympic size), 14 cricket nets, bowling machines and seven turf wickets.

What relevance, if any, have these islands of privilege in a poor community and region? Their existing efforts to relate to the local situation are extremely limited. Bursaries help some pupils enter or remain at the schools, but these assist families who must, because of the contribution they still have to make in almost all cases, be relatively affluent. The R10m. raised by the headmaster of St Andrew's in the USA and Europe to fund such awards helps a small number of people, whereas such a sum could make a vast difference to a far larger number of pupils in township and rural schools. The same applies to the one full boarding award offered by DSG to an African girl from a disadvantaged family in Grahamstown.

Much more valuable, potentially, is the sharing of teaching resources and facilities. St Andrew's founded the Pupil Enrichment Programme in the early 1980s, which brought township children to St Andrew's on Saturdays to 'enhance capacity' in science and maths. This subsequently came to be perceived as paternalistic, and was replaced in the early 1990s with the Teacher Aid Project, which moved help into a township setting. In 2000, as community control in the townships increased, it became the Teachers and Parents Project, but at this point St Andrew's relinquished its involvement at the request of the African community. Some township children were allowed to use St Andrew's sports facilities, but the headmaster stressed that the parameters of such cooperation must be spelt out carefully 'because of different expectations'. DSG bussed in girls from township schools twice weekly to play squash, hockey and other sports, and, like the other private schools, has long had some joint sporting fixtures with township schools (Grahamstown claims the first integrated sports organisation in the country, with schools playing one another, dating from 1988).

Another potential contribution comes from community service by the pupils of these privileged schools. Arguably, however, the benefits to the pupils themselves, in bringing them into contact with the lives led by most South Africans, outweigh the actual contribution that they can make, and it was in these terms that the headmaster of DSG presented his school's community service. At St Andrew's the headmaster pointed out that the boys had little spare time, given the 'frenetic' nature of the school with multiple activities and high expectations; he also mentioned potential problems of litigation and parental objections.

Former White Schools in Grahamstown

The three schools visited in this category, all ex-model C schools, had previously distinctive roles: Victoria Girls' High (VGH) and Graeme College as the only white English-medium secondary schools for girls and boys respectively, and Hoërskool P. J. Olivier (PJO) as the only Afrikaans-medium secondary school. Graeme and PJO also incorporate junior grades. All three have a boarding element (VGH 130, Graeme 112, PJO 80), but with fees a fraction of those in private schools (Table I), and catchment areas within the Eastern Cape, apart from three VGH girls from Lesotho and 20 Ghanaians, Kenyans and other Africans at Graeme. VGH and Graeme in particular have impressive facilities and grounds, offering a wide range of sports, music, drama, design and technology. All three schools achieve or come very close to 100% pass rates in the Senior Certificate; VGH and Graeme also have very high levels of matriculation exemption, but PJO lags far behind (Table II).

All three schools had desegregated much further than the private schools, thanks to fee levels affordable by the black middle class (Table I). At VGH 95% of boarders were African, and at Graeme 45%. In recent years

Graeme has attracted some Afrikaans-speaking whites whose parents want an English-medium education for their children and an environment which has more to offer extramurally. PJO, founded in 1956 for the Afrikaans-speaking minority of whites in Grahamstown, now has spare capacity following the closure of three former employers of Afrikaners – water affairs, the railway and the Afrikaans-Nederlands department at Rhodes University – and the substantial reduction of military personnel stationed in Grahamstown. Its African students are the children of Afrikaans-speaking parents who have joined the rural exodus to Grahamstown. Its white pupils include a small number from relatively poor families, usually because of unemployment.

Fee income enables all three schools to support extra teachers, whilst two of them also continued to benefit from ECED teachers on the redeployment list (Table I). Even without 'excess' teachers, these schools benefit from provincial formula weightings in terms of grades and subjects which give them more quota teachers than their numbers alone would warrant. Graeme College was clear that it would try to retain and pay its 'excess' teachers if and when the ECED eventually insisted on their redeployment. The personal problems inherent in the process are illustrated by the placement letter sent to one Graeme teacher, allocating him to a Xhosa school on the KwaZulu-Natal border, 500 km away: he did not speak Xhosa, his daughter was taking matriculation examinations in Grahamstown and his wife also worked there. The administrative problems of the process produced a revealing comment from the headmaster of VGH:

> Why has it taken so long to redeploy the other three teachers? The administration is not in place ... I have not seen any departmental official ... I don't think I have ever had a reply to my letters yet ... [in effect] this is a private school and run as a private school.

The headmaster of PJO also reported failure to respond to communications on the part of ECED, which had failed over a period of months either to approve the filling of a quota vacancy or to respond to a request to make a substitute appointment to replace a teacher who was seriously ill.

In terms of recruitment, it was clear that none of these three schools adhered strictly to legal requirements. Financial viability was essential for the boarding hostels, so admission of boarders clearly depended on ability to pay, although this certainly did not exclude Africans, as has been seen. Otherwise PJO, with its spare capacity for Afrikaans-speakers, appeared to be easier for Africans and coloureds to enter (though many are no doubt deterred by fee levels) than Graeme and VGH, which are both oversubscribed. In these schools, headmasters used phrases such as 'girls who will benefit' and 'someone who might fit in, on the basis of the school report'. Communication skills and a reasonable fluency in English were mentioned. VGH, while allowing for variations in background, regarded 'ability to cope with the standards' as essential. It had developed a number of unofficial 'feeder' schools, both in Grahamstown and farther afield, including ex-model

C primary schools whose children 'need to continue the type of education they are used to'. In effect, admissions policies of these schools bear comparison with those of private schools. They are not racially discriminatory, but in the absence of monitoring they clearly depart from legal requirements in order to maintain character and standards.

The private school analogy is increased by the fact that these schools are, unlike former African, coloured and Indian state schools, responsible for almost all funding apart from the salaries of quota teachers: utilities, phones and fax machines, computers, repairs and maintenance, furniture and non-teaching staff salaries (with the interesting exception of matrons in the overwhelmingly African VGH boarding houses, reluctantly paid for by ECED after the school secured the intervention of Kader Asmal, the national Minister of Education). There is obvious equity in this arrangement, given the schools' more affluent catchment areas and the higher costs of maintaining their superior facilities. It does, however, confirm their private school *mentality*, which is reflected in the attitudes and justifications mentioned above in relation to recruitment.

Mary Waters: a former coloured school

Opened as a predominantly coloured school in 1940, and located in the coloured area of Lavender Hill, Mary Waters became a high school in 1963 and came under the control of the (coloured) House of Representatives between 1984 and 1994. In 1996 it was decided to broaden the basis of the school by introducing dual-medium instruction – English as well as Afrikaans – and this was done, although formal provincial approval was still awaited. It continued to recruit most Grahamstown coloured children of secondary age, but was now about one-third African. It also had children from smaller Eastern Cape towns as well as the children of military personnel stationed in Cape Town, but no boarding hostel. Accommodation bursaries from the House of Representatives once helped to pay the cost of living with private families, but were no longer available. Provincial maintenance grants, formerly paid to poorer mothers who could prove that the father did not exercise responsibility towards the child, had also been ended.

The school had eight 'temporary' classrooms built 15 years ago, but had little hope of replacing them given the financial problems of the province. The school's location close to informal settlements made it vulnerable to violence, and it used scarce resources to employ a security firm. Three classes were gutted by vandals in 1996, but ECED refused to pay, regarding their replacement as a community responsibility. The school responded with fund-raising efforts in the community and approaches to the private sector which have enabled it to repair some of the damage and acquire some furniture and equipment. The library had to be used as a classroom, so the books were put in store. ECED had failed to deliver textbooks since 1997, and the school was forced to spend money photocopying books. It had no teaching computers, which meant that students had to answer the computo-typing question paper using typewriters (which ECED would not pay to service). The three laboratories were poorly equipped. The school's only sports facilities were two concreted netball courts. There was no sharing of resources with wealthier schools at the time of survey – incidents on the rugby field had soured relations with both Kingswood and Graeme College – so the school had to hire municipal grounds for sports fixtures, though one team had been using an empty field belonging to Kingswood, without permission.

Despite having four teachers on the redeployment register, Mary Waters already had an LTR of 31:1. Its examination results were modest, falling behind those of the best township schools (Table II). Teachers commented that 'it is part of the mindset of our pupils not to be goal-orientated'. The school had a high attrition rate, with five classes in grades 8 and 9 but only two in grade 12. This reflected both poverty and a failure to return after failing grade examinations. African students tended to do better, with a higher proportion going on to higher education. This appeared to reflect a greater screening of African applicants, who were drawn mainly from four ex-coloured primary schools and four township schools. The school tended to lose its star pupils, some of whom have won bursaries at Kingswood and Graeme College; others go to the Technical College.

Despite these shortcomings, Mary Waters was oversubscribed by a factor of 2:1. The fees were doubled to R200 p.a. in 2000, but some parents had offered to double this to get their children in. This probably reflects the calibre and dedication of the staff in a school which remains proud of its history and achievements: the first African student, for instance, is now a High Court Judge.

Township Schools

The four township schools visited in Rini (Grahamstown East) were all 100% African, drawing their pupils largely from local townships and informal settlements. The nominal level of fees (Table I) reflects the poverty of most families in their catchment area. One school, Nathaniel Nyaluza, had nearly 200 parents who had not paid the second instalment, although the headmaster suspected that in some cases the children had spent the money themselves. He predicted that the Parents' Meeting would decide (illegally) to exclude the children whose parents had not paid, and then (as before) 'they will all come and pay'. Nombulelo also had a large amount still owing, but 'many fees come in dribs and drabs'. All four schools sought to supplement their meagre fee income, but the potential is limited in poor communities: activities included shows, concerts and other cultural activities, raffles, hiring out chairs and in one case buildings. Nombulelo was the most successful in this respect, raising 55% of its school budget of just R140,000 in such ways.

All four schools suffered in varying degrees from the poor facilities characterising most township schools. Only one had a functioning library, which was poorly used, and laboratories were poorly equipped except at Nathaniel Nyaluza. Computer provision was wholly inadequate for teaching purposes, ranging from a ratio of 1:95 pupils at Nombulelo to 1:174 at Nathaniel Nyaluza: Nombulelo had obtained its 14 computers from programmes run by Rutgers University and the World Bank, but could not afford Internet access. All schools reported difficulties in obtaining textbooks from ECED, with Nombulelo claiming that it had received none for six years: in 1999 it had spent more than 20% of its budget on producing and duplicating materials. None of the schools had playing fields, although, unlike Mary Waters, some had land available but no money to develop it. In most cases facilities were rented, but Nombulelo benefited from an arrangement with Rhodes University, and had secured sponsorship for cricket nets to be installed, and Nathaniel Nyaluza was able to make some use of facilities at Kingswood and St Andrew's.

Khulitso Daniels suffered from poor 'temporary' corrugated zinc classrooms, erected in 1982, which are uninsulated and so very hot in summer and very cold in winter. ECED had said it had no money for buildings, and parents had paid for repairs themselves, as well as for the installation of electricity in the one brick building, to allow the use of the school's three computers and photocopier, and for burglar bars on the building to protect this equipment. Like Mary Waters, the school also paid for a security firm. ECED was consulting the community about closure of the school.

Examination results varied widely between the four schools (Table II), but none was amongst the worst in the province: in terms of Senior Certificate pass rates in 1999, they ranked 85 (Nombulelo), 176 (Nathaniel Nyaluza), 374 (Benjamin Mahlalesa) and 501 (Khutliso Daniels) out of 909. Nombulelo achieved similar Senior Certificate results to Port Alfred High School (see below) and matriculation exemption results not far behind PJO, despite an LTR of 32:1, whereas Benjamin Mahlalesa seemed to derive little benefit from its LTR of 21:1, swollen by five teachers on the redeployment register. Nombulelo shares the high attrition rate common to most African schools, but this includes the loss of some of its brightest students to VGH and Graeme College, some of them gaining sponsorship, as well as weaker students who move to other schools after failing grades rather than returning to retake with pupils who have been a year or two below them.

Nombulelo clearly benefits from its success, with parents anxious to get their children in, but the headmaster claimed to admit them on a first-come, first-served basis. Nathaniel Nyaluza, in contrast, had received no applications for the coming year at the time of interview, and expected its entry to be smaller than the existing numbers in grades 9-11. This appeared to reflect parents' complaints about the standard of teaching and behaviour of the teachers, which were echoed by the headmaster. He complained of poor control of pupils, absenteeism, poor timekeeping, and leaving classes unattended to take children to extracurricular activities without permission: his appeal to his own staff for greater cooperation had gone unheeded. He attributed the school's relatively good results to his policy of concentrating the most supportive teachers in grade 12. Official procedures for dealing with problem staff offered no solution, given their slowness, the lack of alternative teachers and the inefficiency of the redeployment process. The headmaster, himself African, blamed lack of commitment and professionalism on the lack of whites on the staff, commenting that he had observed the work ethic of white teachers and its effect on the whole school when he had worked in an African secondary school in Northern Province; he attributed the success of Nombulelo to its mixture of white, coloured and African teachers. However, the headmaster of Khulitso Daniels, where all staff are African except for an Indian Head of Sciences, said that all teachers were supportive and doing their best. The headmaster of Benjamin Mahlalesa, which also had just one non-African (Indian) teacher, also had some problems of lateness and absenteeism, but claimed that most teachers were supportive. Many factors could influence variations in the commitment and professionalism of teachers, but demoralisation flowing from poor resources, including lack of textbooks, insufficient information and training on the delivery of new syllabuses and sometimes poor leadership, may all play a part.

Port Alfred Schools

The small coastal town of Port Alfred at the mouth of the Kowie River offers many recreational attractions: beaches and water sports, a harbour and residential marina, angling, golf, hiking trails and a canoe trail. It has enjoyed significant growth in recent years, offering a safe haven for white retirement and second homes, and has also attracted substantial migration of rural Africans who form a substantial majority of the population. The formerly all-white Port Alfred High School (PAHS) will be compared here with one of the African secondary schools, Nonzamo.

PAHS remained two-thirds white (and more so in the senior school), and Nonzamo 100% African. Both schools have local catchment areas, although some Nonzamo pupils from more distant places stay with relatives or rent rooms. The two schools are similar in size, but PAHS has all grades (Table I). Despite the usual vast discrepancy in fee levels, they had the same LTR. Nonzamo had seven teachers on the redeployment list, a reflection of reduced pupil numbers since the building of a second African secondary school in Port Alfred in the early 1990s and the introduction of higher grades in three of its former feeder schools. Three other excess teachers had already left, and another had received a placement in Transkei, but she could not afford to move and could not trust ECED to pay her expenses after the event. PAHS was one teacher under quota, but benefited from 13 teachers paid for by the school (seven of them part-time) and four part-time teachers sponsored by local churches.

Nonzamo was in some respects better off than Grahamstown's African schools. It had four science laboratories with basic equipment, and a library which housed the school's only computer (with Internet access). The school had no playing fields, but free use of the community stadium, and was able to offer seven sports. It supplemented fees with beauty contests and concerts, street collections, small charges for outside use of its facilities (from 2001) and appeals to local companies to sponsor special events. The headmaster described the governing body as very supportive. Although there was some absenteeism in the (all-African) teaching staff, this was not, he claimed, a major problem. The major problem was the very low motivation of the children themselves. The headmaster blamed this (questionably?) on lack of tertiary institutions in Port Alfred, as well as homes without electricity and lack of parental support. Some parents do, however, manage to find the fees to move their children to PAHS, and Nonzamo loses some of its brightest children in this way.

PAHS is *de facto* selective, interviewing applicants and basing entry on ability, but African numbers are increasing. It is a dual-medium school, with 20% of pupils Afrikaans-speaking. No African parents had been elected to the governing body, and they tended not to attend meetings or functions, in part because of transport problems; for the same reason, African pupils found it difficult to stay behind for extramural activities. The school had good sports facilities including a swimming pool, a staffed library with study facilities, and an active cultural life. In contrast to Nonzamo, it had 40 computers. After bad experiences of sharing its resources, PAHS allowed African schools to use its sports grounds only if there was a joint event. The headmaster criticised his two African counterparts in Port Alfred for lack of control and 'a major problem with discipline', and there was some evidence of this when the author visited Nonzamo.

PAHS normally expects a 100% pass rate in Senior Certificate and the 1999 result (89%) was described as 'pathetic' by the headmaster, who attributed it to the effective absence of a head or deputy head for two years. Its matriculation exemption record was more modest (Table II). Nonzamo predictably fell far behind on both counts, although ECED figures show a dramatic improvement in 2001: this is hard to explain and may be an error in the data.

Rural Schools

The two rural schools surveyed were both small schools embracing all grades (Table I). Their isolation ruled out the potential benefits of interaction with wealthier schools or a local university. Shaw Park Combined School near Bathurst was next door to a formerly all-white primary school charging fees of R2400 p.a., now 50% African as a result of bussing African children of professional parents from the former Ciskei and coloured children from Port Alfred. It was struggling to survive with only 50 children, but reluctant to combine with its poor African neighbour which has an LTR twice as high. It did, however, offer some help with office equipment and teaching aids for biology.

Shaw Park itself had lost some of its pupils with the withdrawal by ECED of transport subsidies in 1999; some now walked long distances on foot, starting as early as 5 a.m., and others who relied on lifts were often very late. Unlike many schools in the former Ciskei and Transkei, Shaw Park had a fully qualified staff in whom the headmaster expressed confidence. The school had no library, computers or playing fields, but a local farmer with a playing field for his employees allowed the school to use it free of charge; five sports were available, and there were fixtures with other schools. Imaginative fund-raising events had raised R3080 in 2000, equivalent to about one-third of the school's annual fee income, and R1100 had been spent on a fax machine.

Riebeeck East Combined School occupied good buildings that formerly housed a white school, but was empty until re-used in 1994. It now admits the local coloured and African children in this remote rural area; 30% are Afrikaans-speaking and the rest Xhosa-speaking, but there was absolutely no dividing line and, in the headmaster's words, 'they don't know who they are'. Many coloured pupils were of mixed parentage and spoke Xhosa at home. The school was supposed to be dual medium (Afrikaans and English) but its African teachers (9 out of 13) could not speak Afrikaans very well. The community had requested a change to English as the sole medium of instruction, but the school had not yet decided on this, as English was a third language for most pupils, and its teacher quota benefited from its dual-medium status. The headmaster was reluctant to criticise his staff, but there appeared to be some problems of commitment.

The school had no library and only one ill-equipped laboratory: children had to write examinations without having done any experiments. Unlike most schools, Riebeeck East had received some new books in 2000, for grade 12 which had recently been introduced, but only for three subjects, and it lacked most of the necessary books for lower grades. The one old computer was used only for administration. The municipal field was available for sport. Transport was the school's biggest problem: the headmaster's own van was used to bring most of the teachers to school, and the police occasionally helped with transport for sports fixtures. Transport allowances for children and for teachers unable to live locally were paid by the former House of Representatives, but not by ECED; children walked up to five kilometres.

Parents of children at both schools were predominantly farm labourers; the better-off households were those with a grandparent receiving a pension. Parent members of governing bodies at both schools were reported as making little contribution; at Riebeeck East none had turned up for the previous meeting, and some the headmaster had never seen. The examination results of these small, isolated schools with pupils from very poor families were poor (Table II). The one student obtaining matriculation exemption, at Shaw Park in 1999, could not afford to go to university, but was working to save money and re-applying for bursaries.

Language Issues and 'Race Relations'

The one-way nature of the desegregation process in South African schools mirrors that in residential areas [37], although with greater movement of Africans to formerly coloured schools. With the exception of the unusual situation at Riebeeck East, discussed above, it is only at former white and coloured schools (and essentially in the state sector) that significant desegregation has occurred (Table I); African schools remain unchanged in their intake. More focused research involving participant observation would clearly have been needed to probe relations between children of different 'race' groups in depth, but the issue was explored at each interview.

In no case were serious problems raised: Graeme College had experienced one white–African fight in the past five years, but 'even this may not have been racial'. In all schools children did tend to sit in racial groups in the classroom, unless placed by teachers (as at PJO). The natural tendency for Africans to speak Xhosa to one another encouraged a degree of playground segregation. Sport was seen as bringing children together, and Graeme College had resisted the general tendency to make physical education a casualty of the redeployment process because of its socialising effect in getting pupils to work together physically. The headmaster of VGH believed that children were learning to understand one another's cultures with real breaking down of barriers: he regarded the emergence of teasing across the colour line as positive evidence of more relaxed attitudes replacing an initial wariness. No school reported having, or having yet had, an African head boy or girl, although the last three deputy head boys at Graeme College had been African. Township boys at Graeme visited white homes, and in some cases stayed for weekends, but there was little movement in the other direction. At both VGH and Mary Waters, there were also some good friendships between children of different race groups.

None of these former white and coloured schools currently teaches Xhosa as a matriculation subject. Despite their relative affluence, a common refrain was 'we should like to, but can't afford it'. Port Alfred and PJO taught Xhosa at primary level, and Graeme planned to introduce it at this level as an alternative to Afrikaans. Grahamstown's private schools did offer Xhosa at secondary level, but very few students opted to take it. Both whites and Africans tended to see it as unimportant, albeit for different reasons. Mary Waters had ECED approval to start Xhosa but could not find a teacher, a situation that can only worsen as enrolment in Xhosa courses at universities has reached an all-time low.[38] In one of the most perceptive comments made on the subject, two staff expressed the fear that Africans were in danger of cultural alienation from their own environment: they were moving and speaking in an English-speaking environment, and some of them could hardly write Xhosa. In township schools the most common pattern was for pupils to do Xhosa, English and Afrikaans to matriculation. In some cases Afrikaans was optional, in which case it was more popular than science or maths, often because it was perceived to be an easier subject, albeit a less useful qualification.

Conclusions

The massive inequalities found in the schools surveyed are in themselves no surprise: the vast backlogs of the apartheid legacy, combined with modest economic growth, precluded, and continue to preclude, transformation of schools serving historically disadvantaged groups. Equality of opportunity could only be achieved in present circumstances by ending the practice of charging fees in state schools. Such 'levelling down' would be as unpopular with the black middle class as the white, and would undoubtedly lead to an expansion of the private sector, if this were allowed to survive. The substitution of class divisions for those of race was in practice inevitable. But this does not mean that present policy and practice are incapable of improvement. Partial solutions at least may be found in at least three directions: local initiative, provincial practice and national policy.

Local initiative is important, but not if, as at present, it amounts to the imposition of impossible burdens on poor communities unable to raise significant funds. On the one hand, it needs to embrace far greater sharing of resources – human as well as material – between privileged and deprived schools than now occurs. Provincial policy makers need to reflect on what incentives might be provided to encourage former white schools in particular – private as well as state – to do more in this respect. Decentralisation can also play an important role, if focused on those schools with the capacity to do more for themselves, such as procurement of classroom materials and supplies, maintenance of buildings, supervision of in-service teacher education and reward of performance.[39] The more that these become school-level management responsibilities, the more ECED resources can be concentrated on disadvantaged schools.

At provincial level the specific shortcomings of the ECED have emerged all too clearly. The Department is aware that internal communication is slow, and there is often no clarity on the procedures to be followed: employees from different former administrations often try to follow procedures to which they are accustomed, which results in delays. ECED has been investigating issues of personnel, labour relations and administration at all levels from schools upwards, and has been seeking to implement the recommendations of an internal report since 2001. At the human level the Department is employing Educational Development Officers to provide support, targeting schools with less than 50% pass rates in the Senior Certificate. It is seeking to develop more in-service training for teachers, making use of the many former teacher training colleges which have been closed. There is also an emphasis on 'action research', which brings researchers and those affected together to consider problems and identify solutions. ECED has several donor-funded projects operating in different parts of the province, looking at the development of management capacity at provincial and district level, although these were all concerned with primary schools in 2000. Capacity-building in school governing bodies is a vital need, if a difficult one to fulfil in many communities. It will inevitably be some time before such policies bear fruit, and a further decline in standards in the meantime cannot be ruled out.

Present problems are accentuated by the gap between conception and reality, between political symbolism and implementation, which were noted earlier. In part these appear to derive from the frustration of pursuing idealistic aims, often based on what is regarded as good practice in the most developed countries, without the human or financial capacity to achieve them. There is a fundamental contradiction in South Africa's education policies, insisting on equalisation and redress of opportunities to ensure a more equal distribution of educational resources, without recognising that the need for ever more sophisticated technical and educational skills pulls in the direction of specialisation and selection rather than the construction of a high-quality system for all – a system able to produce an internationally competitive elite of technicians and managers. Outside such an elite, and a small middle class able to use its resources and influence to ensure that their children's schools retain a measure of quality, the poor will be left with an education system geared to low expectations and low-level employment: there will always be a few dramatic success stories, but 'selling the myth that this is a possibility for all can be likened to the logic that promotes the purchase of lottery tickets'.[40] South Africa needs to produce an elite, but the larger part of its education system should be geared to the needs of the urban and rural poor, rather than offloading the consequences of inappropriate policies on to impoverished communities which lack the resources to implement them effectively.

Acknowledgement

This article was first published in *Journal of Southern African Studies*, 30(2), 269-290 (http://dx.doi.org/10.1080/0305707042000215392), reprinted by permission of the publisher (Taylor & Francis Ltd, http://www.informaworld.com).

Notes

[1] British Council funding for this research, as part of a joint project with Rhodes University targeted at sustainable development and resource usage in the Eastern Cape, is gratefully acknowledged. Professor Roddy Fox of the Geography department was a generous host and gave much practical encouragement. I greatly appreciate the ready cooperation of head teachers and other staff at the schools visited. I am also grateful to the Examinations Section of ECED for the provision of examination results. Mrs N. Skenjana, Deputy Permanent Secretary of ECED and Mr Mogolodela, District Manager for Grahamstown, were also very helpful.

[2] E.H. Brookes (1968) *Apartheid: a documentary study of modern South Africa,* 57. London: Routledge & Kegan Paul.

[3] This chapter uses the terms 'African', 'white', 'coloured' and 'Indian' in accordance with common South African usage. This does not imply approval of the policies with which they were associated, but acceptance that they remain, unavoidably, categories for analysis in South African society, and are indeed used as such by the present government. The term 'black' is used to refer collectively to Africans, coloured people and Indians.

[4] South Africa (1997) *School Register of Needs Survey*. Pretoria: Department of Education.

[5] A. Lemon (1994) Educational Desegregation, in J. Brewer (Ed.) *Restructuring South Africa*, 100-101. Basingstoke: Macmillan.

[6] A. Donaldson (2001) Reconstructing Education: reflections on post-apartheid planning, systems and structure, in Y. Sayed & J. Jansen (Eds) *Implementing Education Policies: the South African experience*, 62-72. Cape Town: University of Cape Town Press.

[7] J.D. Jansen (2001) Explaining Non-change in Educational Reform after Apartheid: political symbolism and the problem of policy implementation, in Sayed & Jansen (Eds) *Implementing Education Policies*, 280.

[8] Ibid., 281.

[9] Ibid., 272.

[10] See, for example, W. Morrow & K. King (Eds) (2000) *Vision and Reality: changing education and training in South Africa*. Cape Town: University of Cape Town Press; T. Mda & S. Mothata (Eds) (2000) *Critical Issues in South African Education – after 1994.* Kenwyn: Juta; Sayed & Jensen (Eds) *Implementing Education Policies*.

[11] L. Chisholm & B. Fuller (1996) Remember People's Education? Shifting Alliances, State-Building and South Africa's Narrrowing Policy Agenda, *Journal of Education Policy*, 11, 714.

[12] A. Lemon (1999) Shifting Inequalities in South Africa's Schools: some evidence from the Western Cape, *South African Geographical Journal*, 81, 96-105.

[13] Regional offices have since been abolished, and District Directors appointed for each district to carry out the functions of the former regions at district level.

[14] C. Soudien, H. Jacklin & U. Hoadley (2001) Policy Values: problematising equity and redress in education, in Sayed & Jansen (Eds) *Implementing Education Policies*, 78-91.

[15] Y. Sayed (2001) Post-apartheid Educational Transformation: policy concerns and approaches, in Sayed & Jansen (Eds) *Implementing Education Policies*, 250-270.

[16] T. Mda (2000) Integrated Schooling, in T. Mda & S. Mothata (Eds) *Critical Issues in South African* Education, 43-61.

[17] Soudien et al, Policy Values, 84.

[18] South African Institute of Race Relations (SAIRR), *South Africa Survey 1997-1998*, 486. Johannesburg, SAIRR.

[19] Ibid., 484.

[20] A. Donaldson (2001) Reconstructing Education: reflections on post-apartheid planning, systems and structure, in Sayed & Jansen (Eds) *Implementing Education Policies*, 71.

[21] P. Dickson (2000) 700 E Cape farm schools to close, *The Teacher*, 18 February.

[22] SAIRR (2000) *Fast Facts* No. 8. Johannesburg: SAIRR. http:www.sairr.org.za/members/pub/ff/200206/province/profile/htm

[23] SAIRR (2001) *South Africa Survey 2000/2001*, 530. Johannesburg: SAIRR.

[24] SAIRR (2002) *Fast Facts* No. 6.

[25] Ibid.

[26] SAIRR (2002) *Fast Facts* No. 8. Johannesburg: SAIRR.

[27] Both definitions include those who are economically active (aged 15-64 and available for work) and who have not worked in the seven days prior to interview. The strict definition excludes those in this number who have not looked for self-employment opportunities in the four weeks prior to interview.

[28] SAIRR (2002) *Fast Facts* No. 8.

[29] SAIRR, *South Africa Survey 2000/2001*, 282.

[30] SAIRR (2002) *Fast Facts* No. 6.

[31] Ibid.

[32] C. Taylor (1998) Education, in B.M. O'Leary, V. Govind, C.A. Scwabe & J.M. Taylor (Eds) *Service Needs and Provision in the Eastern Cape*, 45-50. Pretoria: Human Sciences Research Council.

[33] Development Bank of South Africa (DBSA) (1990) *SATVBC Countries: statistical abstracts 1989*. Halfway House: DBSA.

[34] S. Greenberg (1997) Agrarian Reform in Perspective, *Land Update*, July, 6-9.

[35] These very crude estimates were the best that the Town Clerk could provide.

[36] This phrase, used by the Headmaster of St Andrew's College, may be considered a euphemism for 'racist'. The Deputy Headmaster of Kingswood made the same point in similar terms.

[37] See A.J. Christopher (2001) Urban Segregation in Post-Apartheid South Africa, *Urban Studies*, 38, 693-716.

[38] S. Ridge (Professor of English, University of the Western Cape), personal communication.

[39] A. Donaldson (2001) Reconstructing Education, in Sayed & Jansen (Eds), *Implementing Education Policies*, 62-72.

[40] P. Kallaway (1998) Whatever Happened to Rural Education as a Goal for (South African) Development? in W. Morrow & K. King (Eds) *Vision and Reality: changing education and training in South Africa*, 35. Cape Town: University of Cape Town Press.

CHAPTER 7

Language, Literacy and Equality: minority language communities in the Cameroon

BARBARA TRUDELL

This chapter is based on case-study research carried out among three minority language communities of Cameroon's anglophone Northwest Province: Bafut, Kom and Nso' (B. Trudell, 2004). Minority languages are under serious threat of extinction in many parts of the world.[1] The growth of sociolinguistic domains where majority languages are used, fuelled by the influence of global culture and the economic disparities between the world's different peoples, spells the end for thousands of smaller languages over the coming years.[2] For these languages, the process of language shift has gone so far as to be irreversible. Crystal (2000, p. 129) notes that attempts to provide support to threatened languages often come too late in the life of the threatened language.

These Bafut, Kom and Nso' communities range in size from 80,000 to 150,000 members each, and live for the most part in semi-rural, linguistically and culturally homogeneous areas of the Grassfields of Northwest Cameroon. Each of the three hosts a community-based programme of local-language development, carried out largely through mother-tongue education programmes in the local primary schools as well as literacy programmes aimed at adult community members.[3] As these initiatives for local-language development and literacy have been under way for 10-20 years in the three communities, it is possible to examine the actual uses of the written mother tongue in those communities.

Given the relatively small size of the Bafut, Kom and Nso' language communities, the influence of English-language schooling and the pull of urbanised life for the region's young people, it would be reasonable to expect that these languages would also be on the decline. For Bafut, Kom and Lamnso' [4], however, that does not seem to be the case. Instead, use of the mother tongue, particularly the written mother tongue, appears to be increasing in these language communities. The details of, and reasons for, this unexpected phenomenon are explored here.

Social Domains for English and Mother Tongue in the Language Community

In these communities the mother tongue is used for most oral communication. This is true for bilingual as well as monolingual people. The choice to speak English (or Pidgin [5]) is associated with the presence of a non-speaker of the mother tongue. Particular topics, such as technology or development-related concepts, call for the use of specific words or phrases borrowed from English. Certain local institutions, primarily school, mandate spoken English regardless of the language proficiency of the participants. In others, such as local government and commercial institutions, language choice once again depends on the presence or absence of a non-speaker of the mother tongue. However, the default mode of communication in daily life is the spoken mother tongue.

For written text, however, English is the default language. English is the medium for signs, advertisements, and other instances of non-book written text. This is also the case in the local primary schools, where the posters, blackboard writing and exercise books feature English writing.

This divide between oral mother tongue and written English – particularly with the dominance of English in the educational setting – is well known in post-colonial Africa. As Korang & Slemon (1997) note, African nations today comprise peoples speaking many languages, and the question of which group will control the means for representing a people to itself has been settled largely with the 'uncritical acceptance of English and French as the inevitable medium for educated African writing' (p. 252). Indeed, the fact that most African languages have remained unwritten for so long (itself the result of a series of political decisions) has meant that the alternative of written mother tongue often does not exist. In the case of Bafut, Kom and Lamnso', viable written forms of the language were not available until after 1979; written English, meanwhile, has been part of the formal school curriculum since at least 1922.

Not only is the identification of English (and French) with writing evident in national-level education policy and implementation (Ministry of National Education, 1998, 2000), but the prestige of written English in the language communities themselves is evidence of what Griffiths calls the 'impact of concepts of the modern' (Griffiths, 1997, p. 140). English writing is identified with the modern world, and so is privileged over other kinds of inscription, including written mother tongue.

Thus, the uses of written mother tongue in the language communities of Bafut, Kom and Nso' take place in a context in which the mother tongue dominates oral communication and English dominates written text. Instances of written mother tongue use are therefore significant in that they run counter to the norms of language choice.

Acquiring Literacy in the Mother Tongue

In the Bafut, Kom and Nso' language communities, English-language literacy is invariably acquired in formal schooling. Literacy in the mother tongue may be acquired either through the PROPELCA [6] mother-tongue education programme or through an adult literacy programme. In each community, these programmes are run by the language committee. For English-language literates, mother-tongue literacy can also be acquired individually through the use of English-to-mother-tongue 'transition literacy' primers available in each of the three languages.

The PROPELCA programme offers both a *formal* programme, in which the mother tongue is used as a medium of instruction alongside English in grades 1-4, and an *informal* programme in which instruction in mother-tongue literacy is offered in the three higher primary grades (and occasionally in secondary school). Both programmes are intended to result in mother-tongue literacy after three years of study, although the efficacy with which they do so depends partly on the continuity of the instruction from year to year.

The adult mother-tongue literacy programmes are serving both illiterate (i.e. non-schooled) and semi-literate (those who have been to school and are familiar with English reading and writing, yet who cannot actually read English-language text [7]) adult populations. One national literacy programme director puts the proportion of semi-literate to illiterate class attendees at 60:40. The adult literacy programme takes between one and three years to complete.

Attempts to track the numbers of people actually learning to read in Bafut, Kom and Lamnso' are seriously hampered by irregular reporting and uncertain estimates. However, it is estimated that approximately 5000 Bafut, 5000 Kom and 2500 Nso' children and adults are currently participating in programmed mother-tongue literacy acquisition activities, with an estimated one-third of those numbers becoming literate in the mother tongue each year. The trends also show a marked acceleration in participation in the PROPELCA programmes over the past five years.

The PROPELCA and adult literacy programmes each tend to reinforce interest in the other. The NACALCO adult literacy programme director described the attitude of mother-tongue literate parents towards the PROPELCA programme:

> Where literacy classes [8] are, there is an impact on whether
> children go to PROPELCA schools ... [Where adult literacy
> classes had been held,] parents who in fact knew the importance
> of mother-tongue learning were encouraging children to do well at

school. Even sometimes they were talking to the headmasters and saying, 'We know this [PROPELCA] is a good programme'.

The results of PROPELCA classes may also convince a parent to attend mother-tongue literacy classes. Visiting a Lamnso' literacy class in the 1990s, one literacy consultant noted:

> One woman in the class said she was there because her child was attending a PROPELCA school. When that child came home there was an old piece of [English-language] newspaper lying in the house and he picked it up and read 'dy-na-mo.' He had learned to decode syllables. She was amazed, as even much older children [not in PROPELCA classes] could not have done this. That convinced her to come to literacy class.

The language committee, NACALCO and other institutions involved in delivery of mother-tongue literacy programmes operate in a collaborative network in which each institution contributes according to its priorities and competencies. The complementary interests of these institutions (government, churches, denominational education authorities and non-governmental organisations [NGOs]) allow them to collaborate in the various mother-tongue literacy initiatives available in the homelands. Together they have created an environment for local-language development that is based in linguistic research and focused on sustained use of the mother tongue in oral and written forms.

Mother-Tongue Literacy and Language Maintenance

In these language communities the process of learning to read and write the mother tongue has had multiple effects on use and understanding of the language itself. Olson (1994, p. 139) has noted the impact of literacy on language understanding, observing that it is knowledge of the alphabet that makes the speaker aware of phonemes and that a consciousness of the structures of a language is enhanced by learning its writing system. For the Bafut, Kom and Nso' learners, literacy in the mother tongue is accompanied by improved linguistic competence and an increased understanding of the linguistic features of the language. Mother-tongue literacy programmes also provide the platform where language standardisation efforts are taking place.

So in the Bafut, Kom and Nso' language communities, mother-tongue literacy acquisition entails more than simply learning a code for written expression of the language. For the individual learner, a deepened process of language learning accompanies mother-tongue literacy acquisition as well. On a broader scale, the processes of language standardisation which form part of the mother-tongue literacy programmes have implications for the stability and maintenance of the language across the community. Learning to read and write in the mother tongue thus facilitates language maintenance at individual and community levels.

Use of the Written Mother Tongue

How is the written mother tongue actually used in the Bafut, Kom and Nso' communities? This question can be addressed in terms of existing mother-tongue publications, the patterns of use of those publications, and reading and writing behaviours in mother tongue and in English.

Written Texts Available

One indicator of what is read in the mother tongue is the number and type of written texts available in that language. Unlike most European languages, most of the minority languages of Cameroon have a written tradition of only a few decades at most. Indeed, extensive publication and use of local-language materials was not feasible before the establishment of a unified alphabet for Cameroonian languages in 1979.[9]

Table I lists the number of titles that have been published in the Bafut, Kom and Lamnso' languages, by literature type. It should be noted that the existence of the publications listed does not imply that these titles are readily available today to the mother-tongue reader, as is also noted in Table I. In fact, titles produced before 1985 are difficult to find outside of institutional archives.

Literature production in all three languages continues today, primarily through the language committees. In the last few years, Bafut Language Association (BALA) published a post-primer reading book of Bafut folk stories and the 2004 diary. The Kom Language Development Committee (KLDC) has several titles in process: a book on verb tenses in Kom, another on the dynasty of the Fons of Kom, a revision of the guide to the Kom alphabet (a transition primer), a mathematics text for grade 3 and a book of Kom myths and legends. The Nso' Language Organisation (NLO) also has several titles in process: a book on Nso' history, another on Nso' marriage customs, a 'cultural etymology' and translations of three English-language novels by a well-known Nso' author.

The origins of these publications, whether translations or original works, vary with the type of publication. Literature on religious topics is translated material, as are the development titles on AIDS, hygiene, malaria, pesticides and so on. PROPELCA school texts, cultural and language-related topics and all periodical works such as newsletters and diaries are original works. The presence of both translated and original works in the local language is indicative of a shift in the identification of written text with a particular cultural context. Robinson (1997, p. 31) notes that translation is often identified with the influence of a hegemonic culture and with colonial education; indeed, agents of development and Christian missions have for decades used translated materials to facilitate social and spiritual change among the Bafut, Kom and Nso' populations (Sanneh, 1990, p. 70). The dominant position of European culture in the sphere of written language is being challenged, however, as the publication activities of the language

141

committees are establishing the Bafut, Kom and Nso' cultures as viable bases for a body of written literature. As the original works are produced, they are introduced into the written environment of the Bafut, Kom and Nso' communities principally via the PROPELCA programme and the adult literacy programmes.

Still, on the whole the amount of written mother-tongue text in each of these language communities is limited. This insufficiency of relevant reading material hampers efforts to promote the written mother tongue, but production of such material is a logistical and financial challenge.

Literature type	Bafut	Kom	Lamnso'
PROPELCA school texts[a]	5	8	9
Local culture/history/folktales[b]	2	3	15
Development topics[c]	–	6	3
Christian Scriptures[d]	4	6	6
Other religious[e]	–	8	19[f]
TOTAL PUBLICATIONS (non-periodical)	11	31	52
Number of publications (non-periodical) readily available (percentage of total)	9 (82%)	27 (87%)	29 (56%)
News bulletin (produced by language committee)	Occasional	Occasional	Occasional
Diary/calendar (yearly)	Since 1980	Since 1995	Since 1978

[a]These consist of pre-readers, primers, post-primer reading material and mathematics books. Also included are guides to reading the mother tongue, intended for audiences already literate in English.

[b]These include books of folk stories, proverbs, riddles, fables, and descriptions of local cultural phenomena.

[c]These include books on malaria, personal hygiene, AIDS, the treatment of diarrhoea, and the proper use of pesticides. There is also a book in Lamnso' on 'how human rights are violated in Nso'' as well as a book in Kom on the environment.

[d]These include the New Testament in Bafut and Lamnso', individual sections of the New Testament such as the story of Easter, and recently translated Old Testament books of Jonah and Ruth. The New Testament in Kom is soon to be printed.

[e]These include retellings of the parables of Jesus, song books, evangelistic tracts, catechisms and particular Catholic rites.

[f]Most of these publications are by the Kumbo Diocese of the Catholic Church, which has been printing and reprinting various titles since 1976.

Table I. Titles published in Bafut, Kom and Lamnso' languages.

What is Read in the Mother Tongue

Patterns of book purchases. Based on sales figures, the pocket diary and calendar are by far the most popular pieces of mother-tongue literature.[10] In Bafut, 459 copies of the 2002 diary were sold. In Nso', one local publishing firm prints 2000 calendars and 1000 diaries per year, though not all of them are sold; this may be due to competition with Nso' materials which the NLO has produced since 1998, printing 2000 calendars and 500 diaries in 2002 (the latter sold out). In Kom, approximately 1000 diaries are printed and sold each year.

At the other end of the spectrum, the least-sold titles tend to be those on development topics. Most of these have been translated without a clear programme in mind in which to utilise them, nor have they been written in a way that allows them to fit into the school curriculum. Nso' editor Christopher Mengjo termed books such as these 'supplementary books', that is, books which are not necessary to the institutional purpose of either school or church. Mengjo noted that people's current economic situation does not permit the purchase of such materials:

> You only buy [a book] when you need it. People will say, 'I like the book, but the money is not there'.

The presence of text in social environments. The presence of written text in the school environment is also revealing. Based on the proportion of mother-tongue publications which focus on the school audience, and the fact that the school environment is one of the most frequent sites for reading and writing, it is noteworthy that very few books are in fact found there. The primary schools in the homelands are notoriously short of textbooks, in either English or mother tongue.[11] Students have only exercise books into which they copy the teacher's blackboard writing; the teacher may have a copy of the textbook to be taught from, but not always. The blackboard takes the place of textbooks, although with all the different subjects to be taught this way blackboard space becomes quite limited. Classroom observations gave evidence of the dearth of textbooks:

> 33 kids in this class ... The topic is Roman numerals. The children have between 1 and 3 exercise books in front of each of them. No textbooks are in evidence ... Then the teacher gives exercises on the board, converting Roman to Arabic and vice versa.

> On the blackboard (there are two, one covering the front wall and one the back):
> English: conjugations: explanations, examples, exercises
> The Reformation (paragraphs)
> The Empire of Mali
> Continents of the world, oceans of the world
> Chalked on a window shutter: prime numbers 2, 3, 5, ...

In observations of 21 primary classrooms, only one class was observed to have any student books other than exercise books. It was religious instruction class in grade 2 of a Catholic school, where the seven textbooks available were shared among the 33 pupils and then collected by the teacher afterwards in order to 'keep them from being torn'.

143

The dearth of school texts is widely decried by school staff. Yafi Alfred Ndi, a headmaster in Kom, described the problem:

> The parents only complain about money. But when they [the children] come to us, now you take a book, had it been that all have a copy, you have only to open the book and read. But now you are forced to take what is in the book and write it on the board so the children should read. And that is the problem we have. In class [grade] seven, some of the children have a few copies of the required books, especially English and the religious books we emphasise here.

The reason most often given for the lack of textbooks was that parents could not afford them, and indeed the problem has been aggravated since the economic downturn of the early 1990s. It is true that the cost of the primary school textbooks recommended by the Ministry of National Education is prohibitively high, considering that multiple textbooks are required for each child.[12] Yet even PROPELCA textbooks, which cost much less than the English-curriculum textbooks [13], are still a low priority purchase item for parents.

Some teachers believe that the reluctance to buy textbooks is more than simply economic. One grade 3 teacher noted that

> [Parents] don't know the necessity of the child using the book. They don't value the mother-tongue books either; even though they are less expensive they won't buy them.

So when a parent in the homeland does buy a textbook for his or her child, it is considered unusual.

> When you come to a school like this, and you see a child with a copy of an English book, you know at least it is a parent who wants that the child should learn something.

As a result, the reading and writing which are done in primary school classrooms rarely involve books. Rather, text is written by the teacher on the blackboard, and copied by students into their individual exercise books. An entire generation of primary school students in the Bafut, Kom and Nso' homelands has thus engaged in what is essentially bookless learning. The significance of this is amplified by the fact that it is taking place in one of the two principal contexts of literacy practice in society.

In the home, the presence or absence of books appears to be at least partly related to the householders' occupations. Teachers or members of the traditional leadership tend to have more books in their houses than bricklayers or palm wine tappers do.

However, economic distress combined with social expectations about reading has led to a dearth of reading material in any language, either at home or at school. The headmaster of a rural government school in Kom described the situation for many:

> BT: Do children have books in their homes?
>
> Lawyer: [laughs] No, there are no books at home. There are not even tables and chairs to study at in many of their homes. Even in the town, we don't buy much reading material. There is no money any more to buy journals for news – I used to, but since 1993 we cannot afford it. People might just buy the cheap sensationalist newspapers. The children are far from a notion of reading for information, reading to be informed.

The limited presence of books in the home and school, whatever the language, indicates limited use of mother-tongue literature in these contexts.

In the environment of the Christian church, texts of various sorts are key components (J. Trudell 2004). However, the books present in the church are used primarily by a handful of leaders, who either read them out loud to the congregation or refer to them in speaking. The majority of the people present in a church service either listen to text being read out loud or else recite texts from memory. Although perhaps one in ten people carries a Bible, a songbook or a prayer book to church, they do not necessarily use them during the service. In the (few) Muslim mosques in the area, a copy of the Qu'ran is part of the prayer services held; however, its use is restricted to the leader of the service, as few of the congregation read or understand Arabic.

Self-reported reading and writing behaviours. A survey carried out among 36 Kom and Nso' adults who were alumni of the PROPELCA primary school programme asked the respondents what they read and wrote regularly (daily, weekly or monthly). These alumni had all finished primary school, 75% had finished secondary school, and six of the 36 had some tertiary training. Their occupations ranged from farming to teaching school. This group surveyed all reported themselves to be literate in both English and the mother tongue; they are thus among the people in the language communities most likely to engage in regular reading and writing in the mother tongue.

Table II shows that for each category except the religious one, the reported incidence of mother-tongue reading and writing was significantly below that of English. This was especially evident in the education context: once the PROPELCA classes were completed in lower primary school, the formal learning environment for these respondents has been wholly in English.

However, it is noteworthy that the religious reading category has a higher proportion of the total reading in mother tongue than that category does in English: five instances out of 16 total instances reading in the mother tongue, or 31%, compared to five instances out of a total of 65 in English, or 8%. All five reports of religious reading in the mother tongue were specified by the respondents as being the Lamnso' New Testament. Given the limited amount of mother-tongue reading that is being done at all by these 36 respondents, the fact that 31% of it is being done in one religious text is significant.

In addition, the reported instances of reading news periodicals in the mother tongue highlight the potential interest of regular newsletters in the Bafut, Kom and Lamnso' languages. Each of the three language committees has produced such periodicals (Table I), although each committee finds it a financial challenge. The Lamnso' newspaper, for example, has an uneven publishing history:

> The newsletter only went 13 issues, about three or four years. The last one was in mid-2002. It was four pages long and cost 200 francs [cfa, approximately 25 pence]. But people would take it, not buy it, saying, 'You are supposed to be serving the Nso' people!'

The difficulty of recovering production costs has proven to be a significant obstacle to this otherwise potentially popular mother-tongue publication.

Category of written text use	Reading English	Writing English	Reading mother tongue	Writing mother tongue
Formal learning	21	12	–	–
Work (not school-related)	3	5	1	1
Letters	14	26	3	2
News periodicals	12	–	5	–
Religious	5	1	5	1
Personal (e.g. novels, poems)	11	4	2	1
Total	65	48	16	5

Table II. All reported instances of reading and writing on a daily, weekly or monthly basis: English and the mother tongue (36 PROPELCA alumni).

Writing and the Mother Tongue

As a regular use of the written mother tongue, writing is much less common than reading. Even for mother-tongue speakers, writing Bafut, Kom or Lamnso' is more difficult than reading those languages. It is more difficult than English writing as well, particularly for those who have gained their writing skills in an English-medium school. For English literates, writing these languages requires additional skill in representing tone, the glottal stop, and vowel sounds that are not marked in English orthography (Banyee, 1998). The Kom literacy supervisors described the challenge of writing the mother tongue:

> Is it difficult to learn to write [Kom]? Except you are well versed with the mother tongue, it is not easy. You can't just pick it up;

except you have gone through a course it will not be easy for you
to write. You may be thinking that you can write, but when you
take that pen now, you will find that you are writing just a
different thing [i.e. not writing correctly].

Informal uses of mother-tongue writing are uncommon, English being the
preferred medium for note-taking, letter writing or personal communication.
One of the most significant writing behaviours reported by the PROPELCA
alumni (Table II) was letter writing, which accounted for more than half of
the writing events reported. However, this activity was reported to take place
far more often in English than in the mother tongue. The fact that the
recipients of these letters were more likely to be literate in English than in the
mother tongue underscores the dominance of English literacy even within the
language communities.

In addition, the writing experience is largely connected with English-
language school. In that context, student writing takes the form of dictation,
with much classroom time spent copying notes from the blackboard into an
exercise book or completing written examinations. In the 21 primary school
classrooms observed in this study, the closest instance to explicitly practised
creative writing observed was in a grade 7 informal PROPELCA class – in
the mother tongue, not English.

Next the teacher writes a [Bafut] word on the board and asks for
sentences that have that word in it. When a student will propose a
sentence, that student is invited to write the sentence on the
board. Everyone but EVERYONE wants to do this! Their
blackboard writing is a bit cramped and wobbly, but it is legible.
Everyone reads what they have written. Tone marks provide the
most consistent challenge, but some kids also mess up on spelling.

Along with this lack of curricular emphasis on personal, creative writing in
English, the language barrier which English presents for primary school
children in the Bafut, Kom and Nso' areas discourages writing activities
other than those which take the form of copying text.

In addition, the social context in the Bafut, Kom and Nso' language
communities works against the proliferation of writing activity in general.
Literature on the relationship between literacy and society points out that
writing involves processes which suit the cultural values and proclivities of
some societies more than they do others. Kress (1997, p. 17) describes the
difference between speaking as an orientation primarily directed towards
others, and writing as primarily inward-directed reflection.

In speech the needs of the interlocutor are of primary concern;
this is not the case in writing to the same extent. There those
needs are replaced by the development of what the writer thinks is
the appropriate conceptual or other structure of the text. (Kress,
1997, p. 17)

The proclivities of the Bafut, Kom and Nso' language communities – including the literates – lead them to prefer speaking to writing. This evidence bears out Kulick & Stroud's argument (1993) that literacy uses in a community are subject to that community's own unique social patterns. The adult literacy director for NACALCO described people's preference for obtaining information in oral rather than written form:

> Even those who have been to school, they don't read. For example, you have a [written] invitation and you give it to a person. He takes it [speaker holds it to his chest] and says, 'Oh, what are you talking about? Tell me. Oh, when is it? Where is it?' When he has it in his hands!

This association of writing with ineffective communication is not surprising, given that their experience of writing has been primarily in an English-language classroom where their language skills in the medium of instruction were weak.

Thus, the difficulty of writing the mother tongue correctly, the association of writing with English and a cultural preference for oral communication all help to explain the infrequency of writing in the mother tongue.

Nevertheless, signs of enthusiasm for writing the mother tongue can be found. The PROPELCA teachers find that being able to write in the mother tongue gives them a certain prestige with students and parents. One teacher trainee noted the reaction to her new ability to write Lamnso':

> Although I teach both French and English, I discovered I could not even write my own name in Lamnso'. So now I am learning. The other day my first daughter saw me writing a story in Lamnso' and she said to her friends, 'Clap for mother, she is writing in Lamnso'!' The parents where I teach like it quite well; they say, 'Our Madame teaches French, English and Lamnso''.

The one who can write in mother tongue is seen as having 'extra knowledge'. The Kom literacy supervisors explained this perception:

> I can write a thing now, in Kom. You can read English, I can also read [English]. And I can write [Kom] still the same as English; but without knowing the letter of the language, you cannot read ... [As] a teacher, you write things like that [in Kom] and people read [them]; then when they write in Kom they ask [another] teacher now to read, and he cannot.

Teachers and headmasters who work alongside PROPELCA teachers notice their own inability to write the mother tongue or read what the PROPELCA teacher has written; it motivates some to take the PROPELCA teacher training course themselves.

Students themselves enjoy attempting to write in their own language. For the most part this takes the form of writing dictation, as illustrated in this classroom observation:

> The teacher erases the board [which had the day's lesson on it], then asks 'Who can write *Taà* ['father', a vocabulary word for the day]?' Many volunteers to write on the board. Then *Ndè* ['mother']. Then *nsòò* ['field']. Then *mbî* ['goat']. One boy writes it wrong, writing *mdî*. The class says, 'Oooooooh,' and finally another boy volunteers to write it correctly.

Is this interest in writing the mother tongue, catalysed and framed by the mother-tongue literacy programmes, strong enough and pervasive enough to change the attitude of the language communities towards written communication? The data indicate that cultural perceptions of writing, enforced by years of English-language schooling, have not as yet been altered by the presence of mother-tongue writing. However, if the PROPELCA and the adult literacy programmes are able to continue as they are currently operating, the possibility exists for increasingly positive attitudes about writing in the language communities.

The 'Oral Society' and the 'Literate Society': blurring the line?

Arguments about the legitimacy of the oral society/literate society distinction described by Olson (1994) and others have relevance for the Bafut, Kom and Nso' language communities. It would be easy to postulate a connection between their highly contextual, relational social orientation and the consistency with which they choose oral strategies for communication (Tannen, 1985). Nevertheless, Heath's warning (1983, p. 230) against the tendency to classify societies as strictly oral or literate is particularly relevant when the 'oral/literate' classification forms the basis for judgements regarding a people's cognitive or technological capacity.

For the Bafut, Kom and Nso' communities, the debate may be clarified by examining the roles of English and the mother tongue in their learning systems. In these language communities, literate discourses have been primarily formed in the English-language environment of formal schooling. The activities and context of literacy have thus been filtered through a language barrier which forms a total comprehension block for most grade 1 students; as English is acquired, this barrier slowly lowers until by grade 4 or 5 (if the child stays in school that long) content learning is possible. Increased fluency in the English language in later grades allows the formation of literate discourses which are less hampered by a language barrier. Still, the community-wide association of literacy with uncertain comprehension (stemming from their experience in school) reinforces the preference for non-literate strategies for thinking and communication.

This language divide highlights the distinction between literate and non-literate discourse patterns among the Bafut, Kom and Nso' communities, and leads to their identification as 'oral societies' despite the fact that a large proportion of the populations are at least nominally literate in English. Indeed, even well-educated and highly literate members of these communities prioritise oral behaviours over literate ones in daily communication tasks. Assumptions about the supposedly underdeveloped cognitive capacities of oral societies (logical reasoning, historical consciousness, scepticism, and complex organisation; see Brandt & Clinton, 2002, p. 341) are thus applied inaccurately and unfairly to these language communities. In fact, they demonstrate many of the characteristics of 'literate' societies as listed by Brandt & Clinton, but they use reading and writing in specific and restricted ways.

The advantage of mother-tongue literacy learning for these language communities is that it offers the possibility of acquiring literate discourses in a language the student understands. This discourse is still formed around the structures and knowledge practices of formal education, but at least it permits literate behaviour to be associated with complete linguistic comprehension.

Can the development of written mother tongue cause the uses of literacy to broaden in these language communities, thus blurring the line between 'oral' and 'literate' society (Heath, 1983, p. 230)? There is reason to think so, if literate discourses can develop in circumstances that are free of any language barrier. However, the question of whether the dominance of English-mediated schooling would allow such a wide use of the mother tongue for formal education is less easy to answer.

A Silo Model of Social Literacy Use

Over the past 80-plus years of contact with English-language literacy, the Bafut, Kom and Nso' communities have established roles for reading and writing in their own society. The new possibilities presented by the written mother tongue have the potential to alter somewhat the place of literacy in these language communities, but at present the majority of instances of written text use centre on two particular social contexts: the school and the church. These two contexts might be called *silos of literacy practice* (in analogy to the unitary, self-contained structures used for the storage of grain).[14] The term 'literacy practice' refers to 'the socially regulated, recurrent, and patterned things that people do with literacy as well as the cultural significance they ascribe to those doings' (Brandt & Clinton, 2002, p. 342).

In the language communities under study, church and school are the focal contexts for the majority of text-related activities in society – so much so that they form fairly self-contained silos of literacy practice. Such literacy practices may or may not entail what would traditionally be called reading or writing, but they are activities and behaviours which occur specifically in relation to written text.[15] Heath's concept of the *literacy event* is helpful here, defined as a situation or activity in which 'writing is integral to the nature of participants' interactions and their interpretive processes' (Heath, 1982, p. 93).

The church and school silos of literacy practice share a number of characteristics. In each case, the literacy events revolve around a set of written texts which have been produced uniquely for use in these contexts: Scripture and liturgical helps in church, textbooks in school. The literacy events taking place in the church and school silos are multidimensional, involving the presence of written text, oral reading of written text, talk about text, choral recitation of written text and written reproduction of text. These two institutions also require educated people as their leaders; by vocational category, church leaders and teachers have more education – and possess more books – than community members in other vocations. Both silos are also designated sites for teaching mother-tongue literacy: the PROPELCA programme in schools and the adult literacy programmes in church.

In each silo of literacy practice language choice is negotiated, based primarily on the judgement of the people in charge. In the church literacy events, English and mother tongue (and often Pidgin) are used as deemed appropriate by the leadership for reading and speaking.[16] In school classrooms, whether PROPELCA or non-PROPELCA, English and the mother tongue each have their role as determined by the teacher. In the non-PROPELCA classroom, even though the official expectation is that only English will be used and use of the mother tongue has for years been officially discouraged [17], in fact even capable teachers use oral mother tongue when they consider it necessary for pupil understanding.[18] In the PROPELCA classrooms, the use of written mother tongue as a medium of instruction in the early grades is accompanied by oral instruction in English as a subject; in later grades, English comes to dominate the syllabus as time given to mother-tongue medium instruction is slowly phased out.

The normal way to use written text in these two silos is public reading or recitation. However, private or individual uses of text also form part of the church and school literacy silos, although not necessarily inside the physical grounds of the silo. In church, reading of the Scriptures at home is encouraged, particularly when Scriptures are available in the mother tongue. Correspondence-type study programmes are also offered. In school, the instances of individual – though not private – reading and writing observed consisted of writing practice done at the child's desk and then submitted for inspection to the teacher; and silent reading of written questions on the blackboard. Homework is the primary use of reading and writing meant to take place outside of school.

In a few instances, it seemed that written language itself was seen to possess a degree of autonomy unrelated to its actual decoded meaning (as described in Noordman & Vonk, 1994, p. 77). This phenomenon is well known where sacred writings or other texts have been imbued with authority, and is particularly evident when the reader does not speak the language of the text. In this study, a few cases were observed of blackboard writing in English, in which teachers seemed reluctant to change English text once it had been written down. An observation made in a PROPELCA teacher training session illustrated the priority that is given to 'reading what is there' as opposed to making meaning from the text:

> The lesson is on noun–adjective agreement in Kom language. The teacher writes on the board the following statement, and then reads it out loud verbatim: 'Each nouns form adjectives in its own way.' He then hesitates, uncertain about the statement's correctness, but does not correct it.

This teacher trainer knew English well enough to know that this statement was grammatically incorrect; however, having once been written the text seemed not to be subject to change.

These cases were both of English writing, however. Similar kinds of mistakes made in writing the mother tongue were subject to correction. In the same teacher training session, a trainee corrected the teacher's Kom writing:

> The teacher goes to the board and the blank in each [Kom language] exercise is filled in with help from the class. The talk is all in Kom. The exercises are in Kom, although the instructions on the board are in English. *At one point a young student corrects a tone mark [in Kom] which the teacher has written wrong on the blackboard.*

This apparent difference in the way written English and written mother tongue were treated bears out Noordman & Vonk's observation that the language of a text may make it less subject to change; that is, text in a language less familiar to the reader is less likely to be seen as easily manipulated and corrected than is text in a familiar language. Much of the respect for English text and English literacy observed in this study highlights this difference between knowledge of the mother tongue (whether spoken or written) and the lack of fluency in written English.

Other Social Uses of Written Text

Outside these two silos of literacy practice, regular occasions of written text use are few. The print environment in towns centres on businesses and offices, although in many cases it consists only of signs, advertisements or price lists; the more rural the settlement, the less of this print is visible. The act of leisure is rarely seen. Christopher Mengjo, an Nso' editor and publisher, when asked about this phenomenon, described it in terms of cultural values:

> The European sits and reads. The African sits and talks. Even I,
> who write and sell books, when I am sitting in my house, I want to
> go find my friends and talk to them. I do not pick up a book and
> read.

Mengjo's observations point once more to the communicative preferences being acted out by literate members of the Bafut, Kom and Nso' language community. This choice – between private reading and oral social interaction – is primarily a matter of preference, not competence.

The Symbolic Value of Literacy

Alongside the uses of literacy described above, there exists a certain level of respect for reading and written text as symbols of modernity. The ability to decode print is itself seen as mastering a desirable foreign skill. One consultant described the response of an illiterate father to the demonstrated ability of his eight-year-old son (a PROPELCA student) to read a small book in the mother tongue:

> The father said, 'Where did he learn to do that, going from one
> cover to the other without losing his way?' To the father the
> language was not relevant; the fact that this young child could
> manage a book was itself impressive.

Similarly, instances of children sounding out a scrap of English newspaper or even the logo on their father's shoe impress their parents. There is something about unlocking the mystery of print which makes fluent reading a highly respected skill. Joseph Mfonyam, a Bafut linguist and author, expressed the belief that this respect for reading can be used to promote the use of written mother tongue:

> People are tending to see the book culture as ideal; so when they
> see posters and other things in the mother tongue, writing about
> the use of soybeans, etc., people get ideas: 'I read about soybeans,
> and now I am using [what I learned]'.

Respect for books themselves is also evident. They are considered too important to entrust to primary school children, for example. Such an attitude towards books is understandable given their cost; at the same time, allowing the children only limited access to them elevates their symbolic value at the expense of their practical value for learning. The Scriptures are also the object of great respect, and owning a New Testament in English or the mother tongue is considered important in these largely Christian communities. Yet the symbolic value of those books may in many cases outweigh their use as reading material.

153

The Future of Written Mother Tongue

The roles and uses of written mother tongue in the Bafut, Kom and Nso' language communities are framed by the availability of written text in those languages, the means available for acquiring literacy in the mother tongue, and the institutional support in existence for written mother tongue. Social uses of literacy are centred on two silos of literacy practice: the school and the church. Within those silos, there is evidence that the written mother tongue is gaining acceptance. However, these silos of literacy practice are set in a broader social environment in which English dominates the practice of written language, and in which oral language (the mother tongue) is the strongly preferred means of communication. What are the implications of all this for the future of the written mother tongue?

Use and acceptance of the written mother tongue could increase in these communities if the written mother tongue were to move further into the existing silos of literacy practice, or if contexts outside the existing silos were established for which the written mother tongue is essential. The institutions which promote written mother tongue in these three language communities, particularly the language committees, are taking steps in both of these directions.

Increasing the Role of Written Mother Tongue

Increasing the role of written mother tongue in the school context is a primary goal of all three language committees. One way in which this is being done is to increase the sites where PROPELCA is offered. Not only are new primary schools and teachers being sought for the PROPELCA programme, but grades other than primary are being targeted as well. One BALA literacy supervisor is developing a timetable that can be used in the two-year nursery programme. KLDC and NLO personnel offer mother-tongue literacy classes in a few secondary schools where the headmaster permits it.

Another means of increasing the role of written mother tongue in schools is to offer an expanding range of school texts and materials for use by teachers. The NLO, looking to the day when the new law on using local language in schools is officially applied and included in examinations, is preparing Lamnso' materials for use in all seven primary grades and even into secondary school: geography, descriptive publications about Nso' culture, and novels.[19]

Increasing the role of written mother tongue in the church context is another focus of the language committees, particularly in cooperation with the Cameroon Association for Bible Translation and Literacy (CABTAL). Initiatives which incorporate newly-translated portions of the Lamnso' Old Testament into Lamnso' literacy classes are being promoted by the NLO and the Lamnso' CABTAL translation committee. The KLDC actively cooperates with CABTAL personnel in charge of organising literacy/ Scripture use courses in Kom. In BALA, one literacy supervisor has been assigned to focus solely on raising awareness of the possibilities for using the Bafut New Testament in local churches. Shey Ma'wo, an NLO literacy supervisor, has developed a series of Lamnso' Bible study materials and songs which are used by the Lamnso' Choir Association of the Presbyterian churches in the Nso' area. In all these ways, the language committees are working to integrate written mother tongue into the literacy practices of the churches.

Establishing New Contexts for Written Mother Tongue Use

As for the establishment of environments outside the existing silos of literacy practice in which the written mother tongue might play a key role, the language committees are making attempts in that direction also. This is a much more difficult task, however, as it involves modifying social expectations about the proper contexts for the mother tongue and for written text of any kind.

Development initiatives are one area in which the language committees believe written mother tongue use could be expanded. Development NGOs operating in the homelands areas use English-language materials and training, relying on bilingual promoters to convey information to their target audiences orally in the mother tongue. Language committee members believe that the NGOs are aware that this approach is not very effective, and the language committees are poised to exploit this potential niche for mother-tongue publications. In a few instances cooperation is already taking place between development organisations and language committees to produce mother-tongue publications. An AIDS brochure prepared by the Ministry of Public Health was submitted to several Cameroonian language committees (including the KLDC) in mid-2003 for translation into the mother tongue; the plan is to then print it and use it in Ministry programmes. Another development initiative, sponsored by the environmental NGO, Living Earth, involved translation of an environmental education text into the Kom language for use in upper primary school classes. The book was translated by KLDC personnel and published in 2000. However, administrative obstacles blocked the book's use in Kom schools, and its conceptual difficulty makes it unlikely to be used in other contexts. This experience indicates that effective expansion of written mother tongue into the development arena will require materials that are carefully targeted and utilised as part of a larger programme initiative, in order to interest people in purchasing and reading them.

Another potential domain for building new contexts for written mother tongue is that of the existing traditional societies and associations, using the strong support of the traditional authorities [20] to increase interest and use of the written local language. A BALA literacy supervisor described his vision for exploiting this niche:

> We have to go to various meetings. In Bafut we have many
> meeting-groups: the farmers' meeting-group, a group for dancers,
> a group for any other thing. We shall have to approach those
> groups, do literacy work with them, write and have some written
> materials concerning what they are doing. So that if they are able
> to take that written material to help them in what they are doing,
> then our objective will be achieved.

The interest of traditional leaders in using written mother tongue to preserve
and disseminate information within the culture is significant. The only
apparent obstacle to this extension of written mother tongue is the limited
availability of resources – financial and personnel – to write, publish and
distribute such materials.

A third potential new context for use of written mother tongue is the
more general context of leisure and family time. NACALCO's adult literacy
programme director described his own vision for this kind of mother-tongue
reading:

> If the father can stay like this, on a Friday evening he sits down
> and the five-year-old boy is here, and the eight-year-old girl is
> here, and they are reading the story of the tortoise in the language
> and laughing and feeling okay. Is that not a nice family picture?

It is indeed an attractive goal for broadening the environment for mother-
tongue reading. On the other hand, little evidence was found in this study
that would indicate any social move in this direction. Given the societal
patterns of communication described above, it is probable that 'family story
time' these days is more likely to involve oral story telling in the mother
tongue than reading in it. On the other hand, if the parents have forgotten
the stories of the community, reading them from a book in the mother
tongue might be an attractive option.

As for other leisure reading and writing in the mother tongue, the
evidence is mixed. As Table II shows, 80 of the 134 instances of reading or
writing reported by the PROPELCA alumni survey respondents could be
described as private uses of literacy: letters, news reading and personal
reading or writing. However 67 of those 80 instances involved English rather
than mother tongue. Not only so, but observation evidence indicated that, if
leisure reading is taking place, it is not being done in public places such as
restaurants or on public transportation.

Conclusion

The use of the mother tongue, particularly the written mother tongue, is
increasing in the Bafut, Kom and Nso' communities under study. The
growing presence of the mother tongue in primary schools and adult literacy
programmes, and the language committees' efforts to increase the number of
mother-tongue readers and texts, are means by which the local languages are

being strengthened (Crystal, 2000, pp. 136-138). Furthermore, unlike other cases of attempted language recovery (Crystal, 2000, p. 129), these initiatives are taking place while the local language still enjoys popular use and support.

Still, it is important to remember that, for all these positive gains on the part of local language advocacy, maintenance of the local language also depends on the wider influences of the economic and demographic environment, the degree of exposure of the language community to the influence of global society, national education policies (for both government and private education systems) regarding language, and the stakeholders in the current primary school system. Literacy in the mother tongue has potential for affecting learning outcomes for both children and adults, but it needs a supportive institutional and sociopolitical environment to fulfil that potential.

Notes

[1] The Foundation for Endangered Languages notes in its manifesto that 'the majority of the world's languages are vulnerable not just to decline but to extinction'. See http://www.ogmios.org/ manisfesto.htm

[2] Crystal (2000, p. 19) estimates that 50% of the world's languages will be lost in the next 100 years.

[3] Of course the Bafut, Kom and Nso' communities differ from each other in many ways. However, in terms of sociopolitical, linguistic and educational context, the three are comparable and are treated so in this chapter.

[4] Lamnso' is the language spoken by the Nso' people. In Bafut and Kom, the language and the people have the same name.

[5] The English-based Pidgin used in anglophone Cameroon has its roots in the coastal Pidgin developed along the West African coast over the past two centuries or more. In the Grassfields area of Northwest Cameroon, Pidgin is spoken among people who do not share a mother tongue. However, it is not for the most part considered acceptable for use in schools or 'official' contexts.

[6] Operational Programme for Teaching in Cameroonian Languages: a government-approved programme that began in 1981 in four languages of Cameroon. It is currently found in 30 language communities across the country (National Association of Cameroonian Language Committees [NACALCO], 2001).

[7] NACALCO's adult literacy programme director, Noë Ngueffo, believes that many of those who have finished primary school are nevertheless unable to read; he counts these people as 'semiliterate'.

[8] It is significant that there is no distinction made here between English-language and mother-tongue literacy classes; this highlights the lack of such classes in English. To teach literacy to adults in English is a fruitless task in the homelands; those who are illiterate tend to have low English skills as well, since both skills have traditionally been acquired in formal education.

[9] The earliest publications in Bafut were linguistic studies done in the late 1970s. In Lamnso', the Catholic diocese of Kumbo was printing lectionaries and materials for use in Nso' churches as early as 1976. In Kom, the earliest publications consisted of a series of 30 hand-printed booklets on religious and cultural topics, done by an independent missionary in 1968-79.

[10] The Bafut, Kom, Nso' and other language communities of the Grassfields follow an eight-day week based on local market cycles. The pocket diaries and calendars show both the eight-day and the seven-day weeks of the year, and they are for that reason very popular.

[11] It was reported to me that secondary school students tend to have more books than primary students, but I have no hard evidence of this. It was also reported to me that primary schools in the urban areas have the same problem as rural primary schools do, with parents not furnishing their children with school textbooks.

[12] A grade 1 English textbook, produced by Evans Publishers for Cameroonian schools, cost 2500 fr. cfa. This is equivalent to 10% or more of a typical primary teacher's monthly salary. The grade 1 English workbook costs extra.

[13] PROPELCA primers and maths books cost between 500 and 750 francs cfa, less than £1 each.

[14] In this model, the silo of literacy contrasts with the concept of the sociolinguistic domain in that it takes place in a specific type of physical location. The concept of 'domain' is not physically bounded. A silo of literacy practice is also in some ways similar to Gee's Discourse (Gee, 1996), but again it is more narrowly situated. Discourses can be defined by physical location, but are not always so.

[15] These behaviours may include listening to text read aloud, reciting written text which has been memorised, or using written text – such a Bible or a Koran – for symbolic purposes.

[16] English, Lamnso' and Pidgin may all be used in church services, but each has a particular role (J. Trudell, 2004).

[17] A 1958 law mandating English as the language of instruction in primary school (Keller, 1969, p. 73) was not officially repealed, even as PROPELCA was given approval as an experimental programme. This ambiguity regarding official language policy has led to a general sense that use of the mother tongue in primary school is to be discouraged.

[18] This mismatch between official language policy and language choices in the classroom is not uncommon in sub-Saharan Africa. In some cases, the pro-local language policy is never enforced; for example, Mule (1999) decries the continued privileging of English in Kenyan schools, despite legislation about the role of Kiswahili and other indigenous languages in education. In other cases, policy which favours use of a European language is inconsistently applied in the classroom because of the students' lack of fluency in that language; Arthur (2001) notes this behaviour in both Botswanan and Tanzanian schools where English in the official medium of instruction. Ferguson (2003) describes such *code switching* (in this case, using the child's mother tongue as well as the official language of instruction) as a common strategy of classroom teachers in societies where the former colonial language

is the official language of instruction but is not spoken by the students. Ferguson argues that such code switching not only aids cognitive impact, but also helps to create a social and affective environment more conducive to learning.

[19] Well known Nso' author Kengjo Jumbam has written novels in English which are required reading in the national secondary school curriculum; he recently gave the NLO permission to translate those novels into Lamnso' for use in the Nso' schools.

[20] The traditional authority structure remains intact and influential among many of the Grassfields peoples, including Bafut, Kom and Nso'.

References

Arthur, Jo (2001) Perspectives on Educational Language Policy and Its Implementation in African Classrooms: a comparative study of Botswana and Tanzania, *Compare*, 31(3), 347-362.

Banyee (Banboyee), William (1998) *Lamnso' Sound and Spelling Charts*. Bamenda, Cameroon: Nso' Language Organisation.

Brandt, Deborah & Clinton, Katie (2002) Limits of the Local: expanding perspectives on literacy and social practice, *Journal of Literacy Research*, 34(3), 337-356.

Crystal, David (2000) *Language Death*. Cambridge: Cambridge University Press.

Ferguson, Gibson (2003) Classroom Code-Switching in Post-colonial Contexts: functions, attitudes and policies, *AILA Review*, 16, 38-51.

Gee, James Paul (1996) *Social Linguistics and Literacies: ideology in discourse*. 2nd edn. London: Falmer Press.

Griffiths, Gareth (1997) Writing, Literacy and History in Africa, in M.-H. Msiska & P. Hyland *Writing and Africa*, 139-158. London: Longman.

Heath, Shirley Brice (1982) Protean Shapes in Literacy Events: ever shifting oral and literate traditions, in Deborah Tannen (Ed.) *Spoken and Written Language: exploring literacy and orality*, 91-118. Norwood: Ablex.

Heath, Shirley Brice (1983) *Ways with Words: language, life and work in communities and classrooms*. Cambridge: Cambridge University Press.

Keller, Werner (1969) *The History of the Presbyterian Church in West Cameroon*. Victoria, Cameroon: Presbook.

Korang, Kwaku Larbi & Slemon, Stephen (1997) Post-colonialism and Language, in M.-H. Msiska & P. Hyland *Writing and Africa*, 246-263. London: Longman.

Kress, Gunther (1997) *Before Writing: rethinking the paths to literacy*. London: Routledge.

Kulik, Don & Stroud, Christopher (1993) Conceptions and Uses of Literacy in a Papua New Guinean Village, in Brian V. Street (Ed.) *Cross Cultural Approaches to Literacy*, 30-61. Cambridge: Cambridge University Press.

Ministry of National Education, Republic of Cameroon (1998) *Law of Education in Cameroon: Law No. 98/004 of 14th April 1998*. Yaoundé: Ministry of National Education.

Ministry of National Education, Republic of Cameroon (2000) *National Syllabuses for English Speaking Primary Schools in Cameroon.* Yaoundé: Ministry of National Education.

Mule, Lucy (1999) Indigenous Languages in the School Curriculum: what happened to Kiswahili in Kenya? in Ladislaus Semali & Joe Kincheloe (Eds) *What is Indigenous Knowledge? Voices from the Academy*, 227-242. New York: Falmer Press.

National Association of Cameroonian Language Committees (NACALCO) (2001) *Annual Report.* Yaoundé, Cameroon: NACALCO.

Noordman, Leo & Vonk, Wietske (1994) Text Processing and Its Relevance for Literacy, in Ludo Verhoeven (Ed.) *Functional Literacy: theoretical issues and educational implications*, 75-93. Amsterdam: John Benjamins.

Olson, David (1994) Literacy and the Making of the Western Mind, in Ludo Verhoeven (Ed.) *Functional Literacy: theoretical issues and educational implications*, 135-150. Amsterdam: John Benjamins.

Robinson, Douglas (1997) *Translation and Empire: postcolonial theories explained.* Manchester: St Jerome Publishing.

Sanneh, Lamin (1990) *Translating the Message: the missionary impact on culture.* Maryknoll, NY: Orbis Books.

Tannen, Deborah (1985) Relative Focus on Involvement in Spoken and Written Discourse, in David Olson, Nancy Torrance & Angela Hildyard (Eds) *Literacy, Language and Learning: the nature and consequences of reading and writing*, 124-147. Cambridge: Cambridge University Press.

Trudell, Barbara (2004) The Power of the Local: education choices and language maintenance among the Bafut, Kom and Nso' communities of Northwest Cameroon. PhD thesis, University of Edinburgh.

Trudell, Joel (2004) Bible Translation and Social Literacies among four Nso' Churches: an ethnographic study of Scripture use. PhD thesis, University of Edinburgh.

CHAPTER 8

Gatherers of Knowledge: Namibian Khoisan healers and their world of possibilities

CHRIS LOW

The label Khoisan is used in a modern context primarily as a useful folk category. The term has been rejected by San groups because it implies subjugation of San, or Bushmen, by Khoekhoe and propagates old-fashioned and inappropriate Western ideas of homogeneity between distinct people. Barnard's authoritative *Hunters and Herders of Southern Africa* (1992)[1], however, puts a strong case for the legitimacy of making structural comparisons between the various groups that make up the Khoisan on the basis of cultural and cosmological ties. This chapter concerns patterns in healing strategies that exist across the Khoisan and their underlying epistemological and ontological footings. I examine a way of thinking, encapsulated in the phrase 'a world of possibilities', that is prevalent amongst contemporary Khoisan, that is non-scientific and challenged by the imposition of 'Western' rationality through formal education. My findings are based upon 10 months' fieldwork amongst the Nama, Damara, Topnaar, Hai//om, Ju/'hoan and Nharo of Namibia undertaken as part of my doctoral research between September 2000 and September 2001.[2]

Interest in the effects of colonialism on Africans has been a persistent and long-standing feature of colonial discourse. The 'Introductory note' to Schapera's 1930 ethnography *Khoisan Peoples*, for example, emphasises the value of his book to the 'native educationist' as a moulder of 'native' life.[3] Since the 1970s there has been particular academic interest in the effects of colonialism, including the infrastructure of hospitals, churches and schools as moulders of Africans, but with due recognition given to African agency within processes of social transformation and the phenomenon of medical pluralism. There has also been related interest in African healing responses to epidemics.[4] What there has been far less of in both colonial and recent contexts is historical consideration of persistent African ways of thinking and doing medicine. The Khoisan 'world of possibilities' links issues of African thought with historical interest in change and continuity.

My research has included Khoisan from all spheres of contemporary Namibian society – from Nama and Damara occupying high-level jobs in Windhoek to the poorest Khoisan living in 'remote' regions of the country. The main focus of my doctoral study was to assess whether or not there might exist something that could usefully be referred to as a Khoisan medical system. The question, once posed, demanded further specificity in terms of how distinct, persistent and universal such a phenomenon has to be to justify the notion of a 'system'. These underlying questions brought out issues of medical pluralism and transformation of distinctly non-biomedical Khoisan medicine in a colonial and post-colonial context. As my study developed, issues of education came increasingly to the fore in this context of change and acculturation.

It would be naive to envisage a standardised, static, Western derivative of education being carried out across modern Africa. Western paradigms of knowledge and education do, however, continue to try to assert themselves within African schools [5] and the nature of education extended to the Khoisan follows this legacy. Because this chapter reflects my findings, which were not directly related to issues of education, it tends to bring out more questions about the effects of education than it answers. The main thrust of the chapter is to examine the wider and not always positive implications of education in terms of what it actually threatens. I outline some of the distinctive features of Khoisan medicine that are particularly vulnerable to education and other factors of acculturation.

In summary, it seems questionable whether something homogeneous and distinctive enough exists to be usefully thought of as a Khoisan medical system. There are, however, undoubtedly strong and consistent patterns in the way Khoisan think about the body, illness, transference of illness and treatment of sickness. Many of these have strong parallels in other hunter-gatherer and forager cultures. Without wishing to root my interpretation of Khoisan medicine in a simplistic paradigm of environmental determinism, much of my research points towards the important and overlooked role of the sensuous dimensions of environmental experience in shaping Khoisan medical practice and importantly the ideas behind that practice.

Carruthers has observed that the southern African Bushmen home-range fed and shaped their social and economic relationships and perhaps their spiritual world too.[6] Biesele has identified in Bushmen myth and folklore evidence of an 'imaginative substrate' or Bushmen way of thinking that comes from their environmentally attuned hunter-gatherer lifestyle. This way of thinking underpins the creation, transmission and transformation of Bushmen 'traditional' knowledge. At the heart of this hunter-gatherer way of thinking Biesele, like others, recognises a key role of animals. Biesele determines that Bushmen use animals as metaphors and 'to think with'.

Animals are integral to Bushmen folk concepts, including sickness and childbirth.[7] In my doctoral thesis I extend the contents of this imaginative substrate and examine 'wind', 'arrows' and 'smell' as constituents, agents and transmitters of 'potency' found amongst past and present Khoisan. These phenomena are a significant feature of Khoisan ways of knowing the world. Barnard, like Biesele, sees such Bushmen ways of thinking persisting, at least in the short term, despite culture contact, trade and mixed subsistence strategies.[8]

In my current research I am examining the hypothesis that diminishing contact with the rural environment and its resources does not seem to lead to a swift and severe break in persistent healing strategies of either San or 'Khoi'.[9] Khoisan lack of contact with the animals and plants that lie behind many of their therapeutic strategies is absolutely associated with erosion of a hunter-gatherer and forager lifestyle and consequently medicine. The biggest transformer of 'traditional' Khoisan medicine is not, however, access to resources but what challenges their way of thinking.

Morris indicates that animals have become increasingly less salient in the cult rituals and symbolic life of Africans with the spread of Christianity.[10] Changing aboriginal ideas changes the reasoning behind use of animal remedies and associations with animals. Introduced European ways of thinking similarly affect Khoisan relations with the other ingredients of their 'imaginative substrate'. Guenther has pointed to the threat formalised religious education poses to Bushmen ways of thinking.[11] Both taught Christianity and dogmatic education are key challenges to persistent Khoisan ways of thinking. They strain the tolerance for contradiction and personal views and the validity of personal experience that Schapera, Barnard, Guenther and others have identified as a central pole of Khoisan thinking. Additionally poverty or political and economic exclusion from developing Africa seem to tie San and some 'Khoi' to reliance on traditional resource-based medicine in heavily acculturated settlements, such as farms or desert towns. Guenther was surprised by the extraordinary botanical knowledge he found amongst Ghanzi *Nharo* San women living on farms.[12] Their lack of education and poverty seem to have contributed to preservation of their traditional knowledge. If animal and plant resources change, substitutions are found following Khoisan pragmatism and cosmological, epistemological and experiential associations. Biomedicine is accommodated in a context of medical pluralism, which appeals to pragmatic Khoisan, who are essentially unchallenged by alternative view points. Changing familiarity with environmental resources does affect Khoisan medicine, firstly in terms of resource use and secondly in terms of ideas. It is, however, breakdown of their imaginative substrate through education and religious teaching that really changes thoughts behind Bushmen medicine and proves the biggest threat to 'traditional' medical knowledge.

The difficulties and tensions associated with education are something many San are only too aware of. A Namibian Hai//om, Daniel /Kharuxab, for example, stipulated: 'We want education, even though it kills our tradition'.[13] Similarly, David Kruiper, a South African ≠Khomani San, proposed with a sense of despair:

> Ja, the school is the thing that takes our culture away from us. But these children they have to go. They have to go through that so they can come back and write down this culture, before it's all lost. That's all we can do.[14]

Two issues lie at the heart of tensions concerning Khoisan education. Firstly, lack of education leads to exclusion from the positive effects of participation in the contemporary southern African political economy, and secondly, education encourages loss of what is rather inadequately conflated as indigenous traditional knowledge. This traditional loss is in turn tied to loss of identity and dispossession of culture and often land rights.

My search for a Khoisan medical system, something necessarily distinct from Western medicine, concerned what might be lost at the rich cultural interface of modern Africa. In the title of this chapter I used the phrase 'gatherers of knowledge'. I have done so in order to draw attention to a currently popular idea that San not only forage for food but for ideas. This proposition is linked to wider academic understanding that recognises flexibility, fluidity and contradiction found in Khoisan ideas, ontology and cosmology as fundamental Khoisan characteristics. Understanding how Khoisan think is central to issues of learning, creation and transmission of knowledge. In addition to examining the nature of Khoisan medical theory I wish to develop these notions of Bushmen as flexible foraging thinkers within what I feel is a preferable way of thinking about the Khoisan; they live in a world of possibilities.

How we think about the nature, status and transmission of Khoisan knowledge in relation to the Khoisan world of possibilities forms the focus of the proceeding discussion. This is followed consecutively by consideration of ways of knowing, ways of teaching and learning and a brief summary of some of the implications of education.

Background

There has been far more research undertaken amongst the San than the Khoi concerning issues of knowledge. This largely reflects the particular long-term Euro-American popular and academic fascination with the San as some of the world's last hunter-gatherers. This interest has principally concerned later nineteenth-century /Xam Bushmen and post-1950s Bushmen of the Namibian and Botswanan Kalahari, the !Kung, Ju/'hoan and G/wi. It is within these Kalahari groups that the 'imaginative substrate' has been detected. Since the mid-1980s anthropologists have additionally turned attention to Hai//om and Nharo Bushmen who have long lived more acculturated lifestyles on farms and in townships.

Similarly broad brush strokes of interest and approach are detectable in Khoi research. Cape Khoikhoi (modern Khoekhoe) have rightly or wrongly been written out of anthropological interest in 'traditional' culture because of the devastating effects of epidemics on their population and society since the early eighteenth century. Those that survived became culturally indistinguishable as they merged with the working-class descendents of the Cape slave populations and became the basis of the 'Cape coloured' population, visible from around 1900.[15] In the early twentieth century the anthropologist Hoernlé looked for non-European culture amongst Nama around the Cape–Namibian border but found her subjects so acculturated that the exercise was hardly possible.[16] Namibia is, however, a large place and changes that affected Cape and more southerly Khoekhoe populations should not necessarily be assumed to have had sweeping effects on all Namibian Khoi peoples. Lau and other historians of southern Africa have tended to present the introduction of merchant capital and wider colonial changes as a monolithic insertion into all spheres of human behaviour and thought. Often accounts of this nature fail to give due consideration to questions of creation, constitution and transmission of knowledge.[17] Assumptions of universal profound change have detracted interest away from particular groups of Khoi Namibians as in any sense holders of Khoekhoe knowledge. This emphasis of change runs contrary to linguistic evidence that Haacke has found which indicates preservation of older language forms amongst what he still sees as relatively isolated populations.[18] Since Hoernlé there has been some recent work that includes consideration of Nama and Damara medical practices but the focus of research has been very much within towns and has concerned medicine in terms of cultural hybridity and not 'aboriginal ideas'.[19]

Without wishing to underplay the complex patterns of movement, cultural exchange and intermingling that must background any consideration of traditional ideas, I wish to draw attention to the rural Khoi, such as the Damara of the Sesfontein region or even apparently 'urbanised' Nama living in small southern Namibian towns and settlements such as Hoachanas or Gibeon, amongst whom there remains a strong affinity with the environment. Many of the ideas I found amongst such people remain visible in more urbanised situations. Many of their thoughts and practices also tie in intimately with those held by the Bushmen studied by anthropologists and archaeologists who are thought to at least represent windows into, if not reflections of, older African forager ways of thinking about and practising medicine.

Knowledge

Anthropologists have tended to consider Bushmen as distinctive from African agro-pastoralists based on their hunter-gatherer culture and their relative isolation. However, strong links do exist between Bushmen and Khoi ideas of

165

illness and treatment and those of other Africans. That key Bushmen and Khoi concepts seem closely allied to, for example, ideas Evans-Pritchard identified amongst early twentieth-century Azande in Central Africa [20], seems to me to point, possibly, to longer, greater, and more intimate African contact situations than might be recognised. But, more likely, given just as striking parallels with non-African aboriginals, these similarities across Africa say something about cross-over points between biology, culture and participation in indigenous environments. This is a point I will return to. For the moment I wish to draw on cross-cultural similarity to develop how we think about knowledge amongst Khoisan.

Malidoma Somé, a Dagara healer from Burkina Faso, observes that the Dagara believe everyone is born with a purpose. This Dagara conception is similar to that held by many African communities who access the 'spirit world' and see life mediated by spirit forces. Somé identifies the Dagara belief that 'ideas you receive do not come from our imagination, they come from the Spirit World, and it is the spirits who decide what the next step will be ... A person's purpose is to serve, using that which has been put into his or her hands as a gift from Spirit'.[21]

What Somé identifies amongst the Dagara is informative regarding Khoisan beliefs. When I discussed with Damara and Hai//om healers whether or not I should undertake a process of 'opening the body and mind' to become a healer, it was repeatedly stressed that 'if you want these things, there is a reason and you must do it'. What I want was in many senses not controlled by 'I' but bound to a wider world of spirits and purpose. The Bushmen relationship between imagination, spontaneous ideas and ideas given by spirit is also strikingly similar to Dagara spirit ideas. Bushmen healing songs come into the head of the healer from the spirit world, usually when Bushmen sleep but sometimes when awake as well. These thoughts or visitations are from the spirit world. Both Khoi and Bushmen link healing with spiritual intervention in human lives. To be a healer amongst Khoi is a 'gift from God'; not always wanted but a non-returnable gift. Amongst Bushmen one can learn to be a healer but healing power comes ultimately from a spirit, similarly conceived loosely in modern times simply as God.

The Khoisan idea of acquiring healing skill within a greater purpose, which is given to people from the spirit world, seems distinct from secular Euro-American celebrations of knowledge tied to status and skill. In Euro-American contexts there is a respect for 'qualifications' and a broader type of status is granted to those that have them. Amongst Khoisan focus is not so much on special talent or status of the individual. Healing skill does not clearly elevate individuals within a community in a wider context than simply being a person who heals. As Katz says of Bushmen healers: 'The healer is a hunter gatherer who also happens to heal'.[22] Broadly, amongst Khoisan, ability, which is tied to knowledge, does not confer authority in situations other than that immediately associated with a person's field of expertise. Arguably there is respect given to healers but the underlying social context differs from that typical of the 'West' and the respect is contained to matters of healing. The recent emergence of political figures from amongst Bushmen, some of whom are prominent healers, is perhaps associated with increasing social differentiation creeping in with the professionalisation of Bushmen healers.[23] It can also, though, be conceived as a less jarring social transition as healers extend their concern with harmonious social relations into the sphere of lands and livelihoods.[24] That new leaders tend to be healers already involved with community problems, as opposed to other Bushmen, goes some way towards supporting ideas that new knowledge is not sought within contexts of power and status.

Knowledge and Contradiction

Since Livingstone's conversations with a rainmaker in the mid-nineteenth century [25] and contributions from Lévy-Bruhl and Evans Pritchard in the early twentieth century [26], academics have observed and sought to explain contradiction and inconsistency within African and other aboriginal thought processes. Contradiction is a notable feature of Bushmen ideas, myths, folklore and explanations. It is also a feature, though less recognised, of Khoi culture. In a Khoisan context, Gellner's affirmation that in 'traditional society' knowledge has 'no diplomatic immunity' [27] points to, not an indifference to truth or lack of ability to recognise it, but to a culturally mediated personal access to truth which is not contradicted by the personal access of others. In effect this allows multiple truths within both individuals and social groups. But despite the resultant variation regarding what is possible, there exists an underlying consistency in Khoisan ontology, epistemology and cosmology that generates consistency in their healing strategies.

To the Khoisan there is nothing odd about different people having different sorts of knowledge. I asked many informants about apparently fabulous details mentioned in colonial accounts of the Khoisan. I questioned them about such matters as snakestones curing snakebite and snakes with cockerel heads. Rather than denying the possibility of the phenomena, most Bushmen and many Damara replied along the lines of: 'they may do that over there ... we Bushmen [Damara etc.] are all different'. Over 'the other side', they indicated, these things were possible.

Khoisan knowledge is tied to different sorts of interest and associations from the West. Many of these are very rich but different, being related to different day-to-day concerns. 'Why?' is not a Khoisan question. If you ask why something happens or is done, a reply emerges the like of which has long challenged oral historians and anthropologists of Africa: ' It is because of the old people'. A push for further clarity brings out 'the old, old people'. With a further push again informants either become uneasy and uninterested or they start to retreat to familiar or good ways of thinking to explain what has no other explanation. The notion of 'good ways of thinking' was proposed by

Robin Horton in his 1967 discussion of African 'modes of thought'. It appears in another later context with Gentner [28], who examines examples of water being recruited as a way of thinking about electricity. Biesele has similarly determined that Bushmen find animals 'good to think with'.[29] The lives of many Bushmen still intrinsically involve animals, and animals are a key feature of their healing initiatives, their mythology and folklore. Whilst direct familiarity with wildlife is far less common amongst most Nama, Damara and Hai//om, animal influence remains in their folktales and folk knowledge and animal parts or excrement feature in many healing strategies. Elsewhere I have suggested that two further factors, wind and smell, are equally important 'good ways of thinking' for many Khoisan.[30]

To explore how Bushmen made sense of the world Lee asked a group of Bushmen to name as many parts of a car as they could.[31] They used their word for 'tin can' for the body of the car and described the rest of the vehicle in terms of organic features such as eyebrows and feet. This indicates how the familiar is used to explain the unfamiliar. Science demands thinking in terms of cause and effect. What appears a pre-scientific and extra-scientific way of Khoisan thinking is to view phenomena in terms of interconnectedness. Silberbauer identified this type of thinking amongst the G/wi Bushmen.[32]

Critical faculty, speculation and creativity are not strong features of the Khoisan I encountered. This observation is not the same as saying they are not highly knowledgeable, resourceful and imaginative; merely that what they do tends to be heavily mediated by a conservative cultural enquiry. There is not a strong culture of experimentation. This proposition runs somewhat contrary to a notion Guenther emphasises, that Bushmen forage not only in a socio-economic capacity but for ideas.[33] I searched for examples of experimentation amongst my informants. They exist but are few. Some Khoisan said they put unknown plants on arrows and fired them at animals to see what would happen, although this was rare. Some fed unknown plants to dogs to see what would happen. One Ju/'hoan man tried plants around his home on an apparently semi-random basis to treat his tubercular cough.[34] If rural Khoisan have an illness, a primary treatment strategy is to make a plant-based concoction. If their first choice of plant for the treatment is too far away or otherwise unavailable they will pick a nearer available plant that is known to be similar and useful. Very rarely, if familiar plants are not available or do not seem to work, other plants will be looked for and perhaps tested or tried. Why Khoisan choose a particular plant for its healing potential or other qualities depends upon Khoisan ways of knowing plants. How they choose what plants to use is based heavily on appearance and taste, and particularly an association between bitter taste and healing potential. Khoisan do look for alternative solutions but within fairly constrained parameters of behaviour and 'experimentation'. Their behaviour fits Horton's revised model of African behaviour that is typically neither 'open' nor 'closed' but somewhere between the two.[35] Khoisan enquiry is bound within familiar ways of knowing and doing. It is not a scientific but a sensory way of knowing the world.[36]

I conceptualise Khoisan foraging for ideas within the context of a bounded creation of knowledge. The Bushman who 'discovered' plants for his tubercular cough may die and not tell anyone, but others may come across the same knowledge if they continue to be guided by similar Khoisan ways of knowing the world. Knowledge moves in and out of the culture cyclically. The body of Khoisan knowledge is like patchwork quilt that may have parts replaced but it remains essentially recognisable over time.

Ways of Knowing

There are three descriptions that are helpful to discussion of what knowledge Khoisan use, where it comes from and how it is transmitted: prescriptive, creative, transformational. Knowledge from 'old people' is prescriptive, as is knowledge given out by healers and to a lesser extent information passed on by others from within or beyond the household. Prescriptive knowledge follows a hierarchy of resort. The hierarchy is based primarily on popular currency of an idea or practice followed by trial and error through more difficult solutions, such as trying successive plants, and with each failure expending more effort on the search. A decision that the sick person will inevitably die may be accepted soon in the process, particularly in cases of infantile illness, in which case nothing will be done to attempt to save them. Prescribed healing knowledge is generally acted upon without significant personal adaptation of the treatment strategy.

Songs and folklore are important carriers of knowledge amongst Khoisan. In the sense that they tell 'truths' about the world they are prescriptive, but at the same time they accommodate new aspects of life and problems and transform what is known. Although there is little evidence of specific healing details being transmitted through this medium, they have a crucial role in the Khoisan 'imaginative substrate'. In the 1970s Wagner-Robertz transcribed song from a Damara healing dance she witnessed. Her description points to the ingredients of the substrate. Wagner-Robertz identified a particular significance of eagles or vultures to the Damara and proposed that the thought of dying far from one's family and being eaten by vultures was particularly dreadful to the Damara.[37] She described that at the outset of the dance the vulture appears in the songs as a threat to the patient. As the dance progresses the virtues of the bird are increasingly extolled, until eventually the bird is praised as a great expeditious messenger.[38]

The Damara songs that were part of the healing dance culture I encountered were not of this nature. There was no obvious symbolism involving the patient and outside influences. Instead the songs were of short repeated themes concerning knowledge abroad in wider Damara life. One song repeated the theme that lions lived in the local mountain, *!Haoros* [39];

another that 'the ostrich jumps over the net'.[40] Amongst the Hai//om songs included, 'I take the donkey cart to Oshakati', and 'she was too shy'.[41] Lee recorded a song amongst the Ju/'hoan that emphasises the role of healing songs as mediators of hostile social tensions. This is a role that is increasingly important in modern acculturative contexts of social breakdown. Lee's recording includes the lines:

> He lies there dying; while you sit above him wrangling and
> fighting, and arguing and glaring, arguing and glaring, arguing and
> glaring.[42]

Khoisan folklore is, like the songs, both persistent and transforming in the knowledge and imaginative substrate it conveys. As with Khoisan songs, key ideas of healing are supported and reinforced by the imaginative world passed on through the medium. Much of this imaginative world pertains to animals. A particularly pertinent story that is common to all Khoisan concerns the Moon and the Hare. The essential element of the story is an explanation of why the Hare has a split lip based upon the Hare having been entrusted by the Moon to tell humanity that they, like the Moon, will rise again at the end of each day, and hence enjoy immortality. The Hare, however, told people that when they die, they die forever. In so doing the Hare destined humanity to mortality and the fear of death. Out of anger the Moon struck the Hare and split the Hare's lip.[43] The essential element of this story concerns rising. Rising, or the getting up and awakening of any organism, is emblematic of life and has significant implications for Khoisan understandings of sickness and healing potency. Sickness is associated with recumbency, whilst life and activated potency is linked to rising and in a wider sense boiling of healing energy or water, and ripening of plants.[44]

Creative knowledge includes inspirational knowledge arising from dreaming, divining, trancing and intuition. These are culturally determined ways of bringing in 'new' knowledge, as was the 'experimental' search for plant remedies previously considered.

Dreaming plays a varied role in Khoisan life. Many Khoisan will 'just dream' and not ask where it comes from or take special note of a dream. But dreams are also thought to be received from beyond a person. Anyone can dream and the act of being given a dream can be validity enough to justify personal action, although to do so one is, in a sense, both being given a path to follow and setting out a path for oneself. A person who responds to their dreams is a special person. A dream provides a good reason to do something. A Damara woman from Windhoek explained:

> maybe there is a person I massage and that person cannot walk.
> Now in the dreams I hear something tell me: 'If someone comes,
> that person comes now, take him at his arm and push him out like
> that'. And I will do this, and even that polish juice, the red one, if
> someone has got a pain, you can also rub that polish where the
> person has got a pain. It is also okay.[45]

Similarly, another Windhoek resident, Libertina, was inspired by a dream to massage paralysed people with car brake fluid.[46] Damara and Nama who treat people seemed more responsive to dreams than many other Khoisan. A Hai//om healer, Paul from near Otavi, would suck or not suck a sick person's illness on account of his dreams, but this was unusual.[47]

Across the Khoisan there was a sense that dead people come in dreams and bad dreams can harm you. Some Ju/'hoan and Hai//om described this as ancestors or dead relatives firing arrows at the living in their sleep. An elderly Nama lady suggested if ancestors come in your sleep you must tell them to go and rest and leave you alone.[48] Other Khoisan simply described such visitations as dreams. A Nama, Damara and Hai//om treatment for visitations of spirits in the night, or bad dreams, was to burn aardwolf and elephant dung in the house. Aardwolf dung releases a very strong odour and this seems the basis of its use. It is a common healing ingredient amongst Khoi groups and Hai//om. The elephant is known for its appetite for healthy plants. Its urine and dung are used by the Nama, Damara and Hai//om in numerous healing contexts. Both the way my informants discussed bad dreams, and their using fumigating substances to keep bad dreams or spirits away, was associated with an older belief that ancestors, or the wind of ancestors, came in the night and used arrows to attack the living. Arrows being fired by spirits and healers is an idea deeply embedded in Khoisan understandings of potency and sickness. Numerous younger Khoisan who were not familiar with arrows in day-to-day life did not seem to think in terms of arrows. Amongst young people their explanation of bad dreams as 'just dreams', as opposed to real visitations by spirits, stems from their educated biological notions of the role of the brain and the mind. Education and lack of association with arrows and notions of potency is transforming Khoisan relationships with dreams and the spirit world.

Amongst the Ju/'hoan dreaming continues to be a source of inspiration for their healing dance songs. The songs are a gift from a god, ≠Gao N!a. In the 1950s Lorna Marshall unusually encountered one old women who dreamed where animals were and directed the men where to hunt.[49] The Damara of Sesfontein have a particular dreaming practice that I have not come across in any other references. If a person is sick they can go in the night to the hut of a healer and secretly insert a stick into the wall of the hut with a piece of clothing or a $5.00 bill tied to it. This stick is known as an 'anib'. The healer will arise in the morning, emerge from his/her hut and describe pictures or voices that came into their head in the night. The healer's night-time spirit guidance instructs them how to treat the sick person.

Divination is something that has been noted amongst Khoi since the earliest European observers and specifically amongst Bushmen since at least the early twentieth century.[50] Bushmen tend to throw and read knuckle bones or shaped pieces of wood. Damara healers in Sesfontein read the intestines of goats. I did not encounter divination in more urban settings.

Shamanic style trance is a well-known means of accessing the 'spirit world'. After Bushmen trance healing dances people will listen and learn from the healer's experience. After a dance or sometimes after a healer has been travelling out of his body at night, he will tell others of the goings on in another village. I could not clearly establish whether Bushmen used trance states to deliberately discover what plants or animal medicines to use.

It is not widely known that the Damara have also held trance healing dances at least over the twentieth century. In the early twentieth century Vedder remarked that after a trance dance Damara medicine men were watched eagerly by the community for divinatory signs and on return to normal consciousness they gave accounts of their journey in the spirit world.[51] Wagner-Robertz's dance description also involves Damara healers acting in a spirit world in a very similar manner to Bushmen healers. Wagner-Robertz observed that during healing the rainmen called to //Gauab, asking him if the sickness they smelt was the right one and requesting the power to cure it.[52] She described how Damara healers, like Bushmen healers, reported riding to //Gamab on a Kudu antelope. Their blood was 'strongest', meaning most full of potency, when they had been with //Gamab. The dancing healers I encountered around Sesfontein did not readily relate tales of travelling in the spirit world. On questioning, one Damara healer did, however, suggest that a person in trance could tell the community where to find water or healing plants but it was not clear whether this was actually done or he was suggesting it could be.[53]

What might be termed 'intuition' or spontaneous ideas is thought of amongst Khoisan as pictures or words that just come into your head. These sensations will normally be attributed to 'god'. Despite the long missionary presence in Namibia it would be a mistake to assume there had been any 'straightforward' adoption of Christianity and ideas of divinity. There has been a Pastor in 'remote' Sesfontein for over a century. Yet, despite being a regular attendee of the Sesfontein church, my translator told me in reference to the devil: 'You have two gods, we have only one, we do not have this devil'.[54] Missionaries have been amongst Kalahari Bushmen since the 1960s and many Bushmen still have only the vaguest familiarity with Christian belief. When Khoisan talk of things coming from 'god' this may well be couched in Christian terms but there is no precise overlap. One lady of Damara and Nama descent related an episode that points to an overlap between Christian prayer and a different personable way of calling on the spirit world for help. Once, the lady related, at a time when she was suffering from continual sickness, she was out in the early morning collecting wood and she thought, 'today maybe god can give me a plant to drink and feel better'. As she continued walking she came across a plant she had never seen before. She dug it up, took it home, made a concoction and drank it. The plant cured her and to this day she has never seen it or heard of the plant again.[55]

Ways of Learning and Teaching

Bourdieu's notions of 'habitus', Ingold's theories of 'enskillment' and to some extent Lévy-Bruhl's older ideas of 'mystical participation' [56] all provide useful ways of thinking about Khoisan learning outside formal education. Much Khoisan learning comes simply from participation in their culture and environment. At a simple level Khoisan can be envisaged as learning particular sets of skills and ways of thinking relative to both the social and environmental phenomena they encounter and human biological interaction with the world. Placing Khoisan learning in this analytical domain does not make the Khoisan different from other cultures but it does emphasise ties between non-urban environmental influences and aboriginal ways of knowing the world. Lorna Marshall's account of wind, lightning, storms and hail as 'monstrous' events that pose a real threat to the !Kung exemplifies the proximity !Kung have to natural phenomena.[57] Both storms and wild animals pose a very real threat to many Khoisan. This level of involvement with environmental phenomena underpins their imaginative substrate and informs their healing ideas. Many of these healing ideas are passed on through practices learnt by both tacit means [58] and deliberate informal education.

There is no obvious classroom equivalent amongst Khoisan outside school education although group learning or more formal learning situations do exist. Puberty and hunting rituals still survive across the Khoisan, although they are rare and barely visible. These rituals involve revelation of knowledge and personal and group transformation. Since the early nineteenth century 'poison doctors' have been observed amongst Khoisan.[59] These healers, termed *!Gai aob* amongst historic Khoi peoples, still exist amongst Bushmen and Khoi, although their scarcity suggests they are either highly secretive or, more likely, are very rare. These healers allegedly develop immunity from snakebite and scorpion stings by being given increasing doses of poison by a potent poison doctor over a lengthy period of time. This illustrates an essentially Khoisan way of 'being educated'. In Khoisan terms this involves being given a gift, power or attributes that transforms their condition. In this context, which mirrors learning and enskillment in other contexts, the initiate undergoes a process of transformation through administration of poison potency. Through either wanting to become a 'poison doctor' or being directed by spirits, the initiate takes on the snake or scorpion potency. Whilst the gift brings ability in the sphere of poison immunity it does not bring other forms of respect or power even in other realms of healing. It is more a realignment of an individual's relationship with the community rather than a stacking of status points.

Having a specific healing ability or skill was very common across the Khoisan. Individuals would often only treat one or two conditions, such as massage a moved heart back into position or massage paralysed limbs. They did so in accordance with what had been passed to them from elder family members. Few healers had a broad range of skills and in rural areas there were very few who styled themselves in a professional manner; namely, seeing many clients who came from a large area and charging money. The Damara and Nama healers in Windhoek, Swakopmund and Walvis Bay presented the most professional appearance. They tended to draw upon a fusion of 'traditional' animal and plant based remedies, Afrikaans folk and commercial remedies and massage treatment. Treatment strategies were often inspired by 'god' or voices in dreams.

Some parents or grandparents will deliberately try to teach their children and grandchildren. Numerous informants reported that they knew of plant or animal remedies because their elder relatives had at some stage said to them, 'Someday I will die and you must know the plants and animals and how to treat people'. These elders showed the youngsters remedies and how to treat through medical incisions or massage. That only some elders passed on knowledge in this manner reminds us of the importance of personality of family members in terms of both giving and receiving knowledge. Often Khoi fathers or grandmothers seemed to pass on the plant knowledge and the mothers the massage knowledge. Plant knowledge was taught by deliberate outings into the bush to identify healing resources. One Hai//om man described how, when he was very young, his grandmother would march him off into the bush apparently without reason and without water for hours on end. He saw this endurance exercise as a broader part of his Hai//om education and his training to become an adult.[60]

In many instances it was younger informants that knew more about plants than their parents. They suggested that it was their grandparents who had taught them plant knowledge and not their parents. This again points to the difference personalities and internal family relationships make and perhaps to a pattern of grandparents with more time on their hands passing on knowledge. But it is also indicative of a Namibian health service that is perceived as having deteriorated since Independence. Without an adequate supply of medicines many younger Khoisan have fallen back on their 'traditional' knowledge.

Bushmen healers are perhaps the most conspicuous Khoisan teachers. Experienced healers will often guide individuals or small groups of inexperienced Bushmen through a healing dance in order for them to master the power of *n/om* healing potency. In Sesfontein there was clear evidence of money becoming involved in learning to heal, which was not something I encountered elsewhere. For an undisclosed but required sum, one could venture with 'the big rainmen' up to the Kunene River where you are cooked in a pot and then conveyed across the river in the mouth of a crocodile. On successfully reaching the other bank, 'you can see the things that are in people'.[61] Being given the ability to see in this manner seemed to reflect a fusing of Damara ideas of 'rainmen' healers with Herero powers of the 'witchdoctor'.

Earlier I considered the relationship between ideas, spirits and purpose amongst the Khoisan. There is a definite sense amongst Khoisan that if you want something there is a reason for it. If you want to be a healer then that is who you are. Someone who wants to massage can just watch and learn and then work with the massager. Similarly, a trance dancer can learn by watching and trying. This room for the individual leads to a bounded variety in practice as people bring their own way of doing things to common practices. I encountered no evidence of a healer being criticised for not being 'qualified'; doing healing is qualification enough. On the other hand, I did hear of healers who had not received official validation during a recent government initiative to issue healers with notifications of their registration and right to practise. Often these healers had simply missed the meeting at which healers received certificates. Consequently, these healers tried to keep quiet about their healing or had ceased to practise altogether out of fear of the authorities.

There are a number of ways that Khoisan can become healers. These are tied to ideas of spiritually endowed purpose and the personal wanting of something – which is also linked to spirit influence. Numerous Khoisan healers indicated that their parents or grandparents had been healers. This suggests that there is a hereditary element to healing, although whether there was a notion of powers being passed on was unclear. Having healers in the family seems to encourage others to become healers. Inheritance is not, however, a prerequisite to becoming a healer. Amongst Khoi and Bushmen, babies born with the caul intact are considered to be prophets or seers. One can also be given healing ability amongst the Khoi in what is literally termed giving the hand, *//goaba ma*. This normally involves the healer and initiate rubbing palms together or simultaneously making incisions on their wrists. Becoming a healer by undergoing a particular event, which is often dramatic if not traumatic, is a common phenomenon amongst African peoples. Numerous Damara rainmen spoke of becoming healers by being struck by lightning. The more times you were struck, they suggested, the stronger healer you became. Paul ≠Hawabeb, a Hai//om healer, described a series of extraordinary events in his life that eventually led him to the Ju/'hoan to learn how to dance and deal with his changing state. He learnt what he could from the Ju/'hoan but they 'were not his dance steps' so he adapted them and now he heals in his own way – which is in a manner very similar to other Hai//om dance healers. Paul, whose father was a healer, first noticed his life changing when he was a young man and he once became lost out in the fields. Whilst in an agitated state he encountered a lion. Overcome with fear he began to cry. After a very short while, however, he realised that the lion did not wish to attack him but was in fact offering him his tail to hold. Paul took hold of the tail and the lion led him home. Paul explained that lions do not live in the fields where he was lost and wandering.

If a Khoisan person wants to become a healer, or like Paul the gift is being given and they cannot refuse it, they can seek out more experienced healers to teach them. These experienced healers will decide whether or not to 'open' the person before them. Opening the person makes them a ready portal for the spirit world. Experienced healers will assess the strength and nature of the initiate's current healing ability and open them up or give them more powers accordingly. This is done in a number of ways, including dancing, rubbing *sai* or buchu plant powders on certain points of the body and, in one instance I encountered, by stabbing the initiate with 'a knife that does not make you bleed'.[62]

Pluralism

The healer Paul created his own way of healing that borrowed from practices and ideas of Hai//om and Ju/'hoan healers and perhaps Herero 'witchdoctors' – witchdoctor, said in English, being the word used by many such people to refer to themselves. This sort of medical pluralism is a strong characteristic of Khoisan healing. That Khoisan are open to treatments from beyond their immediate 'traditional' culture is perhaps not surprising given that Khoisan culture emphasises pragmatism and their epistemology is tolerant and relatively unchallenged by contradictory ideas.

An example of this tolerance emerged in an exercise I undertook to ascertain Damara ideas of the body. I asked seven members of an extended family unit in Sesfontein, who ranged in age from 5 to 30, to draw and label the human body and I stipulated that they must not refer to each other in the process or use any books they may have. After 20 minutes I collected the drawings and was confronted with perfect copies of annotated anatomical diagrams of the body, taken from an old school biology textbook they had surreptitiously salvaged from a locked trunk. I spent some time discussing these diagrams with each informant, who variously related, in reference to their own diagram, where the organs of the body were and what the function of some of the major organs and vessels is, including the heart, stomach, brain and blood vessels. Before the drawing exercise I had been told ideas by my drawing participants about the contents and function of the internal body that were far removed from those related by them when explaining what they had drawn. They reported, for instance, that the liver was in the centre of the stomach (as it is in a goat hung upside down to be disembowelled), that many organs moved, including the uterus, which may move into the head and make people mad, that blood vessels carried water, that a worm lived in the head of all humans (as it does in livestock) and that testicles could descend to the feet in cold situations. Some suggested that air enters the body through the lungs but also between the legs of women and particularly so when they are vulnerable during car rides or after recently having given birth. Some also thought air enters the body through pores at the base of hair follicles. A matter of hours after the drawing exercise I discussed these non-biological understandings of the body with the informants and they all acknowledge that what they had said prior to the exercise was true. They also affirmed that what they had drawn was also true, as were the biological functions they attributed to the organs pictured. When I pointed to apparent inconsistencies I was greeted with indifference. One particularly bright young man asked me why I asked such difficult questions.

The unproblematic holding of contrary understandings of the body might be explained by a combination of 'poor education', incomplete and uneven 'traditional' understandings of the body and a culture that does not look for 'rationality'. To focus, however, on poor education is to undermine the validity of what becomes lost with 'better education'. It also detracts focus away from the rich hinterland of medical pluralism which informs the health strategies of the majority of Khoisan.

Alternative understandings of illness and treatment are more prevalent than might be suspected. Forty-four year-old Salphina Janjies is a social worker, trained AIDS carer and Sunday school teacher. Her job involves considerable travel to help disadvantaged people at home or in hospitals. Salphina believes that so many people are sick at the present time because they move around so much and mix with different people. It is 'the winds' of different people that are making everyone sick.[63] Salphina's understanding is based upon ideas that run throughout Khoi and Bushmen regarding a relationship between wind and sickness. Despite her familiarity with hospitals and her professional training, a notion of wind underpins her understanding of disease. Salphina is far from alone in this maintenance of an alternative perspective in the face of modern southern African scientific ideas. It is a similar lack of wholesale absorption of 'Western' influence that was evident in my translator's observations regarding Khoisan not believing in the devil. Similarly again, whilst the Sesfontein Pastor was against traditional Damara healing dances, he acknowledged that he treats people by massage because of the messages that are revealed to him in dreams. He thought of these messages as both God given but also 'part of the Damara tradition'.[64] The Pastor's explanation demonstrates a discretion concerning what aspects of tradition should be rejected or retained and it speaks of local accommodation and transformation of 'outside' ideas.

Following global trends, there is a new idiom of respect for traditional medicine within Khoisan communities that has been generated by wider public and governmental interest and support for traditional culture. What is respected, though, tends to be what is implicitly endorsed by science and received notions of rationality. In the southern Namibian town of Gibeon, for example, a women's group was established in 2001 that sought to collect indigenous Khoi healing knowledge from its members and to both preserve it by writing it down and to present it at shows throughout the country. What they focused on was, however, almost exclusively herbal remedies and some animal remedies. This reflects a long-standing colonial and post-colonial bias that privileges these aspects of traditional medicine within proto-scientific paradigms, over massage treatment, healing dances and other unfamiliar practices which to many hold connotations of lesser primitive behaviour and even witchcraft.

By educational appropriation of traditional medicine through the lens of proto-science or superstitious nonsense, the essence of the local and essentially different Khoisan understanding is lost. A good example of appropriation, fusion and potential loss of ideas emerged in a discussion I had with a relatively 'well-educated' and good English-speaking Damara man. I asked him about the practice of Damara making healing incisions in the body and rubbing in plant or animal substances. This is done to protect people from certain conditions, or to imbue them with particular kinds of potency, such as the potency of the Kudu or a snake. Recruiting popular accounts of evolutionary theory mixed with popular scientific medical understandings of inoculation, he explained:

> through the centuries, they call it survival of the jungle, life of the fittest, what actually happened is there are certain people which is very strong, which got immune system very strong and there is diseases in the air, spreading around, germs, meningitis, they call it the backwardness. The children when they are losing life there is something in their brains pulling it. What they do is take this front skin from the resistant person who has the disease but he was not struck down, make cut, squeeze in. They transfer the immune system in other one. I saw it, I saw my daughter, she was six, at soccer field and she cross with somebody and the smile of the body goes into her and she goes into the hospital and she pulls her head back, her eyes go in, on top the brains go in, looked sucked in and she was pulled backward. When we do that thing ..., we cut there and transfer the immune system or front skin, I take her from hospital, they say I can do nothing, [the doctor also had] a black daughter, he said, [you] must look for someone with immune system stronger. I go there and cut and like that, after two hours she is normal. She now is full grown beautiful lady, and the reason is that people do immune thing.[65]

This man fuses a number of traditional ideas with scientific ideas. He refers to traditional Khoisan understandings concerning personal wind entering other people by one person passing by another or smiling at another. He also refers to traditional ideas about curing a sick person by imbuing them with the wind or potency of someone who is a healer or who has had the disease which afflicts the patient. He combines a traditional conception of a particular Damara disease with received ideas of meningitis. Crucially, he collapses traditional wind ideas within modern scientific explanations and practices without acknowledging the essential difference in understanding that lies behind Damara disease and treatment notions and scientific medical paradigms. The only difference he perceives is that encouraged by popular education, that this Damara treatment is a primitive version of inoculation.

With literate educated culture the Khoisan world of possibilities closes down. As Biesele emphasises in her study of Bushmen folklore, rich variability of ideas is characteristic of oral tradition. To write something down encourages comparison and begins to push questions of authenticity. Dictionaries, which are the first step in literacy and education, are particularly responsible for pinning down variety in dialects and word forms and hence relations between ideas. Guenther has identified consistency of ideas as a symptom of acculturation of Nharo Bushmen.[66] Increased familiarisation with biomedicine firstly leads to a new set of alternatives and ideas upon which pragmatic and ideologically open Khoisan healers can draw. As education increases though, for most, the world of the traditional becomes a faint and incomplete story of a primitive past.

Notes

[1] Alan Barnard (1992) *Hunters and Herders of Southern Africa: a comparative ethnography of the Khoisan peoples.* Cambridge and New York: Cambridge University Press.

[2] Chris Low (2004) Khoisan Healing: understandings, ideas and practices, D.Phil thesis, University of Oxford.

[3] Isaac Schapera (1930) *The Khoisan Peoples of South Africa: Bushmen and Hottentots,* v. London: Routledge & Sons.

[4] See, for example: Steven Feierman & John Janzen (1992) *The Social Basis of Health and Healing in Africa.* Berkeley and Oxford: University of California Press; Megan Vaughan (1991) *Curing Their Ills: colonial power and African illness.* Oxford: Polity Press; Terrance Ranger & P. Slack (Eds) (1992) *Epidemics and Ideas: essays in the historical perception of pestilence.* Cambridge: Cambridge University Press.

[5] For an example of this educational cultural meeting point see Helen Verran (2001) *Science and an African Logic.* Chicago: University of Chicago Press.

[6] Jane Carruthers (2003) Past and Future Landscape Ideology: the Kalahari Gemsbok National Park, in W. Beinart & J. McGregor (Eds) *Social History and African Environments,* 258. Oxford: James Currey.

[7] Megan Biesele (1993) *Women Like Meat: the folklore and foraging ideology of the Kalahari Ju/'hoan,* 13. Bloomington: Indiana University Press.

[8] Alan Barnard (2002) The Foraging Mode of Thought, in Henry Stewart, Alan Barnard & Keiichi Omura (Eds) *Senri Ethnological Studies 60,* 5-24. Osaka: National Museum of Ethnology.

[9] I use the artificial European word 'Khoi' as a means of referring to Nama, Damara and Topnaar, as opposed to 'Khoe' which as a linguistic label would include the Hai//om and Nharo Bushmen.

[10] Brian Morris (2000) *Animals and Ancestors: an ethnography,* 24. Oxford: Berg.

[11] M. Guenther (1986) *The Nharo Bushmen of Botswana: tradition and change.* Quellen zur Khoisan-Forschung, 216. Hamburg: Helmut Buske Verlag.

[12] Ibid., p. 235.

[13] Willemien le Roux & Alison White (Eds) (2004) *Voices of the San: living in southern Africa today*, 66. Cape Town: Kwela Books.

[14] Ibid.

[15] Beinart, *Twentieth Century South Africa*, 38.

[16] W. Hoernlé, cited by Alan Barnard (1992) *Hunters and Herders of Southern Africa*, 176.

[17] Brigitte Lau (1979) A Critique of the Historical Sources Relating to the Damara, University of Cape Town BA thesis; Brigitte Lau (1987) *Namibia in Jonker Afrikaner's Time*. Windhoek: National Archives of Namibia.

[18] Wilfred H.G. Haacke (1986) Preliminary Observations on a Dialect of the Sesfontein Damara, in Rainer Vossen & Klaus Keuthmann (Eds) *Contemporary Studies on Khoisan 5.1*, 376, 389. Hamburg: Helmut Buske Verlag.

[19] Deborah Leah Lebeau (1999) Seeking Health: the hierarchy of resort in utilisation patterns of traditional and western medicine in multi-cultural Katatura, Namibia, PhD thesis, Rhodes University; Marion Wallace (1997) Health and Society in Windhoek, Namibia 1915-45, PhD thesis, Institute of Commonwealth Studies, University of London.

[20] E.E. Evans-Pritchard ([1937] 1976) *Witchcraft Oracles, and Magic among the Azande* (abridged). Oxford: Oxford University Press

[21] Malidoma Somé (1999) *The Healing Wisdom of Africa: finding life purpose through nature, ritual, and community*, 3, 79. New York: Tarcher.

[22] Richard Katz (1982) *Boiling Energy: community healing among the Kalahari Kung*, 52. Cambridge, MA and London: Harvard University Press.

[23] Richard Lee (2003) *The Dobe Ju/'hoansi*, 139-140. Melbourne: Wadsworth.

[24] Richard Katz, Megan Biesele & Verna St Denis (1997) *Healing Makes our Hearts Happy: spirituality and cultural transformation among the Kalahari Ju/'hoansi*, 113. Rochester, VT: Inner Traditions.

[25] David Livingstone (1858) Conversations on Rain-making, in *Missionary Travels and Researches in South Africa*, 22-27. London.

[26] Evans-Pritchard, *Witchcraft Oracles, and Magic among the Azande*, 57. Oxford: Oxford University Press; Lucien Lévy-Bruhl ([1910] 1985) *How Natives Think*, 78. Princeton: Princeton University Press.

[27] E. Gellner, cited by Prins, A Modern History of Lozi Therapeutics, in Feierman & Janzen, *The Social Basis*, 344.

[28] R. Horton (1993) African Traditional Thought and Western Science, in R. Horton, *Patterns of Thought in Africa and the West: essays on magic, religion and science*, 213. Cambridge: Cambridge University Press; D. Gentner (1982) Flowing Waters of Teeming Crowds: mental models of electricity, in D. Gentner & A. Stevens (Eds) *Mental Models*, 99-129. Hillsdale: Laurence Erlbaum.

[29] Megan Biesele, *Women Like Meat*, 13.

[30] Low, *Khoisan Healing*.

[31] Lee, *The Dobe Ju/'hoansi*, 153.

[32] George Silberbauer (1981) *Hunter and Habitat in the Central Kalahari*, 132. Cambridge: Cambridge University Press.

[33] Mathias Guenther (1999) *Tricksters and Trancers: Bushman religion and society*. Bloomington and Indianapolis: Indiana University Press.

[34] !Ai!ae ǂ'oma at ǂninihm near Tsumkwe, interviewed 27 August 2001.

[35] R. Horton (1993) Tradition and Modernity Revisited, in R. Horton, *Patterns of Thought in Africa and the West*, 301-346.

[36] For elaboration of the sensory world see David Abram (1996) *The Spell of the Sensuous*. New York: Vintage.

[37] D. Wagner-Robertz (2000) Ein Heilungsritual der Dama Südwestafrika/Namibia, in M. Bollig & W.J.G. Möhlig (Eds) *History, Cultural Traditions and Innovations in Southern Africa*, 12, 64. Cologne: Rüdiger Köppe Verlag).

[38] Ibid., 76.

[39] Andreas !Kharuxab, Sesfontein, 4 April 2001.

[40] Julia Tauros, Sesfontein, 19 July 2001.

[41] Frederick //Awaseb, Tsintsabis, 3 August 2001.

[42] Richard Lee cited by Megan Biesele, *Women Like Meat*, 78.

[43] Alan Barnard (1992) *Hunters and Herders of Southern Africa*, 83; Guenther, *Tricksters and Trancers*, 129.

[44] Cf. R. Lee (1967) Trance Cure of the !Kung Bushmen, *Natural History*, November, 30-37.

[45] Bertha, Katatura, 6 May 2001.

[46] Libertina Garuses, Katatura, 13 April 2001.

[47] Paul ≠Hawabeb, near Otavi, 23 July 2001.

[48] Sophia Hanse, Maltahöhe, 19 May 2001.

[49] Lorna Marshall (1999) *Nyae Nyae !Kung: beliefs and rites*, 48, 74. Cambridge, MA: Peabody Museum.

[50] Isaac Schapera (Ed.) (1933) *The Early Cape Hottentots: described in the writings of Olfert Dapper (1668), Willem Ten Rhyne (1686) and Johannes Gulielmus de Grevenbroek (1695)*, trans. I. Schapera & B. Farrington, xiii. Cape Town; S.S. Dornan (1925) *Pygmies and Bushmen of the Kalahari*, 155-162. London: Seeley, Service & Co.

[51] Vedder cited by Sigrid Schmidt (1986) Present Day Trance Dances of the Dama in SWA/Namibia. Research Reports, *ALASA Khoisan SIG: Newsletter* 4, 10. Pretoria: Department of African Languages, UNISA.

[52] Wagner-Robertz, 'Heilungsritual der Dama', 28.

[53] Abraham Ganuseb, Sesfontein, 7 April 2001.

[54] Suro Ganuses, Sesfontein, 14 June 2001.

[55] Joanna Andon, Maltahöhe, 19 May 2001.

[56] P. Bourdieu (1977) *Outline of a Theory of Practice*. Cambridge: Cambridge University Press; Timothy Ingold (1985) *The Perception of the Environment*. London and New York: Routledge; Lévy-Bruhl, *How Natives Think*.

[57] Marshall, *Nyae Nyae !Kung*, 164.

[58] See, for example, Tola Pearce (1986) Professional Interests in the Creation of Medical Knowledge in Nigeria, in M. Last & G. Chavanduka, *The Professionalisation of African Medicine*, 242-258. Manchester: Manchester University Press.

[59] Schapera, *The Khoisan Peoples of South Africa*, 217.

[60] Werner Classen, Windhoek, 20 March 2001.

[61] Johannes Taurob, Sesfontein, 6 April 2001.

[62] Aibi Haitua, near Otavi, 5 August 2001.

[63] Salphina Janjies (Damara), Mariental, 21 May 2001.

[64] Pastor Theodor Hendriks, Sesfontein, 16 July 2001.

[65] No name, Franzfontein, 15 April 2001.

[66] Guenther, *The Nharo Bushmen of Botswana*, 217.

Notes on Contributors

William Beinart, Rhodes Professor of Race Relations, specialises in southern African history and in environmental history and politics. He also teaches and supervises students on contemporary politics in South Africa. He has recently edited a volume with JoAnn McGregor, *Social History and African Environments* (2003) from the St Antony's conference on African Environments: Past and Present. A second edition of *Twentieth-Century South Africa* (2001) and a book on *The Rise of Conservation in South Africa, 1770-1950* (2003) have been published by Oxford University Press.
Correspondence: Professor William Beinart, African Studies Centre, University of Oxford, 92 Woodstock Road, Oxford OX2 7ND, United Kingdom (william.beinart@sant.ox.ac.uk).

Michael Crossley is Professor of Comparative and International Education at the University of Bristol. He is currently Editor of the journal *Comparative Education* and is a former Chair of the British Association for International and Comparative Education (BAICE). Current research interests include theoretical and methodological scholarship on the future of comparative and international education; research and evaluation capacity and international development cooperation; and educational development in small states.
Correspondence: Professor Michael Crossley, Research Centre for International and Comparative Studies, Graduate School of Education, University of Bristol, 35 Berkeley Square, Bristol BS8 1JA, United Kingdom (m.crossley@bristol.ac.uk).

David Johnson is a Lecturer in Comparative and International Education and a Fellow in African Studies at St Antony's College, University of Oxford. He has conducted a number of studies into education in Africa including in Malawi, South Africa, The Gambia and recently in Nigeria.
Correspondence: Professor David Johnson, Department of Education, University of Oxford, 15 Norham Gardens, Oxford OX2 6PY, United Kingdom (david.johnson@education@oxford.ac.uk).

Anthony Lemon is a Lecturer in Geography and a Tutorial Fellow of Mansfield College, University of Oxford. He is a specialist in the social and political geography of South and southern Africa. His work has sought to demonstrate the spatial character of apartheid planning and its consequences for South Africa's social, economic and political geography, and for that of southern Africa as a whole. Since 1994 he has focused on aspects of post-apartheid reconstruction, including urban desegregation, redistribution within the school education system and electoral geography in relation to nation-building and political and economic stability in post-apartheid South Africa. Secondary research interests include small states and the foreign policy, trade and investment relations of South Africa in a changing global environment. He is currently planning a new book, co-edited with Professor C.M. Rogerson of the University of the Witwatersrand, on the economic geography of southern Africa.

Correspondence: Dr Anthony Lemon, School of Geography, Oxford University Centre for the Environment, University of Oxford, South Parks Road, Oxford OX1 3QY, United Kingdom (tony.lemon@mansfield.ox.ac.uk).

Chris Low is an ESRC research fellow in African Studies, in the School of Interdisciplinary Area Studies, University of Oxford. His research topic is 'Animals in Bushman Medicine', which examines the relationship between Bushmen, animals and medicine from pre-colonial times to the present. He completed his DPhil at Oxford in 2004 on the topic of 'Khoisan Healing: Understandings, Ideas and Practices'.

Correspondence: Dr Chris Low, African Studies Centre, University of Oxford, 92 Woodstock Road, Oxford OX2 7ND, United Kingdom (chris.low@africa.ox.ac.uk).

Michele Schweisfurth is Director of the Centre for International Education and Research, School of Education, University of Birmingham. Within Comparative and International Education her research interests include democratic education, global citizenship and intercultural education, and the professional identity of teachers.

Correspondence: Dr Michele Schweisfurth, School of Education, University of Birmingham, Edgbaston, Birmingham B15 2TT, United Kingdom (m.schweisfurth@bham.ac.uk).

Barbara Trudell has worked in community-based literacy and language development since 1982, in both South America and sub-Saharan Africa. Her current work includes consulting, training, research and advocacy on behalf of local languages across sub-Saharan Africa. Her research interests include the use of African languages in formal and non-formal learning contexts, language policy, and local processes for language development in sub-Saharan Africa

Correspondence: Dr Barbara Trudell, SIL Africa Area, PO Box 44456, Nairobi 00100, Kenya (barbara_trudell@sil.org).

Elaine Unterhalter is a Reader in Education and International Development at the Institute of Education, Univeristy of London. Her specialist research area is gender, education and development. She is the author of *Gender, Schooling and Global Social Justice* (RoutledgeFalmer, 2006) and a wide range of writings on conceptual, empirical, and practice oriented themes. She has published a number of works on gender and the education transition in South Africa and has worked with colleagues at the University of Kwazulu Natal on a six-year ethnographic project looking at changes in two secondary schools.

Correspondence: Institute of Education, University of London, 20 Bedford Way, London WC1H 0AL, United Kingdom (elaine.unterhalter@gmail.com).

Adriaan Verspoor is an independent education consultant specialising in policy analysis and the design and management of education development programmes. He is currently working on a report on the challenges of secondary education development in sub-Saharan Africa. He has been the coordinator and lead investigator of a taskforce on quality improvement in basic education in Africa, launched by the Association for the Development of Education in Africa. He has consulted for a variety of agencies including the World Bank, the Asian Development Bank, the Department of International Development (UK) and the Ministry of Foreign Affairs of the Netherlands. He has field experience in 25 countries in Africa and Asia and has authored and co-authored eight refereed books and journal articles and numerous technical papers and books on education issues in developing countries. He has written a book on the challenges of secondary education development in sub-Saharan Africa which is scheduled to be published by the World Bank in May 2008.

Correspondence: Adriaan Verspoor, 11570 Lake Newport Road, Reston, VA, USA (averspoor@worldbank.org; averspoor @gmail.com).